Recessions and Depressions

Recessions and Depressions

Understanding Business Cycles

Todd A. Knoop

Westport, Connecticut
London

Library of Congress Cataloging-in-Publication Data

Knoop, Todd A.
　　Recessions and depressions : understanding business cycles / Todd A. Knoop.
　　　　p. cm.
　　Includes bibliographical references and index.
　　ISBN 0–275–98162–2 (alk. paper)
　　　1. Business cycles. 2. Economic forecasting. 3. Business cycles—United
　　States—History. 4. Business cycles—History—20th century. I. Title
HB3711.K63 2004
338.5'42—dc22　　　　2004049569

British Library Cataloguing in Publication Data is available.

Library of Congress Catalog Card Number: 2004049569
ISBN: 0–275–98162–2

First published in 2004

Praeger Publishers, 88 Post Road West, Westport, CT 06881
An imprint of Greenwood Publishing Group, Inc.
www.praeger.com

Printed in the United States of America

The paper used in this book complies with the
Permanent Paper Standard issued by the National
Information Standards Organization (Z39.48-1984).

10 9 8 7 6 5 4 3 2

To my loving and supportive family:
Deb, Edie, and Daphne

In the middle of the last century, a great dispute arose among astronomers respecting one of the planets. Some, in their folly, commenced a war of words, and wrote hot books against each other; others, in their wisdom, improved their telescopes and soon settled the question forever. Education should imitate the latter.

—Horace Mann, *Lectures on Education* (1855)

Contents

Illustrations

Figures

TABLES

Preface

It has been said that capitalist economies are like drunks—they have trouble moving in a straight line. While that analogy might be amusing, the real consequences of these economic lurches are often devastating. Not only do recessions and depressions reduce standards of living and increase poverty, but they also undermine the public's confidence in the benefits of capitalism and often even of democracy. Understanding the nature and causes of business cycles in an effort to develop policies to eliminate them is a noble endeavor with potentially extraordinary implications for human welfare.

The study of business cycles has greatly contributed not only to our understanding of economic contractions but also to our understanding of macroeconomics in general. While to the uninformed it might seem that economists are no closer today to understanding business cycles than they were 200 years ago, when business cycle theory is examined within a historical context it becomes obvious that major advances have been made. However, our knowledge is still far from complete. Modern depressions in East Asia, Japan, and Argentina as well as recent recessions in developed nations such as the United States point both to the validity of much of our present theory and also to areas that need to be explored further before economists can completely understand business cycles and enact policies to prevent them.

This book covers the empirics, the theory, and specific case studies of recessions and depressions. This book is written in a nontechnical narrative aimed at upper-level undergraduate students or general readers with some background and interest in economics. As a result, it should have broad interest for use in college courses on business cycle theory, intermediate macroeconomics, and the history of macroeconomic thought, as well as being of interest to a more general audience interested in better understanding economic crises.

While this book does not necessarily challenge any current thinking in the field of business cycle research, it does contribute to the ongoing debate over the nature and causes of recessions and depressions by gathering together the basics of business cycle research and organizing it in an understandable and interesting way. My belief is that this book will encourage a deeper understanding of the issues that surround business cycles for those who read it. In addition, I hope that this book will generate interest in business cycles so that future researchers will want to investigate questions related to economic contractions. To that end, this book clearly points to future avenues for business cycle research. Specifically, more research needs to be conducted using open-economy models that incorporate the effects of exchange rate fluctuations, foreign investment inflows and outflows, monetary policy and inflation, nominal wage and debt rigidities, and the implications of these factors for the balance sheets of firms and banks.

This book grew out of research that I conducted for an upper-level undergraduate course that I taught at Cornell College entitled "Recessions and Depressions." As I was thinking about how to organize this course, I looked for an appropriate text. Somewhat surprisingly, I found nothing that was satisfactory for use in an upper-level undergraduate course on business cycles. No existing book covers the empirics, the theory, and international case studies of recessions and depressions. In addition, no book on business cycles has been written in a nontechnical narrative aimed at the upper-level undergraduate student or the general reader with some background and interest in economics. As a result, when I first taught this "Recessions and Depressions" course, I was forced to rely on primary readings that in many cases were not written at an appropriate level for undergraduates. To help students understand these primary resources, I developed a set of lecture notes for students. These lecture notes were well received by students and by other faculty that reviewed them, encouraging me to write a book that that would allow me to more formally and completely discuss my thoughts on business cycles. I believe that my skills as a teacher have helped me write a book that will not only further knowledge of business cycles but also point to specific areas of business cycle research that might interest many students of economics.

A number of people were of great help to me in writing this book, and I am indebted to each of them. Numerous students in my courses provided feedback, including students in my "Recessions and Depressions" course. I would particularly like to thank Amy Winter, who provided invaluable research assistance and played a big role in this book's timely fruition. Many Cornell faculty also provided feedback, particularly other members of the Economics and Business department. I would also like to thank Cornell College for awarding me a Campbell R. McConnell Fellowship Award, which provided many of the resources needed to produce this book. Finally, I would like to thank and send my love to my exceptionally supportive wife Debra DeLaet and my two daughters, Edie and Daphne, for putting up with an even more distracted than usual husband and dad.

Part I

The Facts of Business Cycles

Why Study Business Cycles?

INTRODUCTION

Consistent with the popular conception of economics as the "dismal science," economists secretly long for recessions and depressions. Not in any real or concrete sense, for as a general rule economists are not sadists and do not enjoy seeing people suffer through the hardships suffered by the citizens of nations that are going through an economic crisis. However, when it comes to the state of economic knowledge, nothing improves economists' understanding of how markets and macroeconomies work more than an economic downturn. The most obvious analogy is to an auto mechanic who learns his craft not by working on cars that are running well but by getting under the hood of autos that have broken down. Much the same can be said of economists. Recessions and depressions are essentially the only substitute that macroeconomists have for an experiment, when markets break down so completely that the underpinnings of the operation of fully functioning economies become more readily apparent. Contractions are an opportunity for economists to pop open the hood and take a look inside the engine of modern economies.

The best example of the learning opportunities economic crises provide is the Great Depression, an unprecedented economic downturn of a massive scale that eventually turned the whole discipline of economics on its ear. The Great Depression played a crucial role both in the development of macroeconomics as a separate field of study from that of microeconomics and also in the development of Keynesian economics, the most fundamental change in the way that economists think about the world since 1776, when Adam Smith published *The Wealth of Nations*. Keynesian economics in turn spawned some of the most radical developments in public policy since the industrial revolution and provided the theoretical foundation for the modern welfare state.

This text will provide in-depth analyses of the following two questions:

1. Why are economies subject to periods of negative output growth (recessions)?
2. How do you explain severe economic contractions (depressions)?

As mentioned, many of the key developments in macroeconomic theory both before and after Keynes have centered on these two questions. The big problem, unfortunately, is that after more than 200 years of debate there is still no general agreement about what causes recessions and depressions. Multiple competing models of business cycles continue to be used among economists. In fact, there is a large disconnect between the models used by academics and those used by private sector economists. This debate over the root causes of business cycles continues to be a key question in the development of macroeconomic thought. The goal of this book is not necessarily to put an end to this debate by providing a definitive answer on why business cycles exist— because there is none at this point—but rather to understand all of the competing theories and factors in the debate.

For an example of how disagreements persist in macroeconomics, consider the U.S. recession of 1990–1991. Some economists have argued that it was caused by an aggregate demand downturn resulting from a reduction in consumer confidence during the Gulf War or by a decrease in the money supply by the Federal Reserve. Others have argued that it was caused by a decrease in aggregate supply brought about by an increase in the price of oil during the war or the delayed effects of tax increases and new government regulations adopted in the late 1980s. To this day, no single cause is generally agreed upon among economists. Another example of the discord among economists is evident in their handling of the East Asian crisis from 1997 to 1999, the most significant international economic crisis since the Great Depression. Economists did not forecast the East Asian crisis. Most disturbingly, there was no agreement at the time among economists about the policies that should have been followed to best deal with the crisis. In fact, the crisis occurred in countries that were previously thought to be model economies that were fundamentally sound. Clearly, there is still much work to be done before economists can come to any sort of consensus about the causes of recessions and depressions.

Given the obvious difficulties inherent in this topic, many people (including many economists) have asked: Why study business cycles if, in the long run, they all average out? The answer is that they are extremely costly to a society, not just in terms of lost income but in terms of disrupted lives—higher suicide and homicide rates, higher poverty levels, and higher divorce rates, among other measures of well-being— with persistent economic, social, and personal effects. Keynes's (1923) response to the question posed at the beginning of this paragraph is one of the classic retorts in all of economics:

> Now "in the long run" this is probably true. . . . But this long run is a misleading guide to current affairs. In the long run we are all dead. Economists set themselves too easy, too useless a task if in tempestuous seasons they can only tell us that when the storm is long past the ocean is flat again.

OUTLINE OF THE BOOK

This book is divided into four parts.

Part I: The Facts of Business Cycles. Chapter 2 describes business cycles both quantitatively and qualitatively. This chapter provides a summary discussion of the duration and depth of business cycles both in the United States and internationally across developed countries, with a focus on six basic facts about business cycles. In addition, the behavior of the components of Gross Domestic Product (GDP) over the business cycle is also described. Finally, this chapter summarizes the cyclical behavior of other important macroeconomic time series variables, including whether each variable is a reliably leading, coincident, or lagging indicator of turning points in a business cycle.

Part II: The Macroeconomic Theory of Business Cycles and Forecasting. The evolution of thought on the nature of business cycles also traces the evolution of a large part of modern macroeconomic theory. In order to comprehend macroeconomics as it is practiced today and where it is headed in the future, it is crucial to understand the theoretical ground already covered and the economic events that precipitated changes in the way we view macroeconomic fluctuations.

The main objective of this section is to cover the evolution of the macroeconomic theory of business cycles. Numerous early business cycle theories were developed before the Great Depression, each of them failing to make a clear distinction between the behavior of individuals and the behavior of economies as a whole. However, these early theories highlight many important characteristics of economic contractions. The study of modern business cycles began with Keynesian economics, which focused on the macroeconomic effects of market failure; after a neoclassical resurgence during the 1970s and 1980s, business cycle research has returned to the study of market failure. However, modern business cycle models have greatly improved upon the microeconomic explanations of why markets often do not work efficiently and the specific roles that various forms of imperfect competition play in output fluctuations. While these new models are more intuitively appealing and are more consistent with the empirical data, they have not yet improved the ability of economists to forecast the future or to act preemptively in order to prevent recessions and depressions.

Part II presents six primary models: the Classical model (Chapter 3), the Keynesian model (Chapter 4), the Monetarist model (Chapter 5), the Rational Expectations model (Chapter 6), the Real Business Cycle model (Chapter 7), and the New Keynesian model (Chapter 8). For each model, the relevant chapter discusses (1) the historical context in which the model was developed, (2) the basic theory behind the model, which includes a description of how the model explains business cycles, (3) the policy implications of the model, and (4) whether existing empirical research supports the model's principal implications. Each model is discussed in a rigorous but nontechnical narrative.

This section concludes with a chapter on macroeconomic forecasting, Chapter 9. Economic forecasting is a difficult topic to cover in a nontechnical book such as this; further, macroeconomic forecasting has a not-so-storied history and a questionable future. This chapter briefly describes the current state of macroeconomic forecasting by discussing the four primary forecasting methods: macroeconomic indicators (such as the index of leading economic indicators and the yield curve), econometric models, structural models, and dynamic general equilibrium models.

Every chapter provides suggested readings that can be used to supplement this text. The purpose of these suggested readings is fourfold. First, they offer readers a chance to expose themselves to some of the seminal, but more accessible, research in the business cycle field. Second, they allow readers to explore the insights of groundbreaking economists in their own words in order to better understand the important contributions these authors made. Third, they give readers an idea about how economists talk to each other, as difficult as it may be to interpret these discussions at times. Finally, these readings give readers the benefit of working through a piece of research and all of its difficulties by themselves. These readings have been chosen because they are written at an appropriate level for an advanced undergraduate reader and are either important articles in the business cycle field or are written by significant authors in the field who are providing an overview of an area of research.

Part III: Business Cycles in the United States. The first chapter (Chapter 10) deals with the Great Depression, primarily from the U.S. standpoint, but also with its international ramifications. While many possible factors will be examined as potential causes of the Great Depression, the primary explanation in this chapter centers on four facts. First, all countries that experienced a depression were on the gold standard and maintained fixed exchange rates. Second, there were severe balance of payment imbalances in place when the gold standard was restored after World War I. Third, asymmetries in the way the gold standard was administered made it unstable. Finally, a massive international deflation was the result of a strict adherence to the gold standard and naïve macroeconomic policy. This chapter explains in detail the theory behind why deflation is so costly, especially in terms of its effects on financial intermediation. It also compares this explanation with traditional Keynesian and Monetarist explanations of the Great Depression. Finally, this chapter discusses the events that initiated the recovery from the Great Depression, principally dropping off the gold standard and re-inflation.

Chapter 11 deals with postwar business cycles in the United States. Following a brief case study of each of these business cycles is a discussion of how postwar business cycles differ from pre–Great Depression business cycles. The basic conclusion of this section is that while there have not been any dramatic changes, postwar business cycles have occurred less frequently and have been slightly shorter than prewar business cycles. Finally, this chapter discusses the role of postwar macroeconomic policy in mitigating (or magnifying) business cycles.

Chapter 12 focuses on the debate over the existence of a "new economy" (i.e., permanently higher productivity and trend output growth) in the United States, which began in response to the robust growth of the mid-to-late 1990s. The principal topics of discussion in this chapter center on productivity growth. How much faster did productivity grow in the 1990s than during the 1970s and 1980s? Why has it been growing faster? How reliable are our measurements of productivity? Are there reasons to think that higher productivity growth will continue in the future? In addition, the 2001 recession and the "growth recession" that followed will be examined. The causes of this economic slowdown and the outlook for the U.S. economy in the future will be debated.

Part IV: Modern International Recessions and Depressions. This section will investigate three economic crises outside the United States. First, the East Asian crisis is discussed, in Chapter 13. After a brief description of other recent currency crises (Mexico in 1994, Latin America in the 1980s, and the European Monetary System in 1992), the East Asian crisis is compared to these previous crises. The critical difference is that the East Asian crisis was actually two distinct crises, in that it was a currency crisis that occurred in conjunction with a banking crisis. The large devaluations that resulted from the currency crisis led to complete collapses of fragile banking systems throughout the region, resulting in capital flight, a massive reduction in financial intermediation, and a severe decline in economic activity. Chapter 13 describes this process in detail. This chapter also investigates the culpability of foreign investors in precipitating the crisis. Finally, recommendations for economic reform in East Asia are discussed and comparisons are made between the Great Depression and the East Asian crisis.

Chapter 14 examines the recent Argentinean crisis and the International Monetary Fund (IMF). The particulars of the Argentinean crisis are eerily similar to those of the East Asian crisis, though there are a few crucial differences. The IMF and the economic reforms it imposes as a condition for receiving aid have become a common target of criticism during recent crises, such as those that occurred in Argentina and East Asia. A detailed discussion of the role of the IMF in ameliorating (or exacerbating) international economic crises is also included in this chapter, in which criticisms of the IMF from the political right, left, and center are examined. The chapter concludes with a brief discussion of the IMF's current attempts to reform itself.

Chapter 15 examines the decade-long recession in Japan. The Japanese economy, including the nature of its inefficient markets and fragile banking system, is characterized. This is followed by an examination of the reasons for deflation in Japan and the failure of macroeconomic stabilization to end this recession. This chapter concludes with a description of economic policy reforms needed to facilitate an end to the Japanese recession.

The main conclusion gained from these international case studies is that the study of depressions is a somewhat different topic than the study of business cycles in general. There are three major distinctions between recessions and depressions (apart from just their size). First, depressions tend to be international in nature, not primarily isolated to just one country. Second, depressions tend to involve the collapse of financial markets in general, and of the banking industry in particular. Third, depressions almost always begin with some sort of macroeconomic policy mistake, in the form of runaway monetary and fiscal policy, misaligned exchange rates, or both. The Great Depression, the East Asian crisis, and the Argentinean crisis all follow this general pattern. The recession in Japan is an intermediate case that is less than a depression but encompasses some of the characteristics of one. Current business cycle research has not yet been able to provide a complete model that adequately incorporates each of these factors. This is in part because most economists have typically focused on explaining business cycles in the United States and other developed countries. As a result, much of our current theory better explains recessions than it does depressions. However, these recent crises have served as a wake-up call to many economists and have spurred much needed research in open-economy models of business cycles that incorporate the macroeconomic effects of market failure, particularly within banking systems.

Chapter 16 is a brief conclusion in which the principal insights gained from the study of business cycles are discussed. This is followed by a list of questions that economists are still struggling to answer, questions that serve as signposts to guide future economic research on business cycles.

Describing Business Cycles

INTRODUCTION

In order to understand why economies are subject to business cycles, it is important to have a good grasp on the empirical regularities (and irregularities) of the key macroeconomic variables that fluctuate as the economy contracts and expands. One purpose of this chapter is to describe the quantitative aspects of business cycles, meaning the depth and duration of both individual and average economic contractions and expansions. The second purpose of this chapter is to describe the qualitative aspects of business cycles, meaning how different macroeconomic variables move in relation to each other during contractions and expansions. Both U.S. and international data will be examined. A good understanding of the business cycle data provides some basic empirical facts that can be used to evaluate the competing theories that attempt to answer the two primary questions posed in this book: Why are economies subject to periods of negative output growth (recessions)? and How do you explain severe economic contractions (depressions)?

BASIC DEFINITIONS

Economists from the Business Cycle Dating Committee of the National Bureau of Economic Research (NBER), the preeminent economic research organization in the United States, date the beginnings and ends of economic contractions and expansions in the United States. To do this, the NBER needs a working definition of what constitutes a recession and an expansion. The NBER defines a *recession* as two or more consecutive quarters of negative GDP growth. This implies that an *expansion* is two or more consecutive quarters of positive GDP growth. The *peak of an expansion* is the point in time at which the level of GDP reaches its maximum before it starts to decline. Thus, the peak of an expansion dates the beginning of a recession. Likewise, the *trough of a recession* is the point in time at which GDP falls to its lowest level before it begins to rise again, meaning that a trough dates the beginning of an expansion. Figure 2.1 graphs real GDP growth rates in the United States between 1948 and 2002 and indicates the dates of peaks (beginnings of recessions) and troughs (ends of recessions).

Table 2.1 provides a complete list of business cycles (measured from peak to peak) in the United States since dating began in 1854. Looking at recent business cycle episodes, there have been ten postwar recessions in the United States. The most recent recession began in April of 2001 and ended in November of that same year. Before this, the United States experienced the longest expansion ever recorded. This expansion lasted more than ten years, from March 1991 to April 2001.

Like any specific definition of a difficult concept, the NBER's definition of what constitutes a recession has been criticized along a number of lines. One problem with this definition is that a lag exists between getting data and making decisions. Output must be falling for at least six months before the NBER will declare a recession. This means that the economy is already at least half a year into a recession before it can be officially recognized as one by economists. This recognition might delay a policy response until it is too late to be effective.

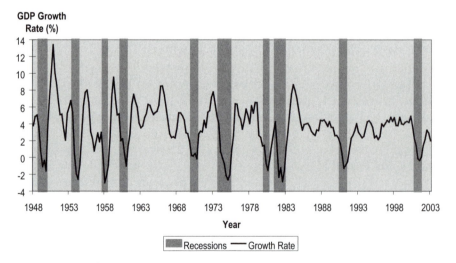

Figure 2.1 Real GDP Growth, Recessions Noted (chained 1996 dollars)

TABLE 2.1   Data on Timing of U.S. Business Cycles

| Trough | Peak | Duration (in months) of | | |
		Contraction	Expansion	Business Cycle
12/1854	06/1857		30	
12/1858	10/1860	18	22	40
06/1861	04/1865	8	46	54
12/1867	06/1869	32	18	50
12/1870	10/1873	18	34	52
03/1879	03/1882	65	36	101
05/1885	03/1887	38	22	60
04/1888	07/1890	13	27	40
05/1891	01/1893	10	20	30
06/1894	12/1895	17	18	35
06/1897	06/1899	18	24	42
12/1900	09/1902	18	21	39
08/1904	05/1907	23	33	56
06/1908	01/1910	13	19	32
01/1912	01/1913	24	12	36
12/1914	08/1918	23	44	67
03/1919	01/1920	7	10	17
07/1921	05/1923	18	22	40
07/1924	10/1926	14	27	41
11/1927	08/1929	13	21	34
03/1933	05/1937	43	50	93
06/1938	02/1945	13	80	93
10/1945	11/1948	8	37	45
10/1949	07/1953	11	45	56
05/1954	08/1957	10	39	49
04/1958	04/1960	8	24	32
02/1961	12/1969	10	106	116
11/1970	11/1973	11	36	47
03/1975	01/1980	16	58	74
07/1980	07/1981	6	12	18
11/1982	07/1990	16	92	108
03/1991	04/2001	8	120	128
04/2001	11/2001	8	—	—
		Averages		
1854-1991 (31 cycles)		18	35	53
1854-1919 (16 cycles)		22	27	49
1919-1945 (6 cycles)		18	35	53
1945-1991 (9 cycles)		11	50	61

Source: National Bureau of Economic Research, www.nber.org/cycles.html

Another criticism of this definition is that it ignores *growth recessions*, or periods of positive but below-average growth. The problem here is that a period of growth that is below *trend*, or the long-run average GDP growth rate, is generally regarded as a recession by the public but not technically considered a recession by economists.

A final problem with this definition is that it defines recessions in terms of quarters. Quarterly data averages out many monthly movements and may provide a misleading picture of the economy. A good example of this occurred during September 2001. Because of the economic disruptions caused by the terrorist attacks, output fell dramatically during September—enough to make output growth negative during the third quarter when it otherwise might not have been negative. Because output growth was also negative in the second quarter of 2001, a recession was officially declared by the NBER. However, output growth in the fourth quarter was positive and strong because a great deal of economic activity that did not occur in September was pushed into October and November. Thus, technically the recession ended as soon as it was declared, and it is not at all clear that GDP had actually been declining for six continuous months, only two consecutive quarters. On the other hand, it could also be hypothetically possible for GDP growth to be negative for six consecutive months but for no recession to be declared by the NBER. If these six months were in three different quarters, measured GDP growth might be negative during only one of these quarters, if output growth in the months before and after these six months was strong enough.

Despite these criticisms, these definitions of recessions, peaks, and troughs are the best that economists have to work with. Lags in getting and interpreting data are impossible to avoid given the difficulties in collecting economic data. Quarterly data is usually preferable to monthly data because monthly data is very costly to collect and its collection relies more heavily on estimation, which makes it less reliable. Defining a growth recession is more difficult than defining a recession using the NBER's definition. This is because the definition of a growth recession relies on measuring growth relative to its trend, and trend output growth is difficult to determine if the trend is not constant over time. As a result, the NBER's definitions of recessions, expansions, troughs, and peaks will be the working definitions used throughout this book.

There is no formal definition of a depression, though an old joke says that a recession is when your neighbor loses their job, a depression is when you lose your job. An informal definition of a *depression* is an economic contraction in which output falls by more than 10 percent. During the era for which we have reliable economic data, the only depression that has occurred in the United States was the Great Depression of the 1930s.

A few additional definitions are extremely useful in characterizing the qualitative relationships between macroeconomic variables over the business cycle. A variable is referred to as *procyclical* if it has a constant positive correlation with GDP, meaning it falls when GDP falls and rises when GDP rises. Some obvious examples of variables that are procyclical are consumption, investment, and employment. A variable is *countercyclical* if it has a constant negative correlation with GDP. Unemployment is an obvious example of a variable that is consistently countercyclical and rises when GDP falls. An *acyclical* variable is one that has no consistent correlation with changes in GDP.

Finally, economists are always looking for macroeconomic variables that can help predict the peaks and troughs of business cycles. A *leading indicator* is a variable that peaks (troughs) before GDP peaks (troughs). For obvious reasons, economists closely watch leading indicators when trying to forecast business cycles. A *lagging indicator* is a variable that peaks (troughs) after GDP peaks (troughs). A *coincident indicator* is one that peaks or troughs at the same time as GDP.

SIX BASIC BUSINESS CYCLE FACTS

What general properties and relationships can be gathered from studying business cycle data? While economists have collected and poured over an inordinate amount of information related to recessions and expansions over the years, six basic facts are crucial to understanding the fundamental properties of business cycles both in the United States and international.

Business cycles are not cyclical. The term *business cycle* is really a misnomer, because it implies that recessions and expansions follow a regular, predictable pattern. They do not. In fact, business cycles vary considerably in size and duration over time. Refer back to Table 2.1. The shortest recession in U.S. history was in 1980–1981 (though it was a very sharp recession) and lasted only 6 months. It was followed by the shortest expansion, which lasted only 12 months. The longest modern recession lasted 43 months, between 1933 and 1937, while the longest expansion ended in 2001 and lasted 121 months, or more than 10 years. Between the shortest and longest recessions and expansions other cycles have exhibited a wide variety of spacing and length. The length of one business cycle is not a reliable indicator of the length of the next business cycle.

Business cycles are not symmetrical. In the United States, expansions average 43 months, while recessions average only 14 months. Thus, expansions are about 3 times longer than recessions on average.

However, output changes tend to be much larger during recessions than they are during expansions.

These asymmetries between recessions and expansions hold internationally as well. Figure 2.2 and Figure 2.3 provide some summary data of business cycles across a small subset of developed countries. Looking at Figure 2.2, notice that across all of these countries expansions last considerably longer than recessions. There is a great deal of similarity across these countries in the length of their recessions. Excluding Spain and Germany, expansions also tend to last roughly the same amount of time across countries. Figure 2.3 presents percentage increases and decreases in industrial production across countries. Recessions tend to be characterized by larger changes in output than expansions. Thus, as a general rule across countries, recessions tend to be shorter but with sharper changes in GDP, while expansions tend to be longer but with more gradual changes in GDP.

Business cycles have not changed dramatically over time. Ten years ago, economists generally believed that business cycles had changed dramatically and were much shorter and less severe during the postwar period than in the prewar period. However, newer and better historical data has given economists a clearer picture of historical business cycles in the United States; this better data suggests that there has only been slight moderation in postwar recessions. A quick glance at the data averages reported at the bottom of Table 2.1 suggests that recessions are somewhat shorter but expansions are significantly longer in the post-

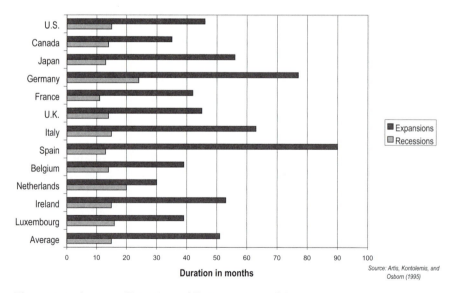

Figure 2.2 Average Duration of Expansions and Recessions

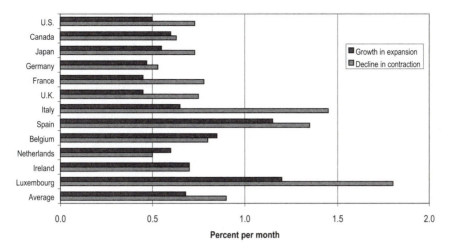

Figure 2.3 Monthly Percentage Increases and Decreases in Industrial Production during Business Cycles

war period than in the past. This means that recessions have been less frequent than they were in previous eras, though this result has been largely driven by two long expansions in the 1980s and 1990s. These issues and the research investigating them will be explored in more detail in Chapter 12, which discusses postwar business cycles in the United States.

The Great Depression and the World War II expansion dominate all other recessions and expansions. GDP fell by 50 percent between 1929 and 1932, while unemployment rose to a peak of 25 percent in 1933. The Great Depression dwarfs the next largest recession that took place during 1973–1975, in which GDP declined by 4.2 percent and unemployment rose to 9 percent. Likewise, the expansion that began in 1938 and continued throughout World War II was unparalleled, with GDP rising by 64 percent between 1941 and 1944. The explanation for this large expansion obviously has a lot to do with the huge increases in government purchases and the massive mobilization of resources that took place during the war. The explanation for the Great Depression is less apparent. Obviously, something unprecedented happened during the late 1920s and 1930s that must be explained in order to have a plausible theory of what causes recessions and depressions. The Great Depression will be discussed throughout this book and will be examined in detail in Chapter 11.

The components of GDP exhibit much different behaviors than GDP itself. The components of GDP are consumption, investment, government purchases, and net exports. Investment and durable consumption are highly volatile and change more than output over the business cycle, while nondurable consumption, government purchases, and net exports are stable and change much less than output over the business cycle.

Table 2.2 presents the components of GDP and their contribution to both average GDP growth and to changes in GDP during recessions. Consumption includes nondurables (like food and clothing), durables (like appliances and automobiles), and services. Both nondurables and services contribute less to falls in GDP than they do to the level of GDP, meaning that they are considerably more stable than GDP as a whole and, in fact, are only mildly procyclical. Durables, however, are significantly more volatile than GDP as a whole, strongly procyclical, and a coincident indicator of peaks and troughs in GDP.

Investment as a whole is consistently procyclical, a leading indicator of changes in GDP, and about 3.5 times more volatile than GDP. Investment includes new residential construction, fixed nonresidential investment (investments made by firms), and changes in inventories. Looking at Table 2.2, we see that each of the components of investment is more volatile than GDP, together accounting for more than 70 percent of the changes in GDP during recessions. Especially important are inventories, which account for less than 1 percent of GDP but 40 percent of the changes in GDP during recessions. Inventories are also a leading indicator of business cycle turning points. Investment clearly plays a crucial role in initiating and propagating business cycles. As a result,

TABLE 2.2   Behavior of the Components of GDP

Component of GDP	Average share in GDP	Average share of fall in GDP during recessions
Consumption		
Durables	8.4%	15.6%
Nondurables	25.8	11.2
Services	29.5	9.1
Investment		
New residential	4.7	20.9
Fixed nonresidential	10.7	11.7
Changes in inventories	0.7	40.6
Net exports	-0.4	-12.3
Government purchases	20.6	3.3

Source: Romer (2001)

investment has also played an integral part in many of the theories of business cycle behavior.

Government purchases include government acquisitions of goods and services but ignore transfer payment programs such as social security and welfare. Government purchases are roughly acyclical and not very volatile.

Finally, net exports are the difference between exports and imports. Net exports are actually a negative share of GDP because the United States has consistently run trade deficits since the mid-1980s. Net exports are slightly countercyclical, meaning that net exports tend to rise during recessions and offset some of the falls in output. However, net exports are not a reliable indicator of peaks and troughs in GDP.

Business cycles are associated with big changes in the labor market. Unemployment is strongly countercyclical, and changes in employment are much larger during recessions than the changes in other inputs into production. Over the long run, increases in the capital stock account for roughly one-third of trend per capita GDP growth, while increases in productivity account for the other two-thirds. Changes in employment account for essentially none of the increases in trend per capita GDP (this makes sense if employment and the population grow at roughly the same rate, which they do). However, during business cycles (times when output is growing at a rate different than trend), the story is exactly the opposite. The capital stock changes very little over business cycles because it is largely fixed in the short run, meaning it contributes little to changes in output over the business cycle. Changes in employment, on the other hand, account for two-thirds of the cyclical changes in per capita GDP while changes in productivity account for one-third of cyclical changes. In other words, during recessions and expansions, changes in employment appear to be driving a large portion of the changes in output. This seems to suggest that any plausible theory of business cycles has to give a prominent role to the cyclical behavior of the labor market.

THE CYCLICAL BEHAVIOR OF OTHER IMPORTANT MACROECONOMIC VARIABLES

As mentioned earlier, economists are always looking for clues to help them forecast the future and to help them evaluate competing models of business cycle behavior. A few of the most closely followed macroeconomic variables are briefly described here.

Unemployment. A worker is classified as being unemployed if he/she is currently without work and has been actively looking for work during the previous four weeks. Total unemployment is strongly countercyclical and is a lagging indicator of both peaks and troughs. Total unemployment lags peaks in output because when the economy first slows down, some workers are still finding jobs (even as new layoffs may be increasing). When the economy begins to improve, the last inputs to be re-added by firms are more workers, so unemployment also lags troughs.

Economists also closely follow two other variables related to unemployment. The first is the duration of unemployment, which is countercyclical and a lagging indicator of peaks and troughs. The second is initial unemployment claims, which are the number of new claims for unemployment insurance. Initial unemployment claims are more sensitive to changes in the business cycle than total unemployment. Unlike total unemployment, which lags peaks and troughs because of lags in the hiring process, initial unemployment claims are a leading indicator because firms anticipate changes in economic conditions and increase layoffs before production falls and decrease layoffs before conditions improve.

Inflation. There are two commonly used measures of inflation. The *GDP deflator* measures changes in the price of all goods produced within U.S. borders and included in GDP. Inflation as measured by the GDP deflator is weakly procyclical, falling during only 5 of the last 10 recessions. It lags peaks and troughs primarily because it includes investment goods and government purchases, the prices of which are slow to respond to changes in economic conditions.

The *consumer price index* (CPI) measures changes in the prices of consumer goods. Like the GDP deflator, it is only mildly procyclical, falling during 6 of the last 10 recessions. Unlike the GDP deflator, changes in the CPI are roughly coincident with business cycle turning points because consumer prices are more sensitive to changes in prevalent market conditions.

It is important to note that while both measures of inflation have been mildly procyclical on average, they have exhibited periods of countercyclical behavior as well. The variability of the cyclical behavior of inflation is a puzzle that economists need to explain.

Real wages. Real wages (*real* meaning adjusted for changes in inflation) do not behave consistently over business cycles, although changes in the real wage do consistently lag behind peaks and troughs in GDP. During the recessions of the 1970s, real wages were procyclical. During the Great Depression, real wages were countercyclical. If measured over the entire length of U.S. data that is available, however, real wages are either acyclical or mildly procyclical.

As mentioned earlier, the volatility of unemployment indicates that the labor market plays a critical role in business cycles. As a result, the behavior of real wages is an integral component of many of the theories examined in this book. Differences in how each of these models views the labor market provide a useful criterion by which to compare and contrast alternate explanations of business cycles. This puzzle regarding the inconsistent behavior of real wages is one that will be referred to repeatedly throughout our discussions.

Interest rates. Both short-term and long-term interest rates are procyclical. However, there are a myriad of interest rates that can be tracked, and some are more reliable predictors of business cycles than others. One of the most reliable is the 3-month Treasury Bill rate, which has fallen during 9 of the 10 postwar recessions. Even though many long-term interest rates are less reliable indicators of business cycles than short-term rates, they probably have a more direct effect on investment decisions and economic activity. In general, short-term and long-term interest rates are lagging indicators of business cycle turning points because inflation is a key determinant of the level of interest rates, which tends to lag business cycle fluctuations.

Capacity utilization. Capacity utilization is the employment rate of capital. For obvious reasons, capacity utilization is procyclical. Its downturns tend to lead peaks because firms typically purchase large amounts of capital during expansions and this capital typically comes on line before a downturn, reducing capacity utilization. On the other hand, capacity utilization lags troughs because firms first reduce inventories and delay new investment projects for as long as possible during downturns.

Output per hour (productivity). Increasing productivity is the primary way that economies improve the standards of living of its citizens over the long run. However, in the short run, the relationship between GDP and productivity is much less clear. Productivity is procyclical, falling during 9 of the last 10 recessions, and it does lead peaks and troughs in the business cycle. However, the reasons for this remain unclear. Do new technologies drive expansions and technological inefficiencies drive recessions? Or could it simply be that firms ask their employees and their capital to work harder during expansions because firms are pushing their capacity constraints, and then allow their workers and capital some slack during recessions because these same constraints are less pressing?

Consumer confidence. The most popular measure of consumer expectations is based on household survey data collected by the University of Michigan's Survey Research Center. An index is generated based on household responses to questions regarding (1) the family's economic prospects over the next 12 months, (2) the United States' economic prospects over the next 12 months, and (3) the United States' economic prospects over the next 5 years. This Consumer Confidence Index is strongly procyclical and a leading economic indicator. However, it is much more volatile than GDP, meaning that the Consumer Confidence Index often provides false signals of business cycle turning points.

Expectations play a key role in many of the explanations of business cycles discussed later in the book because of their importance in influencing investment and consumption decisions. As a result, measures of consumer confidence are very closely watched by economic forecasters.

Stock prices. One of the most visible and closely followed macroeconomic series, stock prices are procyclical and a leading economic indicator of peaks and troughs. The same holds true for two other variables that are key determinants of stock prices: consumer expectations and corporate profits. The problem with using the stock market to predict business cycles is that stock prices are much more volatile than GDP. Stock prices cannot be relied on exclusively when forecasting because of the high probability of false signals.

The money supply. M2 is the most commonly used definition of the money supply and is the summation of currency, checkable deposits, savings deposits, money market mutual funds, small certificates of deposit, and traveler's checks. M2 is strongly procyclical and a leading indicator of peaks and troughs in the business cycle. Federal Reserve policy largely, but not completely, determines the level of M2. The critical issue is this: Do changes in the money supply lead to changes in output, or do changes in output cause the money supply to change in ways that the Fed cannot control? These questions are an important topic for later discussion.

CONCLUSIONS

The empirics of business cycles have not been completely covered in this chapter, but that would be impossible to do. New theories often provide economists with new ideas about things to look for in their economic data. Albert Einstein makes this interaction between theory and empirics quite clear: "It is quite wrong to try founding a theory on observable magnitudes alone. . . . It is the theory which decides what we can observe" (Heisenberg 1971).

The goal for economists interested in why business cycles exist and what can be done about them is straightforward: Find a theory that fits the empirical facts of business cycles as they are understood. While this goal is clear, how to achieve it has not been. A number of different models developed over the past 250 years have attempted to explain the nature and causes of recessions and depressions. Many of these models generate predictions that are consistent with much (though never all) of this economic data. How do we evaluate these competing models? Is a model's ability to match economic data the only measure of its worth? Or do things like logical structure and consistency with microeconomic theory matter just as much? These are just some of the many questions that are dealt with when the macroeconomic theory of business cycles and forecasting is reviewed in the next section.

SUGGESTED READINGS

National Economic Trends, International Economic Trends, and Monetary Trends: These publications are made available by the St. Louis Federal Reserve. They contain a wide variety of current macroeconomic data as well as economic analysis of the current state of the economy. They are available by subscription through the mail or found on the Internet at http://research.stlouisfed.org/publications.

Part II

The Macroeconomic Theory of Business Cycles and Forecasting

3

Early Business Cycle Theories

INTRODUCTION

Before the Great Depression, a number of economic theories laid out the thoughts of early economists about the nature of economic fluctuations. Examining these theories is the first step in evaluating how much progress has been made in our understanding of recessions and depressions. These early theories are very simple, to the point that they are somewhat naive about the way that macroeconomies work as each focuses on a single explanation of what causes business cycles. However, these simple models are interesting not only for what they cannot explain about business cycles but also because of the things they point to as potentially important sources of fluctuations. Many of these early models provided insights that were to be more fully developed in future, more comprehensive business cycle models.

The Classical model is the most important of these early theories and is the primary focus of discussion in this chapter. The Classical model attempts to explain macroeconomic business cycles using microeconomic principles. Its clear, simple insights into the causes of business cycles are still the basis of widely held beliefs among many modern economists. However, the Classical model of business cycles has also been the subject of decades of criticism. As a result, it serves as a useful base model for comparing different modern models of business cycles.

EARLY AGRICULTURAL THEORIES

During times when agriculture was a much more important industry than it is today, economists focused on the cyclical nature of agricultural production to explain recessions and expansions. One of the earliest of these models is the Sunspot theory developed by W. S. Jevons (1884). This theory proposed that low sunspot activity on the surface of the sun was bad for plant growth and agricultural output (which is questionable botany as well as questionable economics). As a result, Jevons believed that the cyclical behavior of economies closely followed the cyclical behavior of sunspot activity. Jevons presented historical evidence that business cycles lasted approximately 10.43 years from peak to peak, while sunspot cycles lasted 10.45 years. In his mind, this correlation proved his theory. However, new evidence was later presented that sunspot cycles in fact lasted 11 years. Jevons tried to salvage his theory by saying that because his theory was so well known by farmers, if farmers expected sunspot activity to change then they would change their behavior accordingly, breaking the link between actual sunspot activity and economic activity. While the sunspot theory is today discredited, Jevon's hypothesis that expectations can be self-fulfilling, meaning that falling expectations can lead to falling output without any real changes in the economy, anticipates later macroeconomic theories that focus on the importance of expectations and how these expectations might affect behavior.

Another influential agricultural theory was the Cobweb theory, first presented by Mordecai Ezekial (1938). This theory attempted to explain how shocks to supply and demand could lead to cyclical fluctuations in prices and output. There are two critical assumptions in the Cobweb theory. First, goods are perishable, so that farmers have to accept the current price and cannot store their output until the next period. Second, the amount farmers plant in the spring is based on what the price was last fall. This means that expectations are backward looking, not forward looking.

Figure 3.1 presents the results of a temporary negative supply shock, in which supply falls from S_1 to S_2 in the fall but returns to S_1 before the spring planting. In the spring, farmers make their planting decisions based on the higher price that existed in the previous fall, P_2, continuing until the upcoming fall. However, because supply has returned to its previous level, farmers find that they have planted too much, based on their assumption that the price would still be P_2 and there is an excess supply. In order to sell all of the crops that are available in the fall, Q_2, farmers must reduce their price to P_3 in order to clear the market. Next spring, farmers plant based on a price of P_3 and produce an amount equal to Q_3 to sell in the fall. Of course, now there is a shortage of crops because P_3 is below the equilibrium price. As a result, the price rises to P_4 in order to clear the market. In the third spring, farmers plant based on the belief that the price will continue to be P_4, and the process continues. Notice that prices and quantities will eventually cycle to-

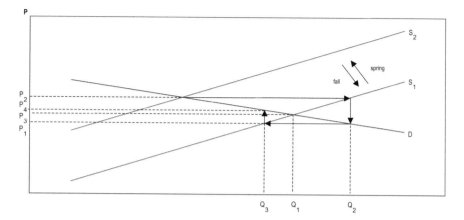

Figure 3.1 Supply and Demand in the Cobweb Theory after a Temporary Fall in Supply

wards the equilibrium price and quantity, but this process takes a long time. In addition, this process is very costly because of the instability created as the market fluctuates between excess supply and excess demand.

The Cobweb theory is not a useful explanation of the behavior of modern markets because of the two questionable assumptions on which it is based. First, most goods in modern economies, even agricultural goods, can be stored. If goods can be stored, producers do not necessarily have to accept the current price, which would smooth cyclical movements in prices and quantities. More important, producers are not nearly as naive as the Cobweb theory assumes. Do individuals really form their expectations of the future based only on what has happened in the past? Or are they forward looking, attempting to anticipate future market conditions? If they are forward looking, equilibrium will be restored much more quickly. Once again the Cobweb theory highlights the important role of expectations in business cycles, which plays an important role in all of the modern macroeconomic theories.

Thomas Malthus (1798) developed one of the best-known models of economic cycles, so famous in fact that the moniker "the dismal science" has stuck with the discipline of economics because of Malthus's discouraging predictions about the future. Malthus observed that in an agricultural society such as the one that existed in Great Britain during the late 1700s, capital was primarily land, and land in an island country is fixed in quantity. In addition, given that agricultural production techniques had largely remained the same over the previous century, Malthus assumed that technological knowledge would also be constant in the future. As a result, Malthus believed that as the population in Britain rose, diminishing returns would quickly set in as the capital-to-labor ratio fell. Over time this would lead to chronic underproduction, falling standards of living, and eventually mass poverty and starvation. However, starvation does have its benefits, namely, that the capital-to-labor ratio would rise, increasing per capita income. As income rose, standards of living and general health would improve. Healthy people have more babies, and the whole process would begin again.

Of course, the problem with Malthus's analysis is that capital and technology are not fixed. Malthus never understood that an industrial revolution was taking place at the time he was writing. As a result, he did not anticipate the extent of improvements in technology and the invention of new forms of capital that have taken place over the last 200 years. Through this omission, however, Malthus's model highlighted the importance of technological change not only in stabilizing economic growth but also in potentially driving business cycles. This latter possibility is the basis of Real Business Cycle models, which are discussed in Chapter 7.

EARLY MONETARY THEORIES

Before the Great Depression, most economies in the world were on the *gold standard*. The gold standard was an international monetary system that required the amount of paper currency in circulation within each country to be backed by a fixed amount of gold. As a result, a country's gold holdings would place an upper limit on the quantity of money supplied within that country. One of the important implications of the gold standard was that the money supply of a country would fluctuate with its trade balance. A country that was running a trade deficit would experience gold outflows, which would eventually necessitate lowering the money supply. On the other hand, a country that was running a trade surplus would see its gold holdings rise and its money supply increase.

Robert Hawtrey (1913) hypothesized that fluctuations in the money supply caused by changes in the trade balance were the cause of business cycles. A country that was running a trade surplus would see its money supply increase. This increased the supply of credit within an economy, increasing investment and output. However, higher output would increase the demand for imports and reduce the trade balance. Eventually, the country would begin to run a trade deficit and see its money supply contract, and the whole cyclical process would take place once again but this time in reverse. Hawtrey's model of monetary business cycles is one in which business cycles are *endogenous*, or internally self-generating. Business cycles are not the result of external, or *exogenous*, shocks to the economy. Hawtrey's solution to preventing these cyclical fluctuations was simple: Abandon the gold standard for *fiat money*, or money that is not backed by a commodity, so that its supply could be stabilized.

The obvious problem with Hawtrey's theory is that business cycles have not ended since modern economies have adopted fiat money. However, by being one of the first to propose that changes in the money supply drive cyclical fluctuations, Hawtrey laid the ground work for modern, more fully developed business cycle models in which monetary policy plays a critical role, such as the Keynesian model (Chapter 4) and particularly the Monetarist model (Chapter 5).

UNDERCONSUMPTION THEORIES

Underconsumptionist economists such as John Hobson (1922) worried that growth in the production of goods within an economy would outpace the growth rate of consumption. Without adequate aggregate demand to absorb these goods, chronic overproduction would exist, which would threaten future economic prosperity and create business cycles.

Why would consumption growth be unable to keep pace with production growth? Hobson's Underconsumption model focused on the fact that households save a larger share of their income as their income rises, meaning that the *average propensity to consume* (consumption divided by income) is countercyclical. As aggregate income in a country increases, the average propensity to consume falls and the gap between aggregate income and total consumption increases. For a while, this gap can be filled with higher levels of investment. However, over time, this increased investment will only aggravate the excess supply of goods and reduce the average propensity to consume even further. Increasingly large excess supplies of goods will eventually necessitate cuts in production and a decrease in aggregate income. However, as aggregate income falls the average propensity to consume rises and the problem of excess supply disappears. This will ultimately lead to an increase in aggregate income and the whole process will start all over again. Thus, like early monetary theories, in Underconsumption models business cycles are endogenous and not initiated by external shocks.

A number of policy solutions were offered by the Underconsumptionists, each aimed at preventing the average propensity to consume from falling over time. One was to redistribute income from the rich to the poor, who have higher propensities to consume. Another was to increase the amount of government purchases within an economy, which would increase the average propensity to consume for the public and private sectors as a whole. These Underconsumption theories were very influential in the development of Keynesian economics (Chapter 4), which also focuses on aggregate demand shortfalls as the primary cause of business cycles. In addition, the fiscal policy solutions proposed by Underconsumptionists were developed more fully in the Keynesian model, resulting in a more complete theory of the proper role of government in stabilizing business cycles.

PROFIT MARGIN THEORIES

A *profit margin* is simply the price minus the average cost of the good. Wesley Mitchell (1927) argued that profit margins are strongly procyclical in imperfectly competitive markets because costs fall during expansions. This happens for a number of reasons. First, firms are able to reduce their inventories, reducing costs. Second, input cartels tend to fall apart during recessions, so the beginning of expansions should be characterized by lower input prices. Finally, larger output means that *economies of scale* can be exploited. Economies of scale refer to conditions when the average cost of production of a good falls as the quantity of the good produced rises. Economies of scale tend to exist in industries with large fixed costs because higher production allows these fixed costs to be spread out over more units, reducing average cost.

Procyclical movements in the profit margin feed expansions and magnify contractions. During good times, rising profit margins increase expected profits and encourage firms to undertake investment projects. However, these projects do not immediately increase the capital stock and capacity. In the meantime, as the economy approaches full capacity, costs begin to rise and profit margins begin to fall. Falling profit margins reduce expected profits and reduce a firm's likelihood of undertaking new investment projects, eventually turning an expansion into a contraction. Once again, expectations play an important role in this model, as they do in all modern business cycle theories. In addition, the recognition in this Profit Margin theory that markets are not perfectly competitive and that imperfect competition may play an important role in explaining business cycles is a crucial component of Keynesian (Chapter 4) and New Keynesian (Chapter 8) economics.

EARLY INVESTMENT THEORIES

For as long as economists have known that aggregate output fluctuates in cycles, economists have also understood that investment is extremely volatile and an important source of economic instability. Investment volatility played an important, but secondary, role in many of the early theories already discussed. In other early theories, investment plays a more central role. Early investment theories of business cycles fall into roughly three categories. Some of these models, such as Hawtrey (discussed previously) and Knut Wicksell (1936), focused on unstable fluctuations in the money supply, which creates changes in investment. In Wicksell's model, changes in the money supply push interest rates either above or below the level required for savings to equal investment. As a result, investment and output fluctuate with changes in the supply of money and bank credit.

A second category of early investment theories, also developed by Wicksell, focused on overinvestment that results from the investment booms and busts that follow the development of new technologies. This theme is later reexamined in more detail by Long Wave theories of business cycles, which are discussed in the next section.

Finally, other early investment theories focused on spending multipliers associated with investment, such as John Clark (1917). Often referred to as Accelerator models, these models center on the possibility that higher investment increases aggregate output, which in turn increases spending, which in turn leads to additional increases in investment and output. Thus, small initial changes in investment can lead to large changes in aggregate output. While these models do not explain why investment would initially change, they do explain why changes in investment can lead to very large changes in output. These Accelerator models and the possibility of spending multipliers, associated not only with investment but also with exogenous changes in consumption and government purchases, were later to become crucial components of the Keynesian model.

LONG WAVE THEORIES

Do economies exhibit extended periods of sustained expansion and contraction? Nikolai Kondratieff (1935) argued from an empirical perspective that prices, interest rates, wages, production, investment, and consumption all fluctuated in short waves and in long waves. Kondratieff thought that economists, by focusing solely on these smaller cycles around an assumed constant trend, were missing the bigger picture, which was that the long-term trend itself was cyclical. Kondratieff identified three long waves using historical data from the mid-1700s to the early 1900s. The first wave expanded between 1780 and 1815 and contracted between 1815 and 1843. The second wave expanded between 1843 and 1875 and contracted between 1875 and 1887. Finally, the third wave expanded between 1893 and 1920 and contracted from 1920 on until 1935, when Kondratieff published his work.

Why might these long waves exist, and what is driving them? Joseph Schumpeter (1939) provided the first and most persuasive explanation of these long wave cycles: technological innovation and creative destruction. Schumpeter argued that technology growth is not constant but comes about as the result of big ideas that are developed sporadically within different industries. Initially, these new technologies are not unambiguously good for economic growth, because new technologies replace old technologies that have already been fully integrated into an economy. During the adoption phase of a new technology, resources are diverted away from proven production processes to unproven processes that may not yet be as efficient or reliable. In addition, workers may not be trained to use new technologies efficiently when they are first introduced, reducing overall productivity. Finally, new technologies make much of the existing capital stock obsolete, effectively reducing the size of the capital stock. This is the basis of Schumpeter's theory of creative destruction, where new technologies initially reduce economic growth and can lead to economic contractions or slowdowns.

As time goes on, innovation begins, as firms and workers learn to work with this new technology in more productive ways. In addition, new capital will have had time to be built. At this point, productivity and aggregate output growth begin to increase. However, this adoption phase can take a very long time—time usually measured in terms of decades and not just in terms of months.

Unfortunately, the growth booms associated with new technologies do not last forever. Once this new technology is fully integrated into the economy, initial growth will be dramatic. Growth will eventually slow as the productivity benefits of the new technology are exhausted. Without a new technological advance, productivity growth and output growth will eventually decline to zero and the economy will experience an extended slowdown. When another new technology is discovered, this creative destruction process will take place and another long wave will begin.

Table 3.1 presents the dates of these long waves and the technological developments hypothesized to be driving these long cycles. Our current wave (the fifth) is believed to be driven by information technology, including things such as better communications technology, the Internet, faster computers, and innovations in software that have broadened the productive use of computers. Notice that each of these waves has gotten progressively shorter over time. The most likely explanation is that firms and workers have gotten more adept at adopting new technologies more quickly. While this means that new technologies are more likely to have a more immediate positive impact on output growth, the downside of quicker adoption is that the productivity benefits from

TABLE 3.1   Schumpeter's Long Waves

Wave	Length	Innovations
First Wave	1775-1835 (60 years)	Water power, Textiles, Iron
Second Wave	1835-1890 (55 years)	Steam, Rail, Steel
Third Wave	1890-1940 (50 years)	Electricity, Chemicals, Internal-combustion engine
Fourth Wave	1940-1990 (40 years)	Petrochemicals, Electronics, Aviation
Fifth Wave	1990-2020 (30 years)	Digital Networks, Software, New media

new technologies are exhausted much more quickly than before. This makes it important that new technologies are regularly developed in order to sustain high rates of growth.

Many economists are skeptical of Schumpeter's long wave hypothesis. These long waves are very difficult to identify empirically. How do you distinguish between a long wave and a permanent change in the trend rate of growth within an economy? How do you separate a downward movement on a long wave from a few recessions taking place coincidentally within a short interval of time? And what is causing the short cycles taking place within these long waves? These are important questions that Schumpeter and his followers have not adequately answered. However, Schumpeter's ideas continue to provoke a great deal of interest among modern economists. This is particularly true among the advocates of Real Business Cycle models (Chapter 7), which focus on changes in technology and productivity as the primary determinant of business cycle fluctuations.

THE CLASSICAL MODEL

The cornerstone concepts of the Classical model were laid out in the first book to treat economics as a distinct field of study, Adam Smith's (1776) *An Inquiry into the Nature and Causes of the Wealth of Nations*. It was further refined by many of the founding fathers of economics such as David Ricardo, Jean-Baptiste Say, and John Stuart Mill. The Classical model is the most fully developed and influential of the early business cycle theories.

The Assumptions of the Classical Model

The Classical model is founded upon three crucial assumptions.

1. *Perfect competition exists in all markets.* This means that all firms and consumers are price takers, wages and prices are perfectly flexible,

perfect information exists about economic conditions, and markets always clear so that excess demand or excess supply cannot persist.
2. *Real values, not nominal values, are used when making decisions.* In other words, money illusion does not exist, and agents adjust all nominal variables by changes in the price level before they act.
3. *The economy is composed of representative agents, or individuals that all have the same preferences and act alike in every way.* When combined with the assumption of perfect competition, the assumption of representational agents means that macroeconomic behavior becomes a simple summation of average microeconomic behavior. In other words, the Classical model does not make any real distinction between macroeconomic and microeconomic behavior.

Output Determination and the Labor Market in the Classical Model

In the Classical model, capital and labor are combined, using a production function to produce aggregate output. Let Y denote real aggregate output, L denote total labor employed, and K denote the total capital stock. The production function can then be written as follows:

$$Y = F(L,K) \tag{3.1}$$

One of the important properties of the classical production function is that each input is subject to *diminishing marginal returns*. Diminishing marginal returns refers to the property that if the quantity of one of the inputs in production is fixed, the additional units of output produced by increasing the other input will get smaller as the quantity of that input rises. In other words, the *marginal product of labor* (the change in output from a change in labor, denoted as MP_L) falls as the quantity of labor rises. Diminishing marginal returns is one of the cornerstone concepts in economics because it implies that a firm's ability to increase output is limited unless it can increase all of the inputs to production.

Diminishing marginal returns play an important role in the Classical labor market. The equilibrium real wage (denoted as $\frac{W}{P}$) in the Classical model is determined by the supply and demand for labor. The demand for labor is determined by firms, which hire labor until the marginal benefit of an additional unit of labor, or the marginal product, is equal to the marginal cost of an additional unit of labor, or the real wage. Diminishing returns imply that the marginal product of labor falls as the quantity of labor rises. Thus, firms will only hire more workers (and accept a lower marginal product) at a lower real wage, meaning that the demand curve for labor must slope downward.

Regarding labor supply, a change in the real wage has two effects. The first is the substitution effect, in which a higher real wage induces more workers to enter the workforce or work longer hours. The second is the wealth effect, in which a higher real wage increases wealth and reduces the incentive to work. The Classical model assumes that the substitution effect of an increase in the real wage is larger than the wealth effect, so that a higher real wage increases labor supply and the labor supply curve is upward sloping.

In equilibrium, real wages adjust in the Classical model so that the quantity demanded of labor equals the quantity supplied. Notice that only the things that affect the quantity of labor, the quantity of capital, or the production function (i.e., things that shift the labor supply or labor demand curves) will affect the level of aggregate output. Thus, changes in output in the Classical model must be driven by changes in these three factors, each of which influences the aggregate supply of goods produced within an economy.

Factors that influence the quantity of labor. Immigration and population growth are two obvious determinants of the quantity of labor supplied within an economy. Public policy is also an important influence on labor supply and labor demand because it can play a role in shaping individuals' incentives to work. For example, income taxes on workers reduce the supply of labor, while taxes on payrolls reduce the demand for labor. Likewise, government regulations that place costly restrictions or requirements on firms (such as health and safety requirements) can also reduce labor demand and the quantity of labor.

Factors that influence the quantity of capital. Anything that encourages firms to invest in capital will increase aggregate output, while anything that discourages investment will decrease aggregate output. Once again, tax policy and government regulations play an important role in shaping the incentives to invest. Public policy also plays a critical role in determining how much households save. Tax policies that favor consumption as opposed to saving (such as an income-based tax system instead of a consumption-based tax system) will reduce the total amount of savings and the quantity of funds available for investment, reducing the quantity of capital. Finally, the discovery of natural resources will increase aggregate output, while wars or natural disasters that destroy capital will obviously reduce aggregate output.

Factors that influence technology. New technologies change the production function of firms, allowing firms to produce more output using the same amount of capital and labor. In addition, new technologies provide firms with incentives to hire more labor and more capital. Anything that improves the incentives to produce and invest in new technologies will eventually increase output growth. For example, the provision of tax incentives and funding for research and development projects, the granting of patent protection, and the provision of educational opportunities are all examples of public policies that encourage new innovation. However, negative shocks to technology are also possible. For example, during the OPEC oil embargoes of the 1970s, higher oil prices made oil-intensive equipment and many oil-intensive technologies too expensive to use, significantly reducing productivity and aggregate output.

Aggregate Demand and Aggregate Supply in the Classical Model

The things that determine real output in the Classical model—labor, capital, and technology—are all factors that affect aggregate supply. Nominal variables, such as the price level, have no effect on these inputs and play no role in determining the level of real output, Y. As a result, there is no relationship between the price level and aggregate output on the supply side of the Classical model, meaning that aggregate supply is a vertical line. The position of the aggregate supply curve is determined by a country's stock of labor, capital, and technology.

What about aggregate demand in the Classical model? The Classical theory of aggregate demand is based on the Quantity Theory of Money Demand originally developed by the philosopher David Hume in the mid-1700s. In the Quantity Theory, money is needed in order to conduct transactions. This implies the following Quantity Theory equation:

$$MV = PY \tag{3.2}$$

P denotes the aggregate price level, so that PY is equal to nominal aggregate expenditure (or nominal aggregate output). M denotes the money supply, and V denotes the velocity of money, or the number of times a unit of money changes hands over a period of time. The intuition behind this equation is straightforward. If money is needed when conducting all trades, for the level of nominal expenditure (PY) to increase, either the supply of money (M) or the velocity of money (V) has to increase as well in order to support this higher volume of trade.

The Quantity Theory is not only a theory of money demand but also a theory of aggregate demand because it states that on the demand side of an economy, a negative relationship exists between the price level and the level of real output. The intuition behind this downward-sloping aggregate demand curve is as follows: holding money and velocity constant, a higher price level reduces the real value of money holdings, which in turn reduces real spending and output.

When these aggregate demand and aggregate supply curves are considered together, two important implications of the Classical model become evident. First, the role of aggregate demand in the Classical model is only to determine the price level. Aggregate demand has no influence on real aggregate output. It is aggregate supply in the Classical model that determines aggregate income and, as a result, aggregate expenditure within an economy. This classical principle that supply creates its own demand is often referred to as *Say's Law*.

Second, given that aggregate demand only influences the price level, changes in the money supply, which shift the position of the aggregate demand curve, only affect the price level. The classical principle that changes in the money supply only affect nominal variables (the price level, nominal wages, nominal output) but not real variables (real output, unemployment, labor, capital, technology) is often referred to as *money neutrality*. Thus, changes in the money supply cannot influence the things that really matter in the Classical model. One strength of the Quantity Theory of aggregate demand is that it provides a simple and accurate explanation for the close correlation that exists between average money growth and average inflation across all countries over long periods of time. Sustained money growth, and nothing else, drives sustained inflation.

Business Cycles in the Classical Model

Business cycles do not exist in the Classical model, at least not in the traditional sense of temporary deviations of output from a long-term trend. All changes in output in the Classical model are permanent and are caused by changes in aggregate supply. As a result, when output falls because of a decrease in aggregate supply, it will not return to its previous level unless something else changes to increase aggregate supply.

So what drives changes in aggregate supply, particularly decreases in aggregate supply that cause economic contractions? Classical economists focused on one primary culprit: government policy, particularly tax policy and government regulation. For example, consider the imposition of a tax on labor income, such as the payroll tax adopted in the United States. Figure 3.2 graphs the effects of this tax, which reduces labor supply, shifts the aggregate supply curve to the left, and decreases aggregate output. The effects of an increase in government labor regulations would also have a similar effect but would reduce the quantity of labor by decreasing labor demand. Figure 3.3 graphs the effects of a tax on savings (or investment). This tax reduces the capital stock, which lowers the marginal product of labor and labor demand. Because of these falls in labor and capital, aggregate supply shifts to the left and aggregate output decreases.

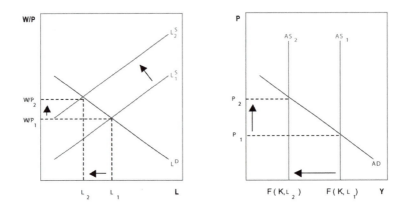

Figure 3.2 Effects of a Tax on Labor Income on the Labor Market and Aggregate Demand and Supply

Markets are perfectly competitive in the Classical model, and if left alone they will work efficiently and maximize output and welfare. As a result, the role of government in the Classical model is essentially a negative one. Anything the government does outside of the basic responsibilities of protecting property rights, providing for national defense, breaking up monopolies, and providing public education will lower efficiency and output. There is no positive role for the government to actively stabilize or manage an economy at the macroeconomic

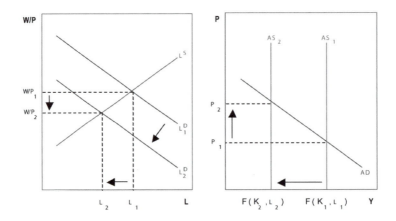

Figure 3.3 Effects of a Tax on Savings (or Investment) on the Labor Market and Aggregate Demand and Supply

level. Even monetary policy in the Classical model is irrelevant to real activity, and its excessive use will only lead to inflation. Hence, the governing philosophy advocated by the proponents of the Classical model is one of *laissez-faire*, or "hands-off." This governing philosophy dominated economic policy debates in the United States and much of Europe during most of the late 1700s and 1800s.

The Classical model has framed the debate on business cycles for most of the last 230 years because of its simple and intuitive explanation of the way that the economic world works. Throughout most of its history, however, even when it was the dominant business cycle theory, the Classical model has come under heavy criticism for a number of reasons. First, the irrelevance of aggregate demand is troubling to many economists. Is it true that things such as monetary policy or exogenous changes in consumption have no direct effect on real output? Second, the assumption of perfect competition has also been questioned. Are prices and wages really perfectly flexible? Do firms and households really have perfect information about existing conditions in the economy? Finally, the assertion that recessions are driven by falls in aggregate supply seemed implausible to many, especially following the events of the Great Depression. It became increasingly difficult to argue during the 1930s that Say's Law was plausible when excess supplies of goods existed throughout the world and unemployment in the United States stood at 25 percent.

CONCLUSIONS

The Great Depression completely changed the study of macroeconomics in general and business cycles in particular. The Great Depression focused the attention of economists on both the costs of output fluctuations and on the inadequacies of their existing theories. However, the more modern business cycle theories that were to be subsequently developed, such as the Keynesian model discussed in the next chapter, looked to these earlier models as a starting point of inquiry. By identifying many of the critical components of business cycles—such as changes in technology, expectations, investment volatility, spending multipliers, the money supply, public policy, the incentives to work and invest, and imperfect competition—these early theories laid the foundation on which much of modern macroeconomic theory has been built.

SUGGESTED READINGS

Robert L. Heilbroner, *The Worldly Philosophers* (1986): A lively and readable discussion of the lives and ideas of the most influential early economists, with chapters on Smith, Malthus, Mills, Schumpeter, and Keynes.

4

Keynes and
Keynesian Theory

INTRODUCTION

In 1999, twenty-seven prominent economists, historians, educators, political scientists, and philosophers were asked the following questions: (1) What books published this century altered the direction of our society? and (2) Which books will have the most impact on thought and action in the years ahead? The most cited book was John Maynard Keynes's *The General Theory of Employment, Interest, and Money* (1936), because of its broad influence on the study of economics and the rationale it provided for more active government involvement in the economy.

Keynes himself was exceptionally interesting for an economist. He was a classically trained pianist, a philosopher, and a member of the Bloomsbury literary group, which also included Lytton Strachey and Virginia Woolf, among others. During World War I, Keynes served in England's treasury department, working on international finance, and was hailed by many as the civil servant most responsible for winning World War I. Keynes's *The Economic Consequences of the Peace* (1920) was an amazingly prescient critique of the peace treaty that ended World War I, which imposed massive reparation payments on the Axis countries and, as Keynes predicted, eventually led to an economic collapse that fueled Hitler's rise to power in Germany. Keynes also worked on England's war financing during World War II. After World War II, Keynes was the primary architect of the Bretton Woods agreement that governed exchange rates and capital flows throughout the world for more than twenty years. Keynes was also a speculator on the foreign exchange market and became a self-made millionaire (although in the process of making his fortune he nearly went bankrupt twice). He was an accomplished mathematician and wrote a book on probability theory. In his spare time, Keynes studied economics and did groundbreaking research in many areas, including consumption theory, monetary theory, and investment theory. *The General Theory* represents the culmination of his work in economics and was Keynes's effort at explaining his complete theory of macroeconomics and the causes of recessions and depressions. Given its publication during the Great Depression, the timing of this book could not have been more auspicious.

Keynes's model was the first truly aggregate model in economics, meaning it was the first model to make a real distinction between macroeconomics and microeconomics. Keynes's model was also the first quasi-general equilibrium macroeconomic model, meaning that it looked at the interactions between the goods, labor, money, and bonds market at the same time. In this chapter, Keynes's principal insights into the nature of business cycles will be examined. In addition, Keynesian theory, which is the name given to subsequent versions of Keynes's theory developed by his disciples, will also be discussed, with a particular emphasis on Keynesian explanations of the Great Depression.

INVOLUNTARY UNEMPLOYMENT IN KEYNES'S MODEL

Keynes's opinion of the Classical theory of business cycles was, to put it politely, not high. Referring to the Classical model, Keynes said in the preface to *The General Theory* "It is astonishing what foolish things one can temporarily believe if one thinks too long alone, particularly in economics (along with the other moral sciences), where it is often impossible to bring one's ideas to a conclusive test either formal or experimental."

Keynes's model of business cycles begins with a critique of the classical labor market. Keynes argued that the classical view of a perfectly competitive labor market was at best naive, at worst insulting and counterproductive. In the perfectly competitive Classical labor market, a representative worker looks for a job in a market where the nominal wage is flexible and instantly adjusts so that the real wage equates labor supply and labor demand. One of the subtle implications of this labor market theory is that only *voluntary unemployment* exists in the Classical model, meaning that only those workers who are not willing to work at the current real wage will be unemployed, while everyone else who wants to work at the current wage can find a job. If this is not the case, nominal and real wages will adjust to make it so.

The problem with this classical view of the labor market is that Keynes believed it could not realistically explain two things that are observed in the real world. First, employment is very volatile. Classical economists explained this volatility by appealing to either changes in people's incentives to work or by changes in the marginal product of labor, but this seemed unreasonable to Keynes because these factors do not fluctuate on a month-to-month basis as employment does. Second, the Classical model has no explanation for *involuntary unemployment*, or the existence of workers who are willing to work at the current wage but are unable to find a job, even at a slightly lower wage. As a result, Classical economists were left to argue that the 25 percent unemployment rate that existed during the Great Depression was simply the result of many workers being unwilling to work for the current wage. Obviously, this was an insulting explanation to those who were standing in breadlines for hours every day.

In contrast, Keynes believed that imperfect competition better describes the way that markets operate. This is particularly true of the labor market, where each worker differs in skill level and, as a result, has to negotiate his or her wage individually. In such a decentralized labor market, workers are not worried about what the economy-wide real wage has to be in order to clear the labor market. Instead, workers worry about their own wages relative to what similar workers are receiving. As a result, there is no guarantee that the aggregate real wage will be at a level where labor demand equals labor supply.

For example, consider a period when the aggregate price level is declining. This will increase real wages because individual workers will be reluctant to reduce their nominal wage and restore labor market equilibrium unless other workers are also reducing their nominal wages as well. If all workers refuse to accept a nominal wage cut without observing others accepting a wage cut first, then wage cuts will take place very slowly. They will only take place after workers observe a significant amount of unemployment, which is the only threat that firms can use to make them amendable to wage cuts. This phenomenon is often called *coordination failure*. Because there is no mechanism for coordinating individual wage negotiations, the end result is nominal wage "stickiness" (as Keynes referred to it), which leads to higher real wages and involuntary unemployment during periods of falling prices. This process is illustrated in Figure 4.1. Involuntary unemployment exists because at the current real wage, which is higher than the market-clearing real wage as a result of the fall in the price level from P_1 to P_2, there are workers who are willing to work but cannot find employment.

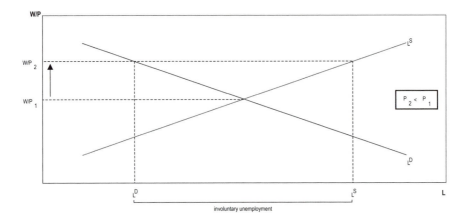

Figure 4.1 A Decrease in the Price Level in Keynes's Labor Market

AGGREGATE DEMAND AND AGGREGATE SUPPLY IN KEYNES'S MODEL

In a world with inflexible nominal wages, a decrease in the aggregate price level increases real wages, which forces firms to reduce employment and output. In other words, aggregate supply in the Keynesian model is upward sloping and not vertical as in the Classical model. The implication is that if labor markets are not perfectly competitive, aggregate demand can have real effects on output and employment. Consider Figure 4.2, in which there is a decrease in aggregate demand. Lower aggregate demand reduces output and the price level from P_1 to P_2, which increases real wages from $\frac{W}{P_1}$ to $\frac{W}{P_2}$. A higher real wage leads to an increase in unemployment. Thus, aggregate demand, not just aggregate supply, plays a role in determining the level of real output and unemployment in Keynes's model. Keynes's model rejects Say's Law, or the principle that aggregate supply determines aggregate demand. This is because nominal wages are not able to fully adjust and balance demand and supply in the labor market.

The simple Quantity Theory model of aggregate demand was satisfactory to classical economists because aggregate demand only influences the price level in the Classical model. However, in a theory where aggregate demand does matter, it requires more attention. Keynes rejected the simple Quantity Theory and argued that aggregate demand is composed of the demands for the individual components of GDP; in other words:

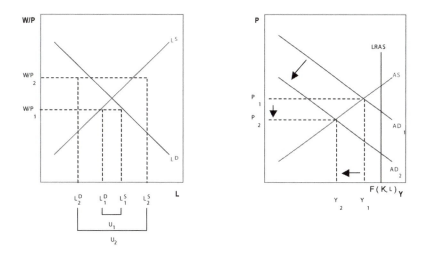

Figure 4.2   A Decrease in Aggregate Demand in Keynes's Model

$$Y^d = C^d + I^d + G^d + (X - M^d) \qquad (4.1)$$

Of these components of GDP, Keynes believed that that the demands for consumption, government purchases, and imports were stable. However, Keynes believed that investment demand is unstable and is the primary source of aggregate demand fluctuations.

The key to understanding investment and aggregate demand volatility is understanding the critical role of expectations. Keynes rejected the classical notion that higher savings automatically leads to higher investment through lower interest rates. Instead, Keynes believed that the levels of savings and the interest rate play only a small role in determining the attractiveness of investment projects. More important in any investment decision is the expectations of the future held by decision makers within firms. Because both the benefits and the costs of investment projects occur in the future, the decision to invest will necessarily depend in large part upon the business conditions that are expected to exist in the future. Expectations also influence stock prices. The stock market is an important source of funding for firms, and stock prices determine the cost of this funding. In Keynes's opinion, stock prices play at least as large a role in the decision to undertake investment projects as interest rates. As a result, through its influence on both the attractiveness of investment projects and on the value of stock prices, investment demand in an economy is primarily determined by expectations. An important implication is that there is no guarantee that expectations will be at a level that will generate enough investment to get the economy to its maximum rate of output. Instead, high savings when business confidence is low will lead to falling aggregate demand, high unemployment, and a recession.

Keynes believed that decision makers in firms and speculators in the stock market form their expectations based on only the flimsiest of conjectures, making these expectations extremely volatile. There are two primary reasons why Keynes believed expectations are erratic. First, in modern corporations it is the executives of firms who make investment decisions, not the stockholders who are the owners of the firm. Executives are much more likely to focus on creating short-term gains that help their immediate job prospects. This leads executives to overreact to both good and bad news. Second, Keynes believed that most executives and speculators are uninformed and instead make their economic decisions based on a herd mentality, meaning that if everyone else is buying, they will buy too. People implicitly count on the fact that there is always a "greater fool" to which any asset can be sold, even if that asset is exceptionally overvalued. This obviously leads both individuals and markets to overreact to new information. Keynes referred to the existence of volatile expectations that were in no way related to economic fundamentals as *animal spirits*. The primary repercussion of animal spirits is that the stock market, investment, and aggregate demand are all extremely unpredictable.

Keynes did agree with classical economists that there is a level of output that is consistent with the full employment of all resources. Keynes referred to this level of output as *potential output*. He also agreed with classical economists that potential output is determined by the total amount of capital, labor, and technology that is available within an economy. However, Keynes's most basic insight is that market mechanisms provide no guarantee that nominal wages, real wages, and expectations will adjust and move an economy towards its potential output; in other words, potential output is more of a theoretically achievable level of output than one that is guaranteed to occur in the long run. Shortfalls in aggregate demand can occur and an economy can get stuck at a point where the current level of production is well below potential output and full employment.

BUSINESS CYCLES IN KEYNES'S MODEL

Business cycles in Keynes's model begin with a change in expectations. Recessions begin with a decrease in business and speculator confidence that reduces stock prices and investment demand. This creates a *multiplier effect*, where lower investment spending reduces aggregate income, which in turn forces households to reduce their spending, which further decreases aggregate income. This process is similar to the one described by the Accelerator model in Chapter 2. As a result, even if there is only a small initial decrease in expectations and investment, the resulting decrease in aggregate demand can be very large. As aggregate demand falls, the price level also decreases, which increases real wages because of nominal wage stickiness. Higher real wages force firms to layoff workers and reduce production. Aggregate output falls below potential ouput. Figure 4.2 graphically illustrates a recession in Keynes's model.

How will this recession end? There are three possibilities. First, it is possible that expectations will rise. However, there is no guarantee that expectations will automatically rebound during a recession. In fact, it is quite possible that a recession will further depress business confidence and further magnify the size of the contraction in output. Second, Keynes believed that wages were not fixed, only sticky. If given enough time, workers will gradually reduce their nominal wage demands as they observe other similar workers taking nominal wage cuts. This will reduce real wages and move the economy back toward full employment. The problem with this approach, however, is that there are no assurances about how long this process will take. Given the difficulties associated with coordination failure, it could take a very long time for wages to fully adjust. In Keynes's opinion, policymakers cannot afford to wait patiently for this process to work itself out in the long run because, in his words, "in the long run we are all dead."

That leaves the third option, which is for the government to attempt to stabilize aggregate demand through the use of monetary or fiscal policy. If falling aggregate demand causes recessions, then enacting a public policy that increases aggregate demand in a timely manner would minimize both the size and the length of contractions. Higher aggregate demand would increase spending, increase the price level, reduce real wages, reduce involuntary unemployment, and possibly restore confidence and increase the stock market and investment.

Three policy options that would increase aggregate demand are available to the government. The first would be for the central bank to increase the money supply. Keynes believed that interest rates are the opportunity cost, or the price, of holding money. Just like any other commodity, a higher supply reduces price, so that a higher money supply would decrease interest rates. Lower interest rates would encourage investment directly and might also reduce the cost of borrowing by driving up stock prices. However, three reasons led Keynes to believe that during economic contractions monetary policy would be largely ineffective. First, as mentioned before, Keynes believed that investment is not very sensitive to changes in interest rates. As a result, changes in the money supply might not lead to any change in investment if expectations remain low. Second, households and banks tend to increase their holdings of money as a precautionary measure during bad times. This is especially true when interest rates are low because there is a low opportunity cost to holding money. Low interest rates also make holding bonds unattractive because interest rates are likely to increase, which will reduce the value of any bonds being held. As a result of these considerations, any change in the money supply during recessions is likely to be hoarded, leading to little change in interest rates, investment, and aggregate demand. Keynes referred to this as a *liquidity trap*. Finally, Keynes was skeptical about the ability of central bankers to manage monetary policy in a timely and proper manner. Given the ineptitude of central bankers during the Great Depression, as elaborated on in Chapter 10, it is not hard to understand Keynes's skepticism.

The second option available to the government for increasing aggregate demand during a recession is to cut taxes. However, when households face economic uncertainty, they tend to save the money from any tax cut and not spend it. In this case, tax cuts will not significantly increase spending and will not generate large spending multipliers.

The final option, and the one advocated by Keynes, is for the government to increase the level of its purchases of goods and services. What exactly these purchases are is of less importantance than the fact that more government spending will increase aggregate expenditure. Only slightly humorously, Keynes suggested the following:

> If the Treasury were to fill old bottles with bank notes, bury them at suitable depths in disused coal mines which are then filled up to the surface with the town rubbish, and leave it to private enterprise on well tried principles of *laissez-faire* to dig the notes up again . . . there would be no more unemployment and with the help of the repercussions, the real income of the community would probably become a good deal larger than it is. It would, indeed, be more sensible to build houses and the like; but if there are practical difficulties in the way of doing this, the above would be better than nothing. (1936)

In other words, only by increasing its purchases, whatever they are, will the government be sure that there will be additional spending within an economy that will initiate the multiplier process and increase aggregate demand enough to return the economy to full employment.

Keynes believed that as a country gets richer, business cycle fluctuations would become larger and take place more frequently. This prediction hinged on the belief that the average propensity to consume of an economy would fall as average income increased. On this point, Keynes shared beliefs similar to those from the Underconsumptionist model discussed in Chapter 3. As a country became richer, falling consumption demand would increase the amount of savings within the economy and also increase the level of investment needed to generate full employment. This higher share of investment in output would lead to increased output volatility. Thus, unlike the classical economists who worried that economies would not save enough, Keynes was concerned that developing countries would begin to save too much, increasing the frequency of economic cycles. In fact, Keynes believed that any policy effort to increase aggregate savings rates would largely be self-defeating because higher savings would reduce aggregate demand and output, in turn leading to a fall in savings. This concept is referred to as the *paradox of thrift*. The only way to avoid lower output and the destabilizing effects of higher savings rates is for public policy to encourage consumption by either increasing the percentage of GDP devoted to government purchases, by redistributing income from the rich to the poor, and/or by taxing savings.

KEYNESIAN ECONOMICS

Paul Samuelson (1964) said that "*The General Theory* caught most economists under the age of 35 with the unexpected virulence of a disease first attacking and decimating an isolated tribe of south sea islanders." Publication of *The General Theory* immediately set off an intense period of research surrounding different aspects of Keynes's model. One challenge facing these economists was that *The General Theory* is not an easy read. This is in part because Keynes largely resisted using equations and empirical data in his analysis, believing that economic processes were too complex to be described by simple equations and that empirical data was often unavailable and unreliable. As a result, Keynes was, either unintentionally or intentionally, vague on many of the finer points of his model. Consequently, even before Keynes had put his thoughts down onto paper, other economists had begun the process of trying to interpret exactly what they thought Keynes meant to say and to communicate it in a way that would be more accessible to non-economists.

The most prominent and influential of these Keynesian models that attempted to place Keynes's theory into a more understandable framework is John Hicks's (1937) IS-LM model. In this model, Hicks developed a quasi-general equilibrium model of aggregate demand that explains how changes in the money market (the LM curve) and changes in the goods and capital markets (the IS curve) influence aggregate demand. This Keynesian IS-LM model is consistent with many of the basic principles of Keynes's model, but with a few important differ-ences that generally separate Keynes's theory from Keynesian theory. First, in the Keynesian IS-LM model, both prices and nominal wages are fixed, not just sticky. Thus, the IS-LM model is best thought of as a model of the very short run before prices and nominal wages have had any chance to adjust. Fixed prices and wages imply that the aggregate supply curve is completely horizontal at the current price level and that changes in output are exactly equal to the size of the change in aggre-gate demand. In other words, the Keynesian IS-LM model is a model of aggregate demand only, and nothing else. Second, Keynesians believe that changes in aggregate demand can be driven by exogenous changes in consumption and not just by changes in investment. Keynesians recognize that the decisions of households to purchase durable con-sumption goods are very similar to the decisions made by firms to purchase investment goods. As a result, both investment and durable consumption are sensitive to changes in expectations, making them very volatile and an important source of fluctuations in aggregate demand.

The third important difference between Keynes and Keynesians has to do with the role of monetary policy in stabilizing output. As men-tioned previously, Keynes did not advocate the use of monetary policy to stabilize aggregate demand. This was in large part because he did not trust central bankers, who he felt enacted policies that played an im-portant role in magnifying the size of the Great Depression. As a result, Keynes spent relatively little time in *The General Theory* discussing monetary policy. On the other hand, Keynesians are very interested in monetary policy because they believe that postwar central bankers are in the perfect position to freely conduct stabilization policy, given their relative independence from political constraints, unlike fiscal policy, which has to be formulated within a complicated political process.

Keynesian interest in monetary policy was also spurred by the work of Arthur Phillips (1958). Phillips investigated the relationship between nominal wage inflation and unemployment growth between 1862 and 1957 in the United Kingdom. He found that a very strong negative correlation existed between these two variables, referred to as the *Phillips curve*. Keynesians immediately modified Phillips's work using U.S. data, but this time focusing on the relationship between price inflation and unemployment. Numerous studies identified a strong negative relationship between inflation and unemployment. To illustr-ate, Figure 4.3 presents inflation and unemployment data in the United States during the 1960s. Keynesians realized that this negative relation-ship was very strong evidence in favor of their model of aggregate demand driven business cycles. To understand why, consider Figure 4.4. Higher levels of aggregate demand in a Keynesian model with an

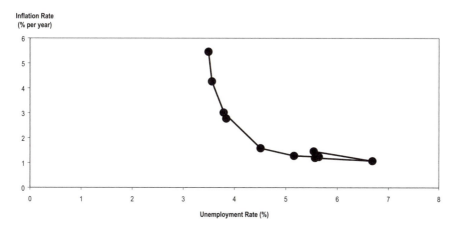

Figure 4.3 Unemployment and Inflation Rates in the United States during the 1960s

upward-sloping aggregate supply curve drive up both the price level and output. Higher prices and output drive down real wages and unemployment, leading to a negative empirical relationship between inflation and unemployment. Thus, this modified Phillips curve is strong evidence of aggregate demand driven business cycles.

Even more important than the empirical support that the Phillips curve offered, Keynesians viewed the Phillips curve as a practical tool that could be used to help central bankers manage monetary policy. If

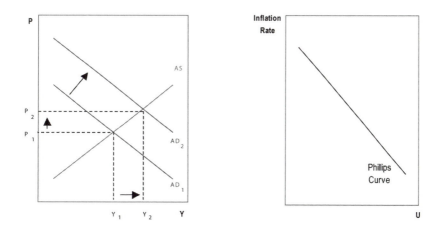

Figure 4.4 The Keynesian Phillips Curve

a stable tradeoff between inflation and unemployment exists, then all that a policymaker has to do is change the money supply until inflation is high enough to get the economy to the desired unemployment rate. Thus, the modified Phillips curve implied that the complexity of stabilization policy could be simplified to a simple inflation rate target.

THE KEYNESIAN EXPLANATION
OF THE GREAT DEPRESSION

The Keynesian model is closely associated with the Great Depression for obvious reasons. Keynesians attempted to fine-tune Keynes's explanation of the Great Depression in order to completely fit the facts of this period.

Keynesians believe that the most important shocks that reduced aggregate demand during the Great Depression originated in the goods market. The initial negative shock was a large decrease in expectations. Why expectations fell so significantly in 1929 is unclear (just as expectations motivated by animal spirits almost always are), but most Keynesian explanations center on an overreaction to overbuilding, overproduction, and the overvalued stock market that occurred during the 1920s. Falling expectations not just reduced investment but also led to a huge decrease in the stock market. The stock market crash in October 1929 initiated a chain-reaction of other bad events. First, it increased the cost of investment, further reducing investment. Second, it reduced wealth, which reduced spending and consumption. Third, the stock market crash spread pessimism throughout the economy, leading to additional falls in expectations, investment, and consumption.

Keynesians believed that falling expectations also played a role in the bank failures that plagued the U.S. economy during the Depression. As the Depression worsened, people began to panic and withdraw their savings from banks throughout the country. These bank runs eventually led to the failure of 20 percent of all banks in the United States during the Depression. Those banks that did not fail were forced to severely restrict their lending, effectively halting financial intermediation and further reducing investment and consumption.

A secondary shock that reduced aggregate demand during the Depression was the refusal of the Federal Reserve and other central banks to stabilize the money supply. As the public and banks began to hoard money as a precautionary measure, bank runs became common, the money multiplier began to shrink, and the money supply began to drop precipitously (this process will be described in more detail in the next chapter). The Federal Reserve, however, stubbornly refused to offset this falling money supply and failed to provide more reserves to banks and more currency to the public. Thus, Keynesians believe that through its neglect the Fed played an important role in reducing aggregate demand, not only by allowing the money supply to fall but also by allowing thousands of banks to fail and financial intermediation to collapse.

Keynesians were, for obvious reasons, highly critical of the laissez-faire policies adopted during the first years of the Depression by governments in the United States and Europe. Their attitude toward these classical policymakers can be summed up in a joke. Q: How many classical economists does it take to change a light bulb? A: Zero. When the conditions are right, the light bulb should change itself.

Keynesian policy proposals to end the Great Depression were aimed at stabilizing the economy through actively attempting to stimulate aggregate demand. Given the ineptitude of the Fed and the high precautionary money holdings and savings rates of the public, Keynesians believed that increasing government spending was the only reliable method of increasing aggregate demand. Not surprisingly, Keynesians were big proponents of the public works programs initiated during the Great Depression in many countries, including the New Deal programs pushed by Roosevelt in the United States. However, given the size of the New Deal programs, which were small relative to the size of the U.S. economy, it was not surprising to most Keynesians that the Depression did not immediately end, though the economy did improve somewhat. The Great Depression lingered on throughout the world until governments increased military spending dramatically before World War II. This is entirely consistent with the predictions of Keynesian economists at the time and is influential evidence in support of the Keynesian theory of business cycles and stabilization policy.

The Keynesian explanation of the Great Depression is reexamined when the Great Depression is considered in more detail in Chapter 10. This Keynesian explanation is compared and contrasted with alternative views of the causes of the Depression.

EMPIRICAL EVIDENCE ON KEYNESIAN BUSINESS CYCLES

As discussed in Chapter 2, stock prices, consumer durables, and consumer confidence are all leading indicators of changes in aggregate output. Investment as a whole is also a leading indicator of output, even though some of the components of investment, such as fixed business investment, lag changes in output because of delays between investment decisions and actual construction. These are very strong pieces of

evidence in favor of Keynesian theory. However, some empirical research has raised questions about the validity of other aspects of Keynesian theory.

Are real wages countercyclical? Figure 4.5 presents data on the price
level, the nominal wage, and the implied real wage during the Great
Depression. Even though nominal wages did fall during the Depression, they did not fall by as much as the price level, leading to an
increase in real wages. This is strong evidence that it was increases in
real wages that drove the high rates of unemployment that existed
during the Great Depression. In other words, unemployment appears
to have been largely involuntary, just as Keynes argued.

However, over different time periods and across different countries,
it is not at all so clear whether real wages are countercyclical. Table 4.1
presents real wage data across thirteen developed countries collected
by Susanto Basu and Alan Taylor (1999). They found that real wages
were basically acyclical during the interwar (1919–1939) and gold standard (1870–1914) eras, but slightly procyclical during the Bretton
Woods (1945–1971) and the floating exchange rate (1971–present) eras.
Thus, looking at a larger subset of countries over a long time horizon,
real wages appear to be acyclical to mildly procyclical. This is hard to
reconcile with Keynes's sticky wage theory of labor markets.

Is inflation procyclical? Procyclical inflation is consistent with aggregate demand driven business cycles and also with the modified Phillips
curve relationship between higher inflation and lower unemployment.
However, empirical data on price cyclicality suggest that prices have

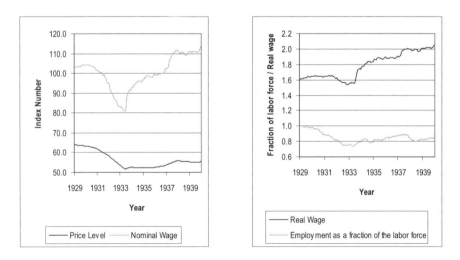

Figure 4.5 The Price Level, Nominal Wage, and Real Wage during the Great
Depression

TABLE 4.1   Real Wage Behavior during Different Periods

	Gold Standard	Interwar	Bretton Woods	Float
Standard Deviation	0.038	0.042	0.042	0.033
Comovement with Output	0.025	−0.06	0.162	0.271

Note: The 13 countries included are Argentina, Australia, Canada, Denmark, France, Germany, Italy, Netherlands, Norway, Spain, Sweden, United Kingdom, and the United States.

Source: Basu and Taylor (1999)

not been consistently procyclical. Figure 4.6 presents output growth and inflation over two time periods, the interwar period (1920–1940) and the floating exchange rate period (1970–1990). Inflation was strongly procyclical in the United States during the interwar period but countercyclical during the recent floating exchange rate period. On average, the correlation between inflation and growth between 1880 and 2000 in the United States is −.03, or an acyclical relationship. In the next chapter, evidence on the corresponding breakdown of the negative relationship between inflation and unemployment will be discussed. The lack of a consistent cyclical relationship between inflation, real wages, and output raises troubling questions about the Keynesian model, questions that future business cycle models would be forced to address.

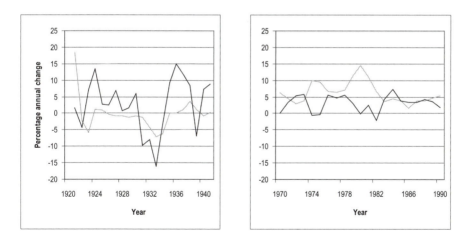

Output: 1920–1940 GNP data, 1970–1990 GDP data
Inflation: price level data is CPI minus food
lighter line indicates percentage annual change in price level
darker line indicates percentage annual change in GDP/GNP

Figure 4.6   Output Growth and Inflation, 1920–1940 and 1970–1990

CONCLUSIONS

What makes a Keynesian a Keynesian? Alan Blinder (1988) claims that the following principles generally define Keynesian economics.

Aggregate demand is volatile and is the source of business cycle fluctuations. This is so primarily because of unstable expectations and their effect on investment, consumption, and the stock market. However, erratic fiscal or monetary policy can also contribute to aggregate demand instability.

Output and employment are more volatile than prices and wages in the short run. Keynesians believe that price and wage inflexibility exists because of imperfectly competitive markets. As a result, changes in aggregate demand can have real effects on output and unemployment.

The movement of an economy to its long-run equilibrium takes place very slowly. Prices and wages only adjust gradually. Because of this, persistent disequilibria in the goods market (resulting in excess supply) and in the labor market (resulting in involuntary unemployment) can exist and be long lasting.

Monetary and fiscal policy can be used to stabilize output. If enacted in a timely manner, increases in the money supply, reductions in taxes, or increases in government spending can be used to offset falls in aggregate demand.

Keynesians are more worried about high unemployment than high inflation. In the Keynesian model, there is a stable tradeoff between lower unemployment and higher inflation. The inflation that results from using stabilization policy is simply the price that has to be paid for more stable output. Keynesians are much more worried about deflation, as occurred during the Great Depression, than inflation.

In summary, both Keynes and Keynesians believe that capitalist economies are inherently volatile and need macroeconomic management in order to avoid destabilizing business cycles that are extremely costly and persistent. Without government intervention, this instability could eventually weaken the public's belief in capitalism and lead to its downfall. Keynes and Keynesians believe in capitalism, but not laissez-faire capitalism. Consider the following quote by Keynes: "It may well be that the classical theory represents the way in which we should like our economy to behave. But to assume that it actually does so is to assume our difficulties away."

Other economists believe that it is the Keynesians who are the Utopians and who are assuming that the world works as they wish it would work. Is stabilization policy in practice as simple as tweaking monetary and fiscal policy until the economy is at full employment? Do economists really understand the economy well enough to properly conduct stabilization policy, or are there reasons to think that they are not so infallible? Is this Keynesian explanation of business cycles consistent with all business cycle episodes, including every aspect of the Great Depression? These are the questions over which the theoretical battle between Keynesians and their critics was joined. However, Keynes so clearly defined the issues relating to the debate that all of the work on business cycles since *The General Theory* can be thought of as a critique of his and his followers' influential models of what causes recessions and depressions.

SUGGESTED READINGS

John Maynard Keynes, *Essays in Persuasion* (1931): A collection of early essays in which Keynes lays out his basic thoughts on the Great Depression, the use of fiscal policy, and the effects of deflation, among other topics. Also included are brief essays on his thoughts about the state of politics in the 1920s and 1930s.

John Maynard Keynes, *The General Theory* (1936): The first three chapters summarize Keynes's primary insights and are the most readable chapters of *The General Theory*.

James Tobin, "Price Flexibility and Output Stability: An Old Keynesian View" (1993): An argument in support of Keynes's continued relevance to modern economics and a critique of Classical and Neoclassical models.

5

The Monetarist Model

INTRODUCTION

During the 1950s and 1960s, monetary policy rose to the forefront of macroeconomic inquiry and business cycle research. As discussed in the previous chapter, Keynes did not spend much time discussing monetary policy in *The General Theory*. This was in part because he thought monetary policy would be largely ineffective during bad times because of the liquidity trap, and also because he was skeptical about the competence of central bankers to engage in timely stabilization policy after their dismal performance during the Great Depression. Keynesians, on the other hand, were very interested in monetary policy, for two reasons. First, Keynesians realized that central bankers are relatively independent and have the unique freedom to engage in stabilization policy largely unencumbered by outside political constraints. Second, the Keynesian Phillips curve, which specifies a constant negative relationship between inflation and unemployment, received a great deal of empirical support during the 1950s and 1960s. One important implication of the Phillips curve is that the complexity of stabilization policy can be simplified to a target simple inflation rate that could be achieved through a well-chosen monetary policy.

The 1950s and early 1960s were the pinnacle of Keynesian influence from both a theoretical and a policy perspective. Not only did Keynesian theory dominate macroeconomic theory, but after John F. Kennedy's election in 1960, many of his Keynesian professors from Harvard moved with him to Washington.

One of the few effective voices of dissent during this period was Milton Friedman, a man who believed in everything that was then out of fashion in economics. Friedman is probably the second most influential economist of the twentieth century and, like Keynes, is a man of many talents. In addition to being a prominent conservative policy guru (Friedman is the source of many influential public policy ideas, including privatization proposals such as school voucher programs), Friedman has done groundbreaking work in the areas of law and economics, consumption theory, and economic history. Friedman is also the father of a unique school of macroeconomic thought referred to as *Monetarism*. Monetarists have the following goal: reassert classical principles in new classical, or *neoclassical*, models that better explain business cycles. A critical component of this neoclassical Monetarist model is the fact that while it accepts the classical principle of money neutrality, it recognizes that it only holds in the long run. In the short run, Monetarists believe (like Keynesians) that fluctuations in aggregate demand can have real effects on output and drive business cycles. Monetarists view the erratic monetary policies followed by misinformed and misguided central banks as the source of these shocks to aggregate demand and the cause of business cycles.

In this chapter, the Monetarist model and its theory of business cycles are discussed. The focal point of this discussion is the proper role of monetary policy and its potential for both stabilizing and destabilizing an economy.

MONETARIST THEORY

The Principles of Monetarism

One of the primary objectives of Monetarism was to reestablish classical concepts in macroeconomic theory. Monetarists believe in three basic neoclassical principles, each based on a traditional classical principle but with a modification.

Prices and wages are perfectly flexible. However, perfect information does not exist. Monetarists believe that perfect competition best describes the behavior of markets, but with the exception that perfect information about the money supply and the price level is impossible because of the secrecy of central banks. Imperfect information means that expectations of the future can have real effects on an economy if these expectations are wrong.

Monetarists believe that firms and households have *adaptive expectations*. Adaptive expectations mean that individuals are not forward looking but backward looking and only change their expectations gradually based on what they have observed in the past. (An example of adaptive expectations at work can be seen on every college campus when the weather suddenly turns cold but many students continue to walk around in shorts and a T-shirt.) Adaptive expectations actually hearkened back to the Cobweb theory, which hypothesized that business cycles were the result of persistent errors in price expectations made by a public that is slow to catch on to any unanticipated change in the economy. In the Monetarist model, nominal wages and the price level are slow to adjust to things such as an unforeseen change in the money supply. Disequilibria in markets can exist not because of any real market imperfections, as assumed by Keynesians, but because of incorrect expectations of what nominal wages and the price level should be to clear the market.

Changes in aggregate demand do not affect real output in the long run, but they do affect real output in the short run. Unlike classical economists, Monetarists assert that money neutrality only holds in the long run, not in the short run. The reason, once again, has to do with imperfect information and price misperceptions. When the public is surprised by a change in the money supply, firms and workers can be fooled into changing their real behavior, meaning money neutrality will not hold. However, firms and households will eventually recognize their mistakes and gradually adjust their expectations. Wages and prices will then adjust and return the labor and goods markets to their long-run equilibriums.

Consequently, changes in aggregate demand can drive business cycle fluctuations. These fluctuations are not permanent but temporary deviations from the long-run rate of aggregate output, which is determined by the full employment of capital, labor, and technology that is available in the economy. Friedman referred to the long-run level of aggregate output as the *natural rate of output*. This concept of the natural rate of output is similar to Keynes' concept of potential output, but the crucial difference is that Friedman believes that the forces that return the economy to full employment are much stronger because wages and prices are perfectly flexible. As a result, the natural rate of output is not some theoretically achievable level of output (like in the Keynesian view), but a level of output that the economy is typically at in the absence of any unexpected demand shocks.

Fluctuations in the money supply drive fluctuations in aggregate demand and are responsible for business cycles. Monetarists adhere to the classical Quantity Theory of money demand and aggregate demand, which states that money is needed in order to conduct transactions. This implies that there is a direct relationship between the amount of money in circulation and the level of nominal aggregate spending in an economy:

$$MV = PY \qquad\qquad (5.1)$$

Remember that V is velocity and represents the number of times a unit of money changes hands over a period of time. Y is real aggregate expenditure, P is the price level, and M is the money supply. In the Quantity Theory, any increase in the level of nominal expenditure (PY) has to be matched by either an increase in the supply of money (M) or a higher velocity of money (V) in order to support this higher volume of trade. The Quantity Theory is a theory of aggregate demand and implies that a negative relationship exists between the price level and real expenditure, holding money and velocity constant (intuition: a higher price level reduces the real supply of money, which leads to a reduction in real expenditure). As a result, changes in this aggregate demand relationship take place only in response to a change in the money supply or a change in velocity. Monetarists believe that the demand for money and velocity are relatively stable if monetary policy is stable, so that changes in aggregate demand are almost exclusively the result of changes in the money supply.

Output Determination in the Monetarist Model

The Quantity Theory equation can be rewritten in percent change terms:

$$\%\Delta M + \%\Delta V = \%\Delta P + \%\Delta Y \qquad (5.2)$$

To understand the intuition behind how changes in the money supply affect aggregate output in the Quantity Theory, consider the following example. Assume that velocity is constant ($\%\Delta D = 0$) and that the natural rate of real output growth is 2 percent ($\%\Delta Y = 2\%$). What will be the long-run effects of 5 percent money growth according to the Quantity Theory? If this 5 percent money growth is completely expected, then output growth will be at its natural rate of 2 percent and inflation will be 3 percent.

Now consider what happens if the Fed increases money growth from 5 percent to 10 percent and this increase is unanticipated by firms and households. The public will suddenly find themselves with excess money holdings because the money supply increased but money demand and velocity did not. The public can get rid of these balances in two ways: They can spend it or they can deposit it in a bank, leading to an increase in bank reserves. Banks get rid of these excess bank reserves by reducing interest rates, which in turn encourages investment and consumption and also stimulates spending. The end result is that if money growth rises by 10 percent then nominal spending growth ($\%\Delta P + \%\Delta Y$) has to rise by 10 percent as well.

However, a key question remains. If nominal expenditure rises by 10 percent, how much of this will be reflected in an increase in inflation ($\%\Delta P$) and how much of this will be an increase in real output ($\%\Delta Y$)? Monetarists contend that inflation will rise only slightly following an unexpected increase in the money supply and that most of the initial change will be in real output growth. Here is where adaptive expectations are important to the Monetarist argument. Because firms did not foresee this increase in the money supply, they think that the demand for their specific product has risen, not that aggregate demand has risen. As a result, firms initially respond to any increase in the money supply and inflation by increasing production. At the same time, workers do not observe why firms are hiring more labor and nominal wages are rising. They think that this increase in the nominal wage is also an increase in the real wage and are fooled into working more. Thus, adaptive expectations imply that the aggregate supply curve in the short run is upward sloping and that unanticipated changes in the money supply have real effects on aggregate output. The slower expectations adjust to this unanticipated change in the money supply, the flatter the short run aggregate supply curve will be and the larger the real effect of an increase in money growth on aggregate output.

However, the real effects of a change in money growth will not last forever. Figure 5.1 provides an aggregate demand/aggregate supply graph of the short-run effects of an increase in the money supply in the Monetarist model and the process by which higher price expectations return the economy to the natural rate of output. Eventually, firms that

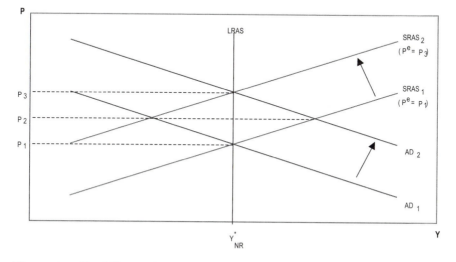

Figure 5.1 The Effects of an Increase in the Money Supply in the Monetarist Model

are increasing their production levels will reach their capacity constraints and become more willing to increase prices. Also, workers will observe that the aggregate price level is rising and that their real wage is falling, causing them to reduce their labor supply, which forces firms to cut back on production. The short-run aggregate supply curve shifts to the left (to $SRAS_2$) as the expected price level increases and the economy gradually returns to its natural rate of output, or the rate of output that is consistent with the full employment of capital, labor, and technology.

Reconsidering the previous example, an unanticipated increase in money growth from 5 percent to 10 percent would lead to at least an 8 percent inflation rate in the long run once the economy returned to its natural rate of 2 percent real output growth (inflation could be higher than this if velocity increases in response to this higher inflation rate). This proposition that in the long run the economy returns to its natural rate of output and that changes in money growth only change the level of inflation is referred to as the *natural rate hypothesis*.

How long is the long run? In Monetarists' minds, the long run is very long. According to Friedman and his research partner Anna Schwartz, it can take up to 10 years before the real effects of an unexpected change in the money supply disappear and leave only higher prices. This process takes so long because the public never has perfect information about the extent of the change in the money supply. They can only learn about monetary policy by observing past inflation rates. This requires a great deal of time and leads to long response lags.

BUSINESS CYCLES AND MONETARY POLICY

The Monetarist model asserts that economic fluctuations are largely the result of unanticipated changes in the money supply that lead to fluctuations in aggregate demand. Expectation stickiness, not price stickiness like in the Keynesian model, means that changes in aggregate demand have real effects on output and unemployment. Recessionary periods in which output growth is below the natural rate are the result of money growth being lower than anticipated. Expansions, where output growth is above the natural rate, are caused by higher than anticipated money growth.

This begs an obvious question: if business cycles are largely caused by unstable monetary policy, then why is monetary policy so unstable? This was the topic of Friedman's (1968) address to the American Economic Association entitled "The Role of Monetary Policy." The principal point of this paper, in Friedman's words, is that "we are in danger of assigning to monetary policy a larger role than it can perform, in danger of asking it to accomplish tasks that it cannot achieve, and, as a result, preventing it from making the contribution that it is capable of making." Friedman argues two seemingly contradictory points in this paper: Monetary policy is powerful, and central bankers should rarely if ever use it.

Goals That Monetary Policy Cannot Achieve

To understand why monetary policy can be destabilizing, Friedman first argues that there are three things that a central bank cannot do.

The central bank cannot control output in the long run. Consider the consequences of a central bank attempting to target a level of aggregate output that is greater than the natural rate of output, such as illustrated in Figure 5.2. If the economy begins at the natural rate of output, the central bank can achieve its target by increasing the money supply and aggregate demand. The problem with this policy is that it will not work forever. Eventually, the public will increase their expected price level, the short-run aggregate supply curve will shift to the left, and the economy will return to its natural rate of output unless the central bank increases the money supply once again. If the central bank is persistent in maintaining this output target, the result will be accelerating inflation rates. Eventually, this high inflation will lead to a public clamor for lower inflation, and the central bank will be forced to accommodate these demands by lowering money growth and aggregate demand, leading to a recession.

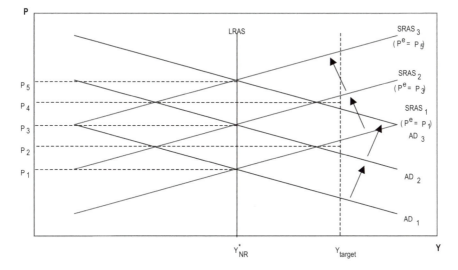

Figure 5.2 The Effects of Targeting an Output Level above the Natural Rate

The seemingly obvious solution is to make sure that central banks do not target output or employment at levels that are above their natural rates. The problem with this solution is that this is easier said than done. The natural rate of an economy is not an observable magnitude. Policymakers always have imperfect information about what the natural rates of output and employment actually are. In addition, these natural rates are not constant but can move with structural changes in the economy such as changes in demographics, changes in productivity, and changes in public policy. To see this, Figure 5.3 presents the unemployment rate in the United States and the estimated natural rates of unemployment between 1960 and 2000. The natural rate has fluctuated between 4.5 percent and 7.5 percent over this period, which is a sizeable range. As a result, targeting the natural rate of output or unemployment can potentially lead to accelerating inflation, if the estimate of the natural rate used by policymakers is too high.

Monetarists believe that there is another practical problem associated with using stabilization policy even if you have perfect information about the natural rate of the economy, and that is that there are time lags between when policymakers identify a problem and when an implemented monetary policy has real effects on the economy. For example, there are lags in the information-gathering process, lags in the decision-making process at central banks, lags in the time that it takes the money multiplier to work, and lags in the time that it takes lower

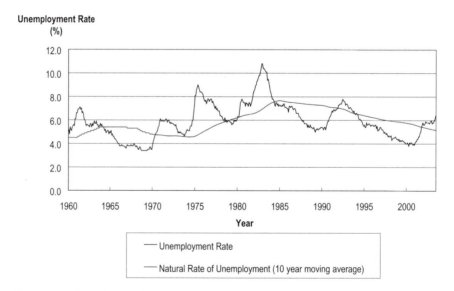

Figure 5.3 The Unemployment Rate and the Natural Rate of Unemployment

interest rates to stimulate aggregate demand and output. As a result, by the time that any policy is implemented and its effects are felt, it may no longer be needed. Friedman referred to this as the "fool in the shower" phenomenon, where cold pipes always make the water that first comes out of the shower cold so that the initial reaction is to overreact and turn the hot water way up, until the water comes out scalding hot. Likewise, in the case of monetary policy, policymakers who are trying to stabilize output will overact to changes in economic conditions because of lags between when the policy is implemented and when the effects of this policy are felt

The central bank cannot control unemployment in the long run. Friedman's natural rate hypothesis also rejects the Phillips curve relationship preached by Keynesian policymakers. Instead, Friedman argues that while a tradeoff might exist between higher inflation and lower unemployment, it is temporary and it is unstable. It is temporary because eventually the public adjusts its price expectations in response to a change in the money supply. Prices and wages then adjust and the economy will return to the natural rate of output. The tradeoff is unstable because the rate at which the public adjusts their adaptive expectations is not observable. Consider Figure 5.4, in which the public increases its expected price level in response to higher actual prices. A higher expected price level means that the central bank needs to set money growth and inflation at higher rates than needed before in order to fool firms and workers into increasing employment. In other words, a higher expected price level shifts the Phillips curve tradeoff upward toward higher levels of inflation for every rate of unemployment and driving unemployment below the natural rate means experiencing even

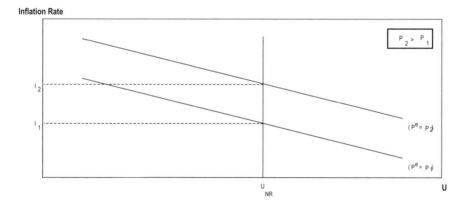

Figure 5.4 The Phillips Curve Tradeoff Changes as the Expected Price Level Increases

higher rates of inflation. Thus, an infinite number of Phillips curves are possible within an economy, each of them consistent with a different expected price level. Without perfect knowledge of expectations, policymakers can never know exactly what the tradeoff between inflation and unemployment is, making monetary policy based on the Phillips curve worthless—or worse, destabilizing.

The central bank cannot control nominal interest rates in the long run. Monetary policy primarily influences output through its effects on interest rates. As a result, traditional operating procedures at most central banks, including the Federal Reserve in the United States, are to target nominal interest rates on a day-to-day basis. However, Friedman argues that targeting nominal interest rates can lead to the same destabilizing inflation problems associated with targeting output and unemployment levels.

Nominal interest rates have two components, the expected inflation rate (the minimum a lender must receive on a loan in order to break even in real terms) and the real interest rate (the real profit rate a lender is expecting on a loan). The central bank can drive down nominal interest rates in the short run by increasing the money supply. The problem is that if the central bank persists in targeting interest rates at low levels by increasing the money supply, actual inflation will rise. This will eventually lead to a rise in expected inflation as well. When interest rates begin to rise because of higher expected inflation, the central bank will be forced to increase the money supply once again if it is committed to its nominal interest rate target. This process will keep repeating itself and inflation will continue to accelerate until public opinion turns against the central bank. Then the central bank will be forced to reduce the money supply in order to reduce inflation, leading to a fall in aggregate demand and an economic contraction. Thus, rigidly targeting nominal interest rates leads to monetary instability and economic fluctuations. By ignoring this distinction between nominal and real interest rates, Keynesians ignore the destabilizing effects of targeting interest rates, just as they ignore the destabilizing effects of targeting output and unemployment.

In addition, targeting interest rates is a bad idea even if Keynesians are right and changes in aggregate demand are driven by exogenous changes in expectations and investment. If changes in investment demand drive business cycles, then interest rates will be procyclical. If the central bank targets interest rates, this would require the central bank to increase the money supply (to lower interest rates) during periods of high aggregate demand and decrease the money supply (to increase interest rates) during periods of low aggregate demand. Thus, interest rate targets force monetary policy to be procyclical and amplify, not dampen, swings in the business cycle.

Goals That Monetary Policy Can Achieve

Monetary policy can prevent changes in the money supply from contributing to aggregate demand fluctuations. Because central bankers insist on using monetary policy to stabilize output, they end up creating a "yo-yo economy," where they let the money supply grow fast in order to increase output but are then forced to cut the money supply and decrease output in an effort to bring down accelerating inflation. Monetarists feel that central banks can avoid these policy swings by changing their goal from economic stabilization to monetary stabilization. Policymakers can do more for economic well-being by doing too little as opposed to trying to do too much.

Monetary policy can be used to achieve price stability. Friedman views inflation as very costly because it distorts the information prices provide and causes markets to operate inefficiently. In addition, unpredictable inflation increases the level of risk in the economy by changing the real value of goods or assets with a fixed nominal price, such as bonds. Friedman believes that sustained inflation is always the result of excess money growth. As a result, Monetarists believe that keeping money growth and the inflation rate at low levels will increase economic efficiency and long run growth.

Monetary policy can be used to offset major economic disturbances. For example, during periods of financial crisis, banking panics, or wars, central banks can provide temporary liquidity to financial markets. However, in the words of Friedman, "In this area particularly the best is likely to be the enemy of the good." In other words, the discretionary use of policy should be used in only the most extreme circumstances in order to avoid its excessive use.

To summarize, Monetarists believe that instead of being a source of stabilization, monetary policy has been a destabilizing force that has led to greater inflation. To correct this, Friedman argues that central banks should control what they can control and target the money supply, not interest rates, output, unemployment, or any other real variable. By adopting a money growth rule that specifies that the money supply increases at a constant rate—say, 5 percent each and every year—central banks will be able to achieve three important goals. First, central banks will be able to avoid sudden swings in policy, which will stabilize economic growth. Central banks will also be able to keep inflation at a low level, reducing the distortions created by inflation and increasing economic efficiency. Finally, central banks will be able to keep inflation steady, eliminating a large source of uncertainty in the economy, which should also increase economic efficiency. This would be a record of success that, in Friedman's opinion, is far superior to the record established by the use of Keynesian stabilization policy. In the words of Friedman:

By setting itself a steady course and keeping to it, the monetary authority could make a major contribution to promoting economic stability.... Other forces would still affect the economy, require change and adjustment, and disturb the even tenor of our ways. But steady monetary growth would provide a monetary climate favorable to the effective operation of those basic forces of enterprise, ingenuity, invention, hard work, and thrift that are the true springs of economic growth. That is the most that we can ask from monetary policy at our present stage of knowledge. But that much—and it is a great deal—is clearly within our reach. (1968, p. 17)

EMPIRICAL EVIDENCE OF MONETARIST BUSINESS CYCLES

Is money growth a leading indicator of changes in aggregate output? Monetarists believe that most business cycles are initiated by changes in the money supply. Friedman and Anna Schwartz, in their book *A Monetary History of the United States* (1963), document business cycles between 1867 and 1960. They argue that all recessions in the United States over this period were preceded by inflation fears from earlier expansionary monetary policy, which forced the Federal Reserve to purposefully contract the money supply and initiate a recession in order to bring down inflation. This includes the Great Depression, during which the money supply fell by nearly one-third. In Chapter 11, postwar business cycles are reviewed on a case-by-case basis. The story told by the Monetarists appears to be consistent with a large number of postwar recessions after 1960 as well. The most obvious example of this was the 1981–1982 recession, which was the most severe economic contraction in the United States since the Great Depression and was clearly the result of a severe contraction in monetary policy aimed at reducing skyrocketing inflation. Christina Romer and David Romer (1994) argue that falls in money growth preceded 6 of the 8 postwar recessions they investigated and that increases in money growth preceded the troughs in output during all 8 of these postwar recessions.

On the other hand, money growth is not a very reliable indicator of aggregate output. Figure 5.5 presents yearly money growth rates, where recessionary periods are shaded. Money growth is much more variable than output growth; in a number of instances, money growth fell quite significantly but the economy did not move into recession. One interesting example of this occurred in the mid-1980s and mid-1990s, when money growth rates declined quite substantially but output growth remained quite strong. Thus, there are reasons to question exactly how close a link there is between money growth and output growth.

Are money demand and velocity stable? According to the Quantity Theory, the relationship between the money supply and nominal income is

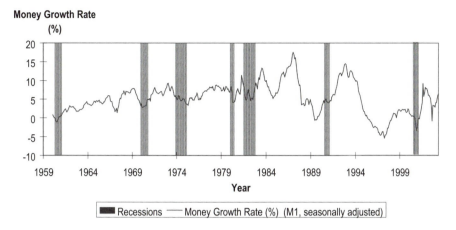

Figure 5.5 Yearly Money Growth and Recessions

stable, assuming velocity is constant. As a result, stable money demand and velocity are critical components of Monetarist theory. Friedman argues that the demand for money is very stable because it is primarily determined by the public's wealth. The only factors that lead to fluctuations in wealth over short periods of time are changes in the inflation rate and changes in interest rates. Higher inflation and interest rates reduce money demand and increase velocity by reducing wealth and increasing the opportunity cost of holding money. However, monetary policy largely determines interest rates and inflation rates. If monetary growth is stable and low, then interest rates, inflation, and velocity will also be stable and low. Thus, Monetarists believe that a constant relationship should exist between money growth and output. If it does not, it is the central bank through its unstable monetary policy that has made it so.

However, there is a great deal of evidence that suggests that money demand and velocity are unstable—so unstable, in fact, that the central bank may not even be able to control the money supply, let alone keep it steady. Consider the M1 definition of the money supply in the United States, which includes the total amount of currency in circulation plus the amount of demand deposits in banks (i.e., bank deposits in which the balance can be withdrawn unconditionally). The Fed does not control M1 directly; it only controls what is referred to as the *monetary base*, which is currency in circulation plus reserves held by banks. Obviously, if the Fed places more bank reserves into the banking system, then M1 will rise. How much it rises depends upon the *money multiplier*, or the ratio of the change in M1 to the change in the monetary base. The size of the money multiplier is based on how much demand deposits change when there is a change in bank reserves. It is not controlled by the Fed, but by the actions of banks, depositors, and borrowers.

To see how changes in money demand can change the money supply, consider two case studies. The first is the Great Depression. Figure 5.6 reports data on the ratio of currency-to-deposits (money holdings by the public) and excess reserves-to-deposits (money holdings by banks). The currency-to-deposit ratio rose significantly during the Great Depression, especially during 1931 and 1932 as banking panics occurred throughout the country. The excess reserves-to-deposits ratio rose gradually and did not rise by more because of the significant levels of deposit withdraws from banks. The effects on the money supply can be seen in Figure 5.7, which presents M1 and the monetary base from 1929 to 1934. The Federal Reserve did little to increase the monetary base during the Depression, but M1 fell by roughly one-third. This was the result of increased precautionary money holdings by banks and the public. As money demand went up, bank deposits, lending, and the money multiplier dropped precipitously, significantly reducing M1. Thus, it appears that much of the fall in the money supply was the result of the Great Depression, not necessarily of a change in monetary policy that precipitated the Great Depression.

The second example occurred during the 1980s and 1990s when financial deregulation spurred a great number of financial innovations in the United States. Some of the financial market changes that took place during the 1980s include ATM systems, interest-paying checking accounts, money market accounts, increased use of credit cards, better information technology, and increased participation in the stock market. Each of these developments significantly changed the public's demand for money and bank deposits. As these variables changed, velocity and the money multiplier fluctuated wildly, and the stable

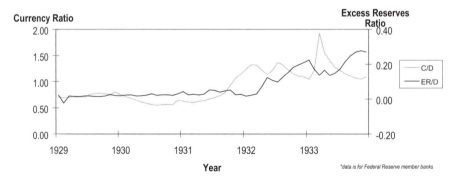

Figure 5.6 Currency-to-Deposit and Excess Reserves-to-Deposit Ratios*

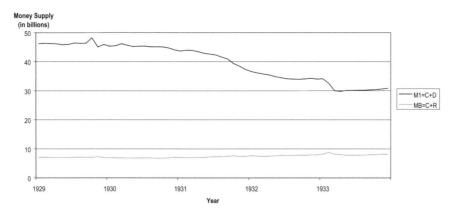

Figure 5.7 M1 and the Monetary Base during the Great Depression

relationship between the money supply and output fell apart. For instance, referring back to Figure 5.5, the money supply fell quite significantly between 1991 and 1995, but the economy experienced fairly strong output growth. As a result, many economists have lost faith in the idea that maintaining a stable money supply is even possible, let alone the notion that a stable money supply can lead to stable output. Gerald Bouey, former Governor of the Bank of Canada, is reported to have said "We didn't abandon the monetary aggregates, they abandoned us" (*The Economist*, April 19, 2004).

Is there a stable tradeoff between unemployment and inflation? Figure 5.8 graphs unemployment and inflation rates in the United States for the

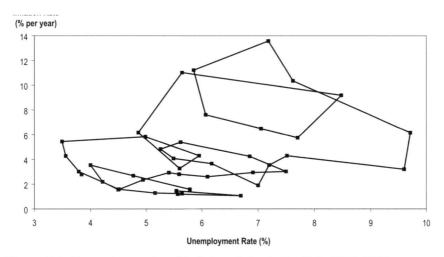

Figure 5.8 Unemployment and Inflation Rates in the U.S., 1960–2002

period 1961–2003. The breakdown of the Phillips curve during the 1970s, during the 1980s, and during the 1990s is very strong evidence in favor of the natural rate hypothesis. As Friedman predicted in 1968, any tradeoff between unemployment and inflation appears to break down the more that policymakers attempt to take advantage of it. However, Figure 5.8 also raises questions about the Monetarist explanation of business cycles. Specifically, the dramatic increases in both inflation and unemployment that took place during 1973–1975 are hard to reconcile with a model in which changes in the money supply and aggregate demand are driving business cycles and in which the public adjusts their expectations slowly due to adaptive expectations. Likewise, how do Monetarists explain the 1990s, when both inflation and unemployment fell rather quickly at the same time? It seems that the Monetarist model cannot.

CONCLUSIONS

The Monetarist theory of business cycles has been largely discredited by the behavior of the money supply during the 1980s and 1990s. Very few economists today believe that monetary cycles are the primary cause of business cycles and that a stable money growth rule would stabilize output growth. However, that does not mean that Milton Friedman's work and the insights of Monetarists have been forgotten. In fact, many aspects of Monetarism continue to be very influential, and include these five major contributions to modern business cycle theory.

Monetarists raised consciousness about the importance of monetary policy. Monetarists are largely responsible for the attention that monetary policy receives today from economists. Criticism of the Federal Reserve and other central banks by Monetarists has greatly improved the transparency of these institutions by forcing them to be more open about their policies and activities. In addition, changes in central bank operating procedures, particularly in terms of abandoning inflexible interest rate targets, are largely the result of Monetarist criticism.

Monetarists reestablished neoclassical principles such as money neutrality and the natural rate hypothesis. Friedman's critique of the Phillips curve and his assertion that the tradeoff between inflation and unemployment is temporary and unstable was a severe intellectual blow to Keynesian economics.

Monetarists highlighted the importance of price expectations and their role in influencing the impact of government policy. This is a theme that is picked up on and expanded in the Rational Expectations model, which are covered in the next chapter.

Monetarists were the first to clearly make a distinction between real and nominal interest rates. As a result, they were able to explain differences in the behavior of short-term versus long-term interest. Monetarists explained how expansionary monetary policy might lead to a decrease in short-term interest rates but at the same time increase long-term interest rates by increasing expected inflation rates. Thus, low interest rates may not be indicative of high money growth but of low money growth, something that cannot be explained in Keynesian models.

Monetarists raised real concerns about the destabilizing effects of stabilization policy. Because of lags in policy and imperfect information about the natural rate of output, Monetarists explained how countercyclical monetary policy could actually amplify business cycle fluctuations. Monetarists were the first to examine Keynesian stabilization policy with a skeptical eye, and this skepticism has played an important part in explaining why most economists now believe in placing some limits on the use of active macroeconomic policy aimed at stabilizing output.

When reviewing each of these contributions, it is clear that while Monetarists may have lost the war, they won many of the battles. Monetarism provided an important critique of simple Keynesian theory and set the stage for future business cycle theories that also focused on the role of government policy in destabilizing economic growth. One of these models, the Rational Expectations model, will be discussed in the next chapter.

SUGGESTED READINGS

Bradford De Long, "The Triumph of Monetarism" (2000): A look at the history of Monetarism and its contributions to modern macroeconomic thought, including its influence on New Keynesian models, which are discussed in Chapter 8.

Milton Friedman, "The Role of Monetary Policy" (1968): One of the most influential papers in modern macroeconomics, in which Friedman states his vision for monetary policy.

Milton Friedman and Anna Schwartz, *A Monetary History of the United States, 1867–1960* (1963): Chapter 7 of this book covers the Great Depression and is a very interesting look into Federal Reserve policy and its ineptitude during the crash.

Thomas Mayer, "The Structure of Monetarism" (1975): A comprehensive discussion of the differences between Monetarism and Keynesian economics.

Joseph E. Stiglitz, "Reflections on the Natural Rate Hypothesis" (1997): A discussion of the natural rate of unemployment, how and why it has changed over time, and its role in the making of economic policy.

6

The Rational Expectations Model

INTRODUCTION

Economists have always believed that what people think about the future affects what they do today. As a result, expectations have long played a major role in business cycle theory, from early business cycle theories such as the Sunspot and the Cobweb models to the two modern business cycle theories we have already discussed: the Keynesian model and the Monetarist model.

However, economists have long held different views about how people form their expectations of the future and how these expectations affect business cycles. Keynesians focus on the role of expectations in generating investment volatility. In the Keynesian model, expectations are subject to extreme fluctuations based on animal spirits and are largely irrational, or at least not necessarily based on real economic fundamentals. Keynesians believe that expectations are self-fulfilling and that volatile expectations drive business cycle fluctuations by influencing the decisions of firms to undertake investment projects and of households to purchase durable consumption goods.

Price expectations play a critical role in generating business cycles in the Monetarist model, where the public forms its expectations adaptively, or backward-looking. These adaptive expectations make price expectations slow to adjust to changes in economic conditions. As a result, changes in monetary policy that affect the actual price level can fool firms and workers into thinking that real conditions have changed, leading them to produce more or less than they would if they had perfect information. Thus, Monetarists believe that lagging expectations and swings in monetary policy are responsible for business cycles.

A big inconsistency is inherent in the way that both of these models treat expectations. The cornerstone of economics is the rational choice model, in which individuals make decisions based on weighing the benefits of an activity against its costs. For example, people are assumed to consume a good until the marginal benefit of another unit of the good equals the marginal cost of the next unit. The logical inconsistency in the Keynesian and Monetarist models is this: Why don't people apply this same rational choice model to their formulation of expectations? These models assume that individuals are rational and forward looking when making all of their other decisions except when selecting their expectations of the future. As a result, these models are in conflict with a well-established microeconomic theory of utility and profit maximization.

The insight of rational expectations, which was first proposed by John Muth (1961), is that this dissonance between how individuals form their expectations and how individuals make their other decisions can be reconciled by simply assuming agents form their expectations based on the rational choice model. In other words, *rational expectations* means that individuals form their expectations by making an optimal forecast of the future using all currently available information. While the public can still make errors, they do not make predictable, or systematic, errors. This simple insight revolutionized modern macroeconomics when Robert Lucas developed a model that incorporated rational expectations into Friedman's natural rate model. This Rational Expectations model raised challenging questions about the causes of business cycles and the benefits of active stabilization policy, both monetary and fiscal policy.

Rational expectations has become a widely accepted component of macroeconomics. This chapter will discuss both the ways that the concept of rational expectations has revolutionized modern business cycle theory and also the empirical support (or lack thereof) for the Rational Expectations model and its explanation of recessions and expansions.

WHAT DOES RATIONAL EXPECTATIONS MEAN?

One of the most important misconceptions about rational expectations regards interpreting the phrase "all currently available information" in its definition. All currently available information means that the public knows (1) all data (past and present) that is cost effective to obtain and publicly known that might affect the variable on which expectations are being formed, and (2) the economic model and how different variables interact. It does not mean perfect information because some information may not be publicly available and because some information may be prohibitively costly to obtain (i.e., the marginal cost of such information is greater than its marginal benefit). Knowing the model simply means that individuals understand how, for instance, changes in monetary policy are likely to affect inflation and their nominal wages.

What if some segments of the public are not rational and do not use all available information when setting expectations? Rational expectations are not invalidated. Those who are rational will take advantage of the profit opportunities created by those who are consistently making predictable mistakes. For example, if certain segments of the public consistently underestimate the future inflation rate, firms will take advantage of these workers by consistently paying them a real wage that is too low compared to those who form their expectations rationally and demand larger increases in their nominal wage. Over time, these irrational workers will figure out that their ignorance is costing them real income and they will change their behavior. By following the lead of other rational workers, they can receive higher real wages and higher standards of living at little cost. This notion—that individuals learn and do what is in their own best interest—is at the heart of the discipline of economics. To assert that individuals do not act rationally is to assert that most of our economics is wrong.

Rational expectations imply that the public is both forward- and backward-looking. In other words, they do not just consider past data on things such as government policy when forming their expectations, but they also consider how the government might respond in the future to new information and how this response might affect the economy. Consider another example. Assume that it is widely known that the natural rate of output growth is 2 percent. Assume that the central bank sets the money growth rate at 5 percent. Because people have information about money growth and they (at least intuitively) understand the Quantity Theory, they will expect a 3 percent inflation rate and adjust their expectations and nominal wage demands accordingly.

Now suppose that the central bank raises money growth to 6 percent in an effort to increase output growth above 2 percent and that the public knows what the central bank is attempting to do. Under adaptive expectations, the public would not adjust their expectations until they saw actual inflation begin to rise. As a result, this change in the money supply would have real effects on output growth until inflation expectations caught up with actual inflation. But under rational expectations, the public knows that money growth of 6 percent will eventually lead to inflation of 4 percent. They anticipate this higher inflation and immediately increase their expected inflation rate and immediately increase their nominal wage demands. Money neutrality is restored very quickly, and real output growth remains at 2 percent. Thus, the central bank's ability to increase output above the natural rate has been greatly restricted. In fact, if the public has good information about monetary policy, then monetary policy cannot affect real output growth, even in the short run. Only by surprising the public through acting unpredictably will monetary policy have real effects.

LUCAS'S RATIONAL EXPECTATIONS MODEL

The idea of rational expectations had floated on the fringes of macro-economics for most of the 1960s. It was not until Lucas (1972) showed how rational expectations could be integrated into a macroeconomic model that economists began to understand its full ramifications.

Lucas's Rational Expectations model is based on Friedman's natural rate model, which was discussed in the previous chapter on Moneta-rism. In this model, there are a large number of firms and workers who operate within markets with perfectly flexible prices and wages. The only market imperfection is one of information: Firms and workers cannot observe changes in aggregate demand and the aggregate price level; they can only observe the price of the good that they produce (their *own-price*). The only substantive difference between Friedman's and Lucas's model is that the public has rational expectations and not adaptive expectations.

How do firms and workers respond when they see their own-price increase? There are two extreme scenarios that can be followed. The first is that firms and workers view this as entirely the result of an increase in aggregate demand and inflation. In this case, the public increases its expected price level. Firms will not produce more as their own-price rises because they believe their relative price is staying constant. Like-wise, workers will not be willing to work more as their nominal wage increases because they believe that their real wage is constant. In this case, there are no changes in any real variables such as aggregate output or employment.

The second extreme scenario is that firms and workers keep their expected price level constant and treat this increase in their own-price as entirely the result of an increase in their relative price from an increase in the demand for their good. In this case, firms will produce more. As workers see their nominal wage increase, they also believe their real wage is increasing and will work more. As firms produce more and workers work more, aggregate output increases.

Lucas's original and important insight was to show that rational individuals who maximize profits and utility will respond to any increase in their own-price as if it were partially the result of an increase in inflation and partially the result of an increase in their relative price. In other words, rational agents will not respond according to either of the extreme scenarios discussed above but instead will make some compromise between these alternatives. As a result, any increase in the aggregate price level will to some extent fool firms and workers into increasing real output and employment, although not by as much as in an economy populated by agents who form their expectations adaptively.

In this Rational Expectations model, the following *Lucas supply equation* describes how aggregate output is determined:

$$Y_t - Y_{NR} = \alpha(P_t - P_t^e) + u_t \tag{6.1}$$

Y_{NR} is the natural rate of output, P_t is the expected price level, and u_t represents exogenous real supply shocks that can also change the level of output. The intuition behind this equation is straightforward. Assuming no supply shocks ($u_t = 0$), if an increase in aggregate demand and the aggregate price level is completely anticipated ($P_t = P_t^e$) then output will always be at its natural rate ($Y_t = Y_{NR}$). However, an unexpected increase in aggregate demand and the price level ($P_t > P_t^e$) fools firms and workers into producing more and increases aggregate output above its natural rate ($Y_t > Y_{NR}$).

How much aggregate output increases in response to an unexpected increase in aggregate demand (which is based upon the value of α in the Lucas supply equation) is determined by how many people are tricked into thinking that an increase in the aggregate price level is an increase in their relative price. Lucas shows that if people are rational then the real response to an increase in the own-price becomes a function of how volatile monetary policy and aggregate prices have been in the past and how volatile they are expected to be in the future. In a country that has a history of variable inflation, there may be little real impact from an unexpected change in money growth (i.e., α will be low). On the other hand, in a country with a history of monetary stability, an unexpected change in money growth is more likely to have real effects on output (i.e., α will be high). Of course, if the central bank tries to take advantage of this fact and systematically increases money growth in an effort to increase output growth, the public will adjust its behavior and the central bank will quickly lose its power to influence output (i.e., as α falls and expected price variability rises).

BUSINESS CYCLES IN THE RATIONAL EXPECTATIONS MODEL

Business cycles in the Rational Expectations model are temporary deviations from the natural rate of output caused by unanticipated changes in aggregate demand. For example, consider the effects of an unanticipated decrease in money growth by the Fed. This reduction in the money supply reduces aggregate demand. Firms mistakenly view this fall in aggregate demand, at least in part, as a decrease in the individual demand for their good and respond by cutting production and reducing nominal wages and employment. As workers see their nominal wages fall, they mistakenly believe that this is also a reduction in their real wages and reduce their labor supply. Until firms and workers realize that their own-price fell because aggregate demand fell, output and employment will remain below their natural rates and the economy will be in a recession. However, in a world of rational agents, this period of time should not be a long one. People will quickly realize that they have been operating under mistaken expectations. Firms and workers will adjust their production and labor supply accordingly, prices and wages will correct themselves, and the economy will return to its natural rate.

How can changes in aggregate demand be unanticipated if expectations are rational? Once again, remember that rational expectations do not mean perfect expectations. There are three very important reasons why changes in money policy are difficult to observe. First, most information on monetary policy only becomes available after a lag. There is also significant revision in monetary data, with initial estimates often differing significantly from subsequent data. Second, central banks often make temporary adjustments in the money supply to respond to temporary changes in market conditions. For example, the Fed may temporarily increase the money supply during periods of bad weather because the check-clearing process slows down. Even for expert "Fed-watchers," it is often difficult to separate permanent changes in the money supply from temporary changes. Third, the Fed and other central banks have historically been very secretive organizations. Until recently, the Fed never released press statements indicating when they were changing monetary policy. Proponents of the Rational Expectations model argue that one of the reasons the U.S. economy has been more stable recently has been the Fed's new openness, which has provided the public better information about monetary policy.

Rational expectations has radical implications for stabilization policy. Systematic, or predictable, policies will always be anticipated by the public, which will adjust its expectations and their actions in anticipation of any change. The only way that a policymaker can influence real variables is if changes in policy are unanticipated by the public. In other words, the only way for policymakers to increase real output is for them to be secretive and unpredictable. Of course, the problem is that stabilization policy by its very nature cannot be unpredictable. Stabilization policy will not be able to stimulate output during recessions if everyone knows exactly how policymakers are going to respond beforehand.

In fact, if taken to its logical extreme, the Rational Expectations model implies *policy irrelevance*, or that all government policies that are observable will be completely ineffective. This holds not just for monetary policy, but for fiscal policy as well. Consider a deficit-financed tax cut aimed at stimulating aggregate demand. If the public is rational, it will realize that these deficits will have to be paid for in the future by individuals with higher taxes (if not by themselves, then by their heirs). As a result, it will likely save this entire tax cut and aggregate demand will change very little or not at all. Likewise, a deficit-financed increase in government spending will also be matched by an increase in household saving, leading to at most a minimal change in aggregate demand. This notion of deficit irrelevance is often referred to as *Ricardian Equivalence*, in reference to the classical economist David Ricardo, who first formulated this concept. Unless these changes in fiscal policy are unanticipated, they will not have real effects; but if changes in policy are unanticipated, it cannot be the case that stabilization policy is serving the goal of stabilizing output, only destabilizing output.

Another important implication of rational expectations is that without an understanding of how people adjust their expectations in response to changes in economic conditions, which in any given circumstance may be impossible to predict, any forecast of the future based on data from the past will be unreliable. This is referred to as the *Lucas Critique*, and it raises important questions about stabilization policy because forecasting is an integral part of policy formation for two reasons. First, accurate forecasts of downturns are critical so that policy can be enacted in a timely manner. Second, the eventual effects of changes in policy must be understood in order for these policies to be conducted on the proper scale. If the effects of policy are different under different sets of expectations, it may be impossible to correctly predict the impact of stabilization policy on the economy. This would result in a level of variability in the timing and effectiveness of policy that would seriously diminish the ability of policymakers to stabilize output.

To summarize, the Rational Expectations model implies that government policy cannot play a positive role in the economy. In fact, by being a large source of economic uncertainty, changes in government policy destabilize the economy and drive swings in the business cycle. Because of this, rational expectation proponents strongly believe in laissez-faire fiscal policies and rules-based monetary policies.

EMPIRICAL EVIDENCE ON RATIONAL EXPECTATIONS

Are price expectations unbiased? Unbiased expectations mean that, on average, expectations are correct and that errors are not consistently made in one direction or another. Many studies have investigated whether the Michigan Survey of Consumer Sentiment, which includes a question about the public's expected inflation rate, is an unbiased estimator of actual inflation. These studies have generally found that although there is a large amount of forecast error, this measure of expectations is in fact unbiased. A number of studies have also investigated a survey of economists' expected inflation rates, called the Livingston survey, and have generally found that these expectations are biased (the irony here is thick). However, all of these studies are based on survey data, which is very subjective and unreliable, and can be biased by only a few individual responses.

Victor Zarnowitz (1985) conducted a comprehensive study of professional forecasts of inflation. He found that 44 percent of the 2,350 inflation forecasts examined were biased either positively or negatively. However, professional forecasts of other macroeconomic series were much more accurate, with only about 10 percent of these forecasts being biased. While this study raises questions about the validity of rational expectations, just how many forecasts have to be biased before we can reject rational expectations remains unclear.

How do people respond to extreme disinflations? According the Keynesian and Monetarist models, any attempt to reduce inflation by reducing money growth will lead to a significant recession. In the case of a *hyperinflation*, which is defined as inflation of greater than 1,000 percent a year, how can a government hope to reduce inflation without causing a complete economic collapse? Thomas Sargent (1986) investigated two hyperinflations that took place in Germany and Poland after World War I, from which some data are reported in Table 6.1. First consider Germany, where inflation fell from over 42 billion percent in 1923 (that is not a typo) to 12 percent during 1924. At the same time that inflation

TABLE 6.1   The End of Hyperinflations in Germany and Poland

GERMANY	Inflation Rate	Index of Production
1921	155%	77
1922	7,488	86
1923	4.2×10^{10}	54
1924	12	77
POLAND	Inflation Rate	Number of Unemployed
1921	136%	98,000
1922	819	116,255
1923	44,359	86,003
1924	0.19	127,936

Source: Sargent (1986)

was plummeting, industrial production actually rose significantly. In Poland, inflation fell from 44,000 percent to less than 1 percent during 1923. While unemployment rose in Poland, it did not rise by nearly as much as any Monetarist or Keynesian would predict. The only way to explain these results is to recognize that the public adjusted their price expectations and nominal wages in response to these severe monetary contractions much more quickly than any model of adaptive expectations would predict. This is persuasive evidence in support of rational expectations.

Another economic episode that has received a great deal of attention from economists is the 1981 recession in the United States. This recession was caused by a large decrease in the money supply initiated by the Fed in an effort to reduce inflation, which had risen to nearly 10 percent. Figure 6.1 presents inflation and unemployment rates between 1979 and 1987. Inflation fell from 9.9 percent in 1981 to 3.6 percent in 1983, during which the United States experienced its worst unemployment since the Great Depression. Rational expectations proponents argue that this recession was not so severe as anticipated, given the size and steepness of the decline in inflation. In addition, this recession was relatively short, lasting only 16 months. Critics of rational expectations charge that this monetary contraction was widely announced by the Fed and taken seriously by the public. The fact that a severe recession still took place raises serious questions about the validity of the Rational Expectations model.

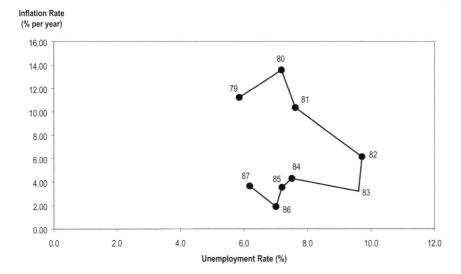

Figure 6.1 Unemployment and Inflation Rates in the United States, 1979–1987

Does output volatility differ across countries? As discussed earlier, the Rational Expectations model predicts that changes in aggregate demand and the price level are more likely to lead to large changes in real output within countries with a history of stable inflation. In other words, in terms of the Lucas supply equation in (6.1), α should be higher in countries with a reputation for steady inflation. Lucas (1973) tested this hypothesis for 18 countries for the period 1952–1967. The results for 7 of these countries are reported in Table 6.2. Countries with a history of variable inflation, such as Argentina and Paraguay, have low estimated values for α, meaning that changes in aggregate demand had little real effect on output, just as Lucas predicted. Likewise, countries with a history of stable inflation, such as the United States and West Germany, had high estimated values for α. However, the correlation between inflation history and α is not perfect. Note that α is lower in Canada than in West Germany, even though prices were less variable in Canada. Likewise, α is lower in Argentina than in Paraguay, even though price variance was considerably higher in Paraguay. However, taken as a whole, Lucas's study is strong evidence in favor of rational expectations and indicates that the reputation established by policy-makers plays an important role in shaping the public's response to changes in aggregate demand.

Laurence Ball, N. Gregory Mankiw, and David Romer (1988) conducted another cross-country empirical study. They found that the real effects of aggregate demand shifts both across countries and over time within one country were smaller when average inflation was higher. What is surprising about this study is that it actually raises questions about the Rational Expectations model. Why should average inflation matter, when it should be the variability of inflation that affects whether a change in aggregate demand is unexpected? This evidence suggests that the real effects from these demand shocks are not the result of the

TABLE 6.2   Estimates of the Real Effects of Aggregate Demand
Shocks, 1952–1967

Country	α	Var(P)
Argentina	0.011	0.01998
Paraguay	0.022	0.03192
Italy	0.622	0.00044
UK	0.665	0.00037
Canada	0.759	0.00018
West Germany	0.820	0.00026
United States	0.910	0.00007

Source: Lucas (1973)

public being fooled but are more likely caused by other forms of market imperfection, such as inflexible wages and prices.

Do anticipated changes in aggregate demand have real effects? A number of studies have attempted to classify aggregate demand shocks from fiscal and monetary policy into those that should have been easily predicted by the public and those that were unpredictable. These studies have uniformly found that both predictable and unpredictable shocks have real effects on output. In addition, price changes from the predictable demand shocks tend to lag behind changes in output by 2–5 years. These results are hard to reconcile with a model of rational expectations and perfect competition in which output fluctuations are driven by firms and workers who are temporarily fooled into changing their behavior.

Recently, the Federal Reserve has moved towards more openness in its operations and in its announcements of changes in monetary policy. By any definition, most changes in the money supply today should be anticipated by the public. And yet markets, policymakers, and the public all believe that changes in the money supply have real and long-lasting effects on output and unemployment in the future. When are people being irrational—when they form their expectations or when they believe that changes in monetary policy have real effects on the economy?

CONCLUSIONS

Economist Robert Gordon has referred to the Rational Expectations model as economics "in which theory proceeds with impeccable logic from unrealistic assumptions to conclusions that contradict the historical record" (1976, p. 185). Even the preeminent proponent of rational expectations, Robert Lucas, has acknowledged that some of the implications of the Rational Expectations model, such as policy irrelevance, are not validated by what we observe in the real world. Few economists today believe that observable changes in policy are irrelevant to real economic activity and that only unexpected changes in policy influence output. Likewise, nobody today thinks that the Rational Expectations model can adequately explain both the depth and persistence of business cycles. The assertion that the Great Depression could be caused by a great big misunderstanding takes implausibility to a whole new level.

However, this does not mean that the concept of rational expectations has been abandoned. In fact, rational expectations has become one of the cornerstone concepts in modern macroeconomics along with such concepts as the natural rate hypothesis. Rational expectations have significantly advanced our understanding of business cycles in three important ways. First, rational expectations have corrected an important contradiction that had existed in macroeconomics by asserting that people don't just act rationally when making a decision about whether or not to buy orange juice, but they also act rationally and use all currently available information when forming their expectations of the future. Research on rational expectations has also focused attention on the importance of information in economics. "What do firms and workers know and when do they know it?" is now a fundamental question that must be addressed in all economic models. Finally, rational expectations has once again raised important questions about the ability of government policy to stabilize the economy and moderate, not amplify, business cycles.

What economists have increasingly come to question is not the idea of rational expectations but the Rational Expectations model in which individuals form their expectations within near-perfectly competitive markets (the exception being imperfect information) with perfectly flexible prices and wages. Rational expectations in an imperfectly competitive model of the economy can have much different implications. For example, consider a model in which people have rational expectations but firms and households face constraints on the amount of funds that they can borrow regardless of their future ability to pay the money back. In this model, any tax cut may not get saved to pay future taxes (which would lead to policy irrelevance) but instead could be spent in lieu of getting a bank loan. The result would be that tax cuts would increase consumption, investment, and real output growth. This would be a rational response to borrowing constraints. In fact, the initial size of the change in aggregate demand would be larger if expectations are formed rationally than if firms and households were slow to adjust to these tax cuts because of adaptive expectations. In other words, it is not necessarily rational expectations but the Rational Expectations model of perfectly flexible markets that generates what many economists consider to be implausible results.

Thus, as an idea, rational expectations continue to play an important role in business cycle theory. For example, it is a crucial component of Real Business Cycle models, discussed in the next chapter, and New Keynesian economics, discussed in Chapter 8. It is interesting to note that the primary objective of New Keynesian models is to show exactly how models with rational expectations and other microeconomic fundamentals can still exhibit Keynesian results if markets are imperfectly competitive. However, the Rational Expectations model has largely been abandoned as an all-encompassing model of business cycle behavior.

SUGGESTED READINGS

Robert E. Lucas, "Rules, Discretion, and the Role of the Economic Advisor" (1980): Lucas's arguments in support of Friedman's rules-based monetary policy and how rational expectations reinforce Friedman's skepticism about the effectiveness of stabilization policy.

Robert E. Lucas, "Some International Evidence on Output-Inflation Tradeoffs" (1973): A cross-country study of the real effects of changes in the price level in which Lucas finds empirical evidence that supports rational expectations.

Rodney Maddock and Michael Carter, "A Child's Guide to Rational Expectations" (1982): A conversation about rational expectations.

7

Real Business Cycle Models

INTRODUCTION

Real Business Cycle models were developed in the 1980s, but really represent the culmination of a movement towards reestablishing classical principles in business cycle theory that began in the 1960s. This process began with the Monetarists, who agreed with Keynesians that business cycles were driven by aggregate demand shocks. However, Monetarists argued that Keynesians ignored the natural rate of output and that changes in demand were driven not by animal spirits but by unstable monetary policy. As a result, Monetarists found themselves arguing for limited government and laissez-faire policies, cornerstone beliefs of Classical economics.

The Rational Expectations model took Monetarist arguments one step further by asserting that only unexpected changes in policy can drive business cycles. The Rational Expectations model incorporated a stronger form of the natural rate hypothesis in which only erratic government policy could have real effects on output, eliminating any possibility that stabilization policy can be beneficial. Thus, the belief in rules-based, laissez-faire policies was held even more strongly among the advocates of this neoclassical model.

Real Business Cycle models took this neoclassical movement to its logical, if circular, conclusion by returning to all of the fundamental principles of the Classical model. Real Business Cycle models assert that the natural rate hypothesis holds in the long run and in the short run because markets are perfectly competitive and individuals have perfect information. Aggregate demand is irrelevant to real economic activity and money neutrality always holds. Only aggregate supply, which is a function of the amount of labor, the amount of capital, and the aggregate level of technology in an economy, determines the level of real output in an economy. As a result, in Real Business Cycle models, only changes in aggregate supply generate business cycles. Government policies that create market distortions and reduce the incentives to work, invest, or innovate are the primary culprit in initiating reductions in output.

Interest in aggregate supply and its role in business cycles was spurred by two phenomena during the 1970s and 1980s. First, ideology played a role. Not only did Real Business Cycle models build on the neoclassical resurgence of the 1960s and 1970s, but they also dovetailed nicely with a political movement referred to as *Supply-Side economics*, which is often associated with Ronald Reagan, who became president of the United States in 1981. Supply-Side politicians assert that aggregate supply determines output and that the primary focus of policymakers should be on the negative effects of government taxation and regulation. In fact, Supply-Side politicians believe that taxes are so costly in terms of reducing the incentives to work and invest that cutting taxes will actually increase tax revenue. This is because tax cuts lead to extremely large increases in aggregate output.

Even more important, aggregate supply rose to the forefront of business cycle theory during the 1970s because of oil price shocks. The Organization of Petroleum Exporting Countries (OPEC) placed an embargo on the United States in 1973, quadrupling the price of oil within a matter of months. Another large increase in the price of oil took place in 1979 after the Iranian revolution. These two large increases in oil prices led to large reductions in aggregate supply. This is in part because these increases in the price of oil made much of the existing oil-intensive capital stock too expensive to operate, effectively reducing the level of capital available to firms. In addition, oil is an input into the production of every single good in modern economies (if for no other reason than oil is needed to transport goods from here to there). As a result, increases in oil prices led to significant increases in the marginal cost of production across every single industry.

The result of these large decreases in aggregate supply was unprecedented *stagflation*, or rising unemployment and inflation at the same time. Stagflation runs exactly opposite to a Phillips curve view of the economy, where inflation and unemployment move in opposite directions. The Keynesian, Monetarist, and Rational Expectations models, which primarily focus on aggregate demand shocks as the cause of recessions, had no plausible explanation for these events. However, the Classical model, with its focus on aggregate supply shocks, did.

As a result of these ideological and empirical realities, economists in the 1980s were primed to modernize the Classical model in an effort to provide a more plausible explanation of business cycles. How and how well Real Business Cycle models accomplished this goal is the subject of this chapter.

DESCRIBING REAL BUSINESS CYCLE MODELS

The main difference between the Classical model and a Real Business Cycle model is in the level of detail that is incorporated into the economic analysis. While both are models of perfect competition in which the economy is always in equilibrium, Real Business Cycle models are much more rigorously specified and explicitly include modern microeconomic principles such as marginal analysis. In other words, Real Business Cycle models are characterized by individuals who maximize their utility and firms who maximize their profits subject to budget constraints. What makes these macroeconomic models and not simply well-specified microeconomic models is the assumption of *representational agents*, or the assumption that all individuals have the same preferences and act alike in every way. Likewise, all firms face the same production functions, cost curves, and budget constraints. As a result, macroeconomic behavior becomes a simple summation of microeconomic behavior.

Real Business Cycle models are actually based on Neoclassical Growth models, which have been used extensively in macroeconomics since the 1950s to investigate issues related to long-run growth across countries. Real Business Cycle advocates assert that the same models that economists use to investigate the long-run growth behavior of economies can be used to investigate their short-run cyclical behavior as well.

The typical Real Business Cycle production function takes the following form:

$$Y_t = F(K_t, L_t, u_t) \text{ where} \tag{7.1}$$

$$u_t = \delta + u_{t-1} + \varepsilon_t \tag{7.2}$$

This is similar to a classical production function but with one important difference: u_t, which represents changes in aggregate productivity. These productivity shocks follow a *random walk process*, given in equation 7.2, where δ is a constant and ε_t is a random variable that captures exogenous shocks to productivity. This random walk process implies that any random change in productivity from a change in ε_t will have permanent effects on productivity and, as a result, on aggregate output. Positive values of ε_t will lead to permanent increases in output and negative values of ε_t will lead to permanent falls in output. The implication is that business cycles in Real Business Cycle models are not temporary deviations from the natural rate of output; instead, they are changes in the natural rate of output itself. A contraction in output will not end until a series of positive productivity shocks occur to offset previous negative shocks.

Intuitively, where do these productivity shocks come from? Real Business Cycle proponents argue that they can come from a number of sources, as follows.

Changes in the price of important inputs into production, such as the price of oil. Higher input prices can increase the costs of production and also reduce the productivity of capital by making a portion of the capital stock too expensive to operate. Large oil price increases in the United States preceded recessions in 1973–1975, 1980, and 1990–1991. On the other hand, low oil prices such as those that existed throughout most of the 1980s and 1990s are typically associated with periods of increasing productivity and output. The price of other important raw materials such as steel, food, and coal can also contribute to changes in aggregate productivity.

Changes in technology. While we typically think about changes in technology occurring at a constant rate, technology actually increases in fits and starts much as Schumpeter asserts in his theory of creative destruction, discussed in Chapter 3. Schumpeter argues that new technologies initially decrease productivity by pulling resources away from existing technologies that are highly productive because firms and workers have learned how to use them efficiently. Eventually, this new technology will increase once workers and firms better learn how to use it, but this process could take a number of years, potentially even generations. Once this happens, however, productivity growth will not remain permanently high because at some point diminishing returns to this new technology will set in. At that point, productivity growth will begin to fall until some other new technology is developed to take its place and begin the cycle all over again. Thus, Schumpeter viewed technology as a random, cyclical process that drives cyclical movements in output. Real Business Cycle proponents typically agree, although they would emphasize that these fluctuations in technology can explain not only long waves but business cycles as well.

Changes in government taxation and regulation. Taxes lower aggregate productivity by reducing the incentives to work, to invest in new capital technologies, and to invest in education. For example, consider the effects of highly progressive income taxes. These taxes are most likely to affect those who are more highly educated, reducing the benefits of obtaining an education. Likewise, those who have the largest incomes also tend to save the largest fraction of their income, so progressive income taxation could reduce total savings and also total investment. Through these channels, changes in the tax code have an indirect effect on fluctuations in aggregate productivity.

New government regulations can also be highly distortionary. Worker safety standards, food and drug regulations, regulations on natural resource exploration, and many other government programs are viewed by many as unnecessary constraints on markets and productivity.

Wars and natural disasters. Consider the effects of the terrorist attacks of September 11, 2001. By forcing the U.S. government to increase security requirements on airlines, roads, international travel, and the like, these terrorist attacks have in all likelihood significantly reduced overall productivity within the U.S. economy. Wars often negatively impact the price of oil and other important inputs to production and lead to the destruction of both labor and capital.

Natural disasters tend to have their primary impact on the capital stock of an economy, and while their effect on aggregate productivity tends to be initially large, it also tends to be short lived.

Demographics. Workers most productive years tend to be during middle age, when workers' experience is at its peak and their physical condition has not deteriorated. As the population of a country gets older—which is happening across most developed countries such as the United States, Europe, and Japan—some impact on aggregate productivity is likely. On the other hand, other demographic factors, such as the continued tendency of women to join the labor market, have undoubtedly increased aggregate productivity because women are increasingly better educated than their male counterparts. However, most demographic changes take place gradually over a period of years, making them an unlikely cause of business cycles.

BUSINESS CYCLES IN REAL BUSINESS CYCLE MODELS

In Real Business Cycle models, recessions and expansions are driven by cyclical changes in aggregate productivity. When a number of negative shocks from various sources occur simultaneously, output is likely to fall to a permanently lower level. The more frequent and the larger these shocks, the bigger the change in output will be.

It might seem strange that random shocks to productivity can create business cycle swings. Shouldn't every negative shock be quickly offset by some positive shock? The answer is, no. Economists and statisticians have long known that if you flip a coin 20 times, cyclical patterns will emerge. There will be series of heads that follow each other just as there will be series of tails. If productivity is a random variable, then it is not surprising that economies exhibit cyclical patterns. Persistent business cycles can come about as a result of the luck that is inherent in any random process.

Different Real Business Cycle models have highlighted other real reasons for business cycle persistence. One of the most influential Real Business Cycle models is the "time-to-build" model developed by Finn Kydland and Edward Prescott (1982). In this model, the long periods of time that it takes to construct capital make changes in output highly persistent. Other Real Business Cycle models have focused on the interplay between industrial sectors in an economy. In a model developed by John Long and Charles Plosser (1983), shocks to one industry spread slowly to other industries through changes in the demand for their products. This process takes time and can explain how recessions and expansions gradually build and then gradually end.

Real Business Cycle models have clear prescriptions for how stabilization policy should operate. First, business cycles are efficient in Real Business Cycle models. In other words, they do not represent lost output, as suggested by aggregate demand theories. Instead, they are an optimal response to real changes in the economy. As a result, stabilization policy is unnecessary. Instead, government policy should focus on supply-side policies aimed at increasing the productive capacity of the economy. The best way to do this is to follow a laissez-faire approach to government intervention in the economy.

Unemployment is also efficient in Real Business Cycle models because it is completely voluntary. Involuntary unemployment is not possible because labor markets are perfectly competitive. Voluntary unemployment rises during recessions because real wages fall in response to negative productivity shocks that reduce the demand for labor. While this might strike many as implausible, Real Business Cycle proponents would argue that the concept of involuntary unemployment was developed by economists to justify why some people do not want to take low-paying jobs. Can't a recently laid-off manager always find a job somewhere, even if it means working at a fast-food restaurant? Such a person might be saying that he or she cannot find a job, but what is really happening is that he or she is unwilling to take a large cut in pay.

Even more surprisingly, standard Real Business Cycle models argue that money is neutral and never has real effects on the economy. Central banks control inflation, but they cannot influence output because the money supply influences only aggregate demand and not aggregate supply. As a result, Real Business Cycle proponents typically ignore monetary policy and argue for rules that will keep money growth and inflation low.

Government can influence output through fiscal policy in Real Business Cycle models, but not in the way envisioned by Keynesians. Keynesians believe that lower taxes and higher government spending stimulate output by increasing aggregate demand. Real Business Cycle economists believe that lower taxes and higher government spending stimulate output by increasing aggregate supply. Lower taxes increase aggregate supply by increasing the incentives to work and invest in capital, education, and technology. What is not so obvious is why higher government spending would increase aggregate supply. The Real Business Cycle argument is that higher government spending increases government deficits. The public realizes that these higher deficits will have to be paid off in the future with higher taxes, so they begin to work more now in order to accumulate the wealth needed to do this. This increase in labor supply increases aggregate supply and output. Consequently, these "supply-side" arguments, where everything that affects the economy does so through its effects on aggregate supply, turn traditional Keynesian views of macroeconomic policy completely upside down.

EMPIRICAL EVIDENCE ON REAL BUSINESS CYCLE MODELS

Do changes in productivity lead changes in output? Aggregate productivity is a difficult thing to measure. A widely used method of estimating aggregate productivity was developed by Robert Solow (1956) and uses the following production function:

$$Y_t = A_t K_t^{\alpha} L_t^{1-\alpha}$$ (7.3)

This production function is in *Cobb-Douglas* form. It is easy to show that this production function exhibits both *constant returns to scale*, meaning that doubling both capital and labor will double output, and *diminishing marginal returns*, meaning that holding one input constant, the increase in output gotten from increasing the other input falls as the quantity of that input rises.

A_t in this production function represents aggregate productivity. While aggregate productivity is not observable, all the other variables in equation 7.1 can be directly measured. One way to think about A_t is that it is the growth in output that cannot be explained by growth in inputs. As a result, taking output growth and subtracting out capital growth and labor growth, making sure to weight their contributions to output based on the value of α, will leave you with an estimate of A_t. This measure of aggregate productivity is commonly referred to as either the *Solow residual* or *multifactor productivity*.

Figure 7.1 presents the Solow residual and output growth in the United States from 1948–1990. Obviously, there is a close correlation between these two variables, with the Solow residual slightly leading changes in output. (The relationship between multifactor productivity, output growth, and the robust growth experienced in the United States during the 1990s is discussed in more detail in Chapter 12 on the "new economy.")

There is a huge problem, however, with using the Solow residual to measure changes in aggregate productivity. The Solow residual is not a direct but an implied measure of productivity. It is an "everything but the kitchen sink" estimate—everything other than input growth that affects output growth gets lumped together into the Solow residual. Some of the changes in the Solow residual might reflect changes in technology and other advances in productive efficiency, but some of the changes in the Solow residual might be caused by changes in factors that are not accounted for, such as unmeasured changes in the quality of capital or labor. As a result, the Solow residual includes much more than just exogenous changes in aggregate productivity.

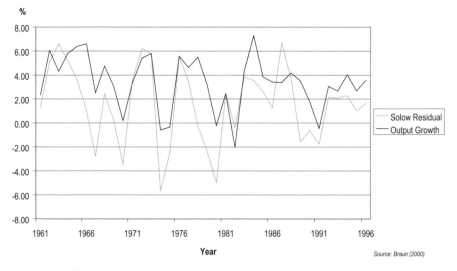

Figure 7.1 Solow Residuals and Output Growth

For example, changes in worker effort can make the Solow residual respond to changes in aggregate demand even when there has been no change in aggregate supply. To understand why, consider a firm undergoing a decrease in demand during a recession. If this firm thinks that this downturn will be short, it is likely to resist laying off workers because of the costs involved. As a result, the firm's workers will find that they have less to do and worker effort and productivity will decrease. On the other hand, during periods when business is unusually strong, the firm will ask these same workers to increase their efforts in order to meet higher demand. In other words, firms agree to smooth workers' employment in exchange for workers changing their effort during busy and slack times. This process is often referred to as *labor hoarding*.

A clear example of how labor hoarding and changes in labor effort can affect aggregate productivity occurred during World War II when productivity growth, as measured by the Solow residual, grew at a remarkable 7.6 percent a year on average. This large increase was not caused by any new technology. Instead, it was caused by large increases in the demand for government purchases and by workers working harder because they felt their efforts contributed to the war effort. This suggests that procyclical changes in the Solow residual can be driven by changes in aggregate demand and do not initiate, but are the result of, fluctuations in output. As a result, critics of Real Business Cycle models would argue that the fact that changes in productivity lead changes in output does not necessarily mean that business cycles are aggregate supply driven.

How well do Real Business Cycle models mimic business cycle data? Because Real Business Cycle models are completely specified versions of real economies, they can be used to simulate the real world and their behavior can be directly compared to actual business cycle data. There are three steps to such a simulation. First, the researcher constructs the model and programs the relevant equations into a computer. Second, the model is calibrated, meaning parameter values are chosen so that the model matches certain long-run properties of a given economy. Third, the model is subjected to shocks, such as productivity shocks estimated by the Solow residual or changes in taxes and government spending, and the behavior of key business cycle variables can be observed.

Table 7.1 presents business cycle data for the U.S. economy in the first column. This data includes the standard deviation of output, the standard deviation of other variables relative to output, and the correlation of these variables with output. In the second column, the same data generated by a Real Business Cycle model is presented. This Real Business Cycle model incorporates labor taxes, capital taxes, consump-

TABLE 7.1   Business Cycle Data for the U.S. Economy and a Real Business Cycle Model

	U.S. Data[a]	RBC Model[b]
Std. Deviation of Output	1.73	1.48 (0.17)
Std. Deviation Relative to Output:		
Total Consumption	0.49	0.55 (0.06)
Hours Worked	0.79	0.71 (0.04)
Investment	3.10	3.47 (0.25)
Productivity	0.49	0.44 (0.04)
Correlation with Output:		
Total Consumption	0.75	0.68 (0.10)
Hours Worked	0.87	0.92 (0.02)
Investment	0.89	0.93 (0.02)
Productivity	0.60	0.78 (0.06)
Corr(real wages, hours)	0.10	0.48 (0.11)

[a] In this data, investment (from 1954-1989) refers to gross fixes investment and durables, consumption is defined as nondurables and services, prices are measured by the GDP deflator, and the hours data are taken from the household survey which includes total employee hours in all industries. Productivity is defined as output divided by hours. Each of these series is expressed in terms of constant 1982 dollars. All series have been deflated by the 16 and over population and were smoothed using the Hodrick-Prescott filter with a smoothing parameter of 1600.

[b] The second moments for the model economies were computed by calculating 100 sets of 244 observations from which the first 100 observations were eliminated in order to control for initial period bias. The number of quarters over the period 1954:1-1989:4 then corresponds to the number of observations in each simulation, which is 144. Each series was smoothed using the Hodrick-Prescott filter, which is the same filter used in calculating the U.S. data. The mean of these samples are reported above, with the sample standard deviations reported in parentheses.

Source: Knoop (2003)

tion taxes, Solow residual productivity shocks, and government spending shocks. Each is chosen to be consistent with the U.S. economy. Comparing the results, the similarities are striking. While output is not quite variable enough and the correlation between productivity and output is too high, for most variables this Real Business Cycle model mimics the U.S. economy quite well.

Critics would argue that such results are not persuasive. If you have estimates of productivity shocks that are closely related to changes in output (even if there is no causation), it should not be surprising that putting these shocks into any sort of model will generate results that are close to what are observed in the real world. The key question is this: Where do these productivity shocks come from? Real Business Cycle proponents would argue that these productivity shocks primarily reflect exogenous changes in technology, government regulation, taxation, and input prices. Critics would argue that it is falling output that causes productivity to fall endogenously and not the other way around.

To better understand why many economists are so skeptical about Real Business Cycle models, consider its explanation of the Great Depression. Real Business Cycle theorists are forced to argue that the Great Depression was caused by a reduction in aggregate productivity and aggregate supply, even though we know that prices fell during the Great Depression, which is inconsistent with a decrease in aggregate supply. What was the source of this fall in productivity? The most commonly mentioned culprit is the Smoot-Hawley tariff, which was imposed in 1930 and increased tariffs on imports by 40 percent. However, this was during a time when imports were only about 6 percent of GDP. To put it politely, this explanation is a bit of a stretch.

Are real wages procyclical? This question about the cyclicality of real wages was also raised during the discussion of Keynesian economics in Chapter 4. The evidence presented in Figure 4.5 suggests that real wages were strongly countercyclical during the Great Depression. Table 4.1 presents real wage correlations with output collected by Basu and Taylor (1999) across 13 countries for the period 1870–1999. They found that real wages have been only slightly procyclical during the postwar era and basically acyclical over the entire period. A large number of other studies have basically supported the conclusion that over long periods of time real wages are mildly procyclical to acyclical within the United States. These results raise red flags because Real Business Cycle models need large procyclical changes in the real wage during business cycles in order to generate large changes in voluntary unemployment.

In addition, quite a bit of empirical evidence suggests that even when real wages do change, labor supply is inelastic and does not change by enough in response to changes in the real wage to explain cyclical movements in employment and the number of hours worked (for an example of such a study, see a paper by Joseph Altonji [1986]). Referring back to the last row of Table 7.1, the Real Business Cycle model generated a correlation between real wages and hours worked of .48 while in the actual data this correlation is much closer to zero at .10. Thus, the empirical evidence on acyclical real wages and labor supply inelasticity suggests that it is something other than procyclical changes in real wages that is driving swings in employment. In other words, cyclical changes in employment do not appear to be entirely voluntary.

Does monetary policy influence real output? The 1981–1982 recession was clearly caused by a large contraction in money growth initiated by the Fed to reduce inflation. How do you explain the 1981–1982 recession in a Real Business Cycle model? The answer is that it is not possible in standard Real Business Cycle models that assert money neutrality.

Any number of empirical studies examining the relationship between money and output could be cited here, but the commonsense answer to this question of whether monetary policy influences real output is yes. Even though it is true that some of the strong positive correlation between the money supply and output results from the money supply responding to changes in output (for more detail about why this is the case, see Chapter 5), it is also clearly true that changes in the money supply have real effects on output, at least in the short run. While the public, policymakers, businesses, and markets all believe this to be the case, it is only the most extreme Real Business Cycle advocates who do not.

CONCLUSIONS

Real Business Cycle theory defined much of the cutting-edge business cycle research during the 1980s and its influence, though lessened, continues in modern macroeconomic theory. Economists today pay much more attention to supply factors such as productivity, capacity utilization, and input prices when investigating business cycles than they did previously.

While the supply shocks of the 1970s and the resurgence of interest in neoclassical economics played important roles in the popularity of Real Business Cycle models, another extremely important factor in their appeal to economists is that they are based on microeconomic principles—principles such as utility maximization, profit maximization, and market equilibrium. In many economists' eyes, Real Business Cycle models are both elegant and theoretically consistent. The fact that the study of both long-run growth and short-run business cycles could be merged into one unified macroeconomic model is also incredibly appealing to economists.

N. Gregory Mankiw (1989) argues that any good theory has to be both internally and externally consistent. By internally consistent he means that the theory has to be intuitively plausible and understandable. Because they are explicitly based on microeconomic theory that is widely accepted and has withstood the test of time, neoclassical models such as Real Business Cycle models are internally consistent. However, to be externally consistent a theory has to be able to match the empirical facts. As we have discussed, by asserting that only aggregate supply matters in determining output, that money is neutral, that unemployment is entirely voluntary, and that productivity shocks are the only cause of business cycles, the predictions of Real Business Cycle models do not seem to fit the facts of business cycles as we currently understand them. Keynesian economics, while failing to meet the objective of internal consistency because of its lack of microeconomic rigor, does considerably better at being externally consistent with the empirical data. Can economists develop a model that is both consistent with microeconomic theory but can also explain the facts of recessions and depressions in a plausible manner? New Keynesian models, the subject of Chapter 8, aim to achieve such a reconciliation between neoclassical and Keynesian economics in an attempt to provide a unified theory of business cycles.

SUGGESTED READINGS

Robert E. Lucas, "Unemployment Policy" (1978): A neoclassical critique of the concepts of involuntary unemployment and full employment. Lucas argues that stabilization policy aimed at eliminating involuntary unemployment is likely to distract policymakers from the more legitimate goal of increasing economic efficiency through maintaining low inflation and reducing government regulation.

N. Gregory Mankiw, "Real Business Cycles: A New Keynesian Perspective" (1989): Criticisms of Real Business Cycle models and methodology. Mankiw ends with arguments in support of New Keynesian models, which are the subject of Chapter 8.

Charles Plosser, "Understanding Real Business Cycles" (1989): A comprehensive review of Real Business Cycle models and methodology. In this paper, Plosser works through the details of a basic Real Business Cycle model.

8

New Keynesian Models

INTRODUCTION

During the 1980s, economists began asking themselves a very important question: Can models be developed that incorporate rational expectations and the natural rate hypothesis, but still exhibit Keynesian
properties such as market failure, excess supply, and involuntary unemployment? This question was only natural given the decline of the
Monetarist, Rational Expectations, and Real Business Cycle models in
the late 1980s. Real Business Cycle and Rational Expectations models
fell out of favor because fewer economists believed their policy conclusions. In addition, new data increasingly challenged the neoclassical
assumption of perfect price and wage flexibility. However, economists
continued to believe in the concept of rational expectations and they
continued to be attracted to the microeconomic fundamentals incorporated in Real Business Cycle models.

Monetarism declined in popularity among economists for two additional reasons. First, the stagflation of the 1970s was clearly not caused
by monetary policy, so the belief that changes in the money supply were
the sole source of all business cycles seemed increasingly difficult to
support. Second, the close relationships between the monetary base, the
money supply, and output broke down during the 1980s. It seemed
increasingly implausible to argue that policymakers should adhere to
simple money growth rules when money demand, M1, and M2 were so
unpredictable. However, most economists continued to believe in the
natural rate hypothesis and that monetary policy plays an important
role in both stabilizing and destabilizing output.

"New Keynesian economics" is the name given to a new group of models that were developed to fill this void. New Keynesian models borrow the concepts of market failure and price inflexibility from Keynesian economics, the natural rate hypothesis and a focus on monetary policy from Monetarist economics, the concept of rational expectations from the Rational Expectations model, and a belief in the importance of developing models with microeconomic foundations from Real Business Cycle models. New Keynesian researchers have attempted to develop new and widely varied models in which market failure is generated by individuals engaging in optimizing behavior (not just through assumed, or ad hoc, behavioral assumptions). The ultimate goal of New Keynesian models is to better describe both the sources of imperfect competition and the role that market failure plays in business cycles.

WHAT NEW KEYNESIANS DO NOT BELIEVE

It is important to keep in mind that the term "New Keynesian" refers to multiple models with a common theme. In fact, there is no single model that can truly be called representative of this entire school of thought. As a result, it is often unclear exactly what New Keynesians believe in and what separates them from old Keynesians. N. Gregory Mankiw (1992) describes what he believes to be their core beliefs by stressing the six disagreements New Keynesians have with old Keynesians. On each of these points, notice how New Keynesians have adopted principles from previous business cycle theories.

New Keynesians do not believe that reading The General Theory *is the best way to understand business cycles.* New Keynesians believe that *The General Theory* is very ambiguous and that a big reason for this ambiguity is its lack of rigor, especially when it comes to explaining the microeconomic foundations of macroeconomic behavior. For example, Keynes claimed that nominal wages are sticky downward. Why? If the answer is imperfect information and coordination failure, why don't people form their expectations rationally instead of basing their wage demands only on what their wages are relative to other workers? If the answer is wage contracts, then why do workers sign contracts if they lead to costly unemployment? By skipping over a number of the "Why?" questions, Keynes and his followers left many of their conclusions open to questioning. New Keynesians want to answer these questions based on detailed and specific models in which individuals engage in optimizing behavior (i.e., behavior that is consistent with microeconomic theory).

The lessons of the Classical model are helpful. Keynes dismissed the Classical model as a special case of his general theory. New Keynesians do not dismiss Classical economics so readily. Especially important to New Keynesians is the idea that a natural rate of output and unemployment exist and that these natural rates are determined by capacity (i.e., aggregate supply) in the long run.

Economies are not threatened by saving too much. Keynes's *paradox of thrift*, where economies can stagnate because of saving too much and consuming too little, is simply not observed in reality. Contrary to Keynes, there is a positive relationship between higher savings and higher investment across countries. New Keynesians believe that higher savings lead to more capital formation and higher output in the long run. As a result, they are more likely to worry about a country that does not save enough as opposed to one that saves too little.

High inflation is not the cost of low unemployment. New Keynesians believe in the natural rate hypothesis and do not believe that there is a long-run tradeoff between inflation and unemployment. In other words, the Phillips curve is not a part of New Keynesian theory, only old Keynesian theory.

Monetary policy can be used as a tool to stabilize output, while fiscal policy is much less useful. Old Keynesians believe in big fiscal policy multipliers, but in reality these large multipliers do not appear to exist. When added to the political difficulties of trying to use fiscal policy in a timely manner to stabilize the economy, most New Keynesians do not advocate its use to offset business cycles. On the other hand, despite Keynes's worry about a liquidity trap, New Keynesians believe that monetary policy can be an effective tool for output stabilization, but only if used correctly by policymakers.

Policymakers should favor rules over discretion. Keynesian aggregate demand management has an inflationary bias and is also subject to the simultaneous problems of policy lags, a lack of accurate forecasting, and the Lucas Critique. Because of this, New Keynesians are generally proponents of policy rules. This is not because they believe that systematic monetary policy cannot influence output (like in the Rational Expectations model). Instead, they believe that the inherent difficulties in enacting the correct policies at the right time make effective stabilization policy much easier in theory than it is in practice.

WHAT NEW KEYNESIANS DO BELIEVE

New Keynesian models generally fall into one of three categories: models of price inflexibility, models of nominal and real wage inflexibility, and models of imperfect information and risk. Although widely varied, it is important to understand what these New Keynesian models have in common. Each is a model of imperfect competition, and in each model this imperfect competition leads to some form of market failure and persistent disequilibria that can play a role in generating business cycles.

Models of Price Inflexibility

A sizeable amount of empirical data (some of which will be discussed later) suggests that prices are not perfectly flexible but are slow to adjust to changes in supply and demand. If the prices of goods are rigid, then recessions can originate from disequilibria in the goods market, as opposed to relying on inflexible wages in the labor market as Keynes did. New Keynesian models focus on four primary explanations of price inflexibility.

Delivery and service considerations. Firms can respond to changes in market conditions in many ways besides changing prices. For example, consider a period of high demand when firms' resources are stretched. Instead of increasing prices, firms can lengthen delivery lags or cut back on other services associated with the goods they sell. This way, customers do not have to pay a higher price and firms do not have to increase capacity. On the other hand, during periods of low demand when resources are slack, firms can shorten delivery lags and improve services. They can then avoid cutting prices while still providing something of value to their customers. Hence, this group of models recognizes that price is just one margin on which firms can adjust their operations in response to changes in demand and still satisfy their customers.

Firms incur menu costs when changing listed prices. Many firms are price setters and not price takers. As a result, prices for many goods are not determined by auctions or negotiation, as assumed in perfectly competitive models, but instead are chosen by firms trying to maximize profits. Often these prices are posted and fixed for a period of time. The primary reason for this is that firms and customers do not want to negotiate every price. Haggling takes time, and as our standard of living has increased, our time has gotten more valuable. Any small amount of money saved by customers through bargaining would likely be outweighed by the wasted time. In addition, higher wages mean that firms are reluctant to hire workers to negotiate prices. For these reasons, customers and firms alike in the United States have increasingly preferred to bargain over only the biggest ticket items, such as cars and houses, and list the prices of other goods. (This is one reason why haggling over prices is more common in poorer countries than in richer countries.)

Posted prices mean that costs are incurred by a firm every time it changes a price. The costs of changing prices are often called *menu costs,* alluding to the costs a restaurant would incur when it changes prices and has to print new menus. However, menu costs apply to a whole range of prices that are publicly posted, such as those in department stores, catalogs, and advertisements.

Why do menu costs imply price inflexibility? Because even small menu costs give firms some incentive to resist changing their prices. Until the change in revenue from changing a price is sufficient to offset the menu costs, firms will not change the price. While this might only imply a small amount of price inflexibility at the individual firm level, Mankiw (1985) has shown that it is possible that even small menu costs lead to significant price inflexibility at the aggregate level and can create persistent surpluses or shortages that lead to significant fluctuations in aggregate output. The menu costs associated with negotiating changes in prices can also explain why many suppliers and retailers operate under fixed-price contracts with their customers.

Many prices are based on markup-pricing strategies. For price-setting firms with a large number of goods (department or grocery stores for instance), an easy and intuitive pricing method is *markup-pricing*. Markup-pricing refers to choosing a price that is simply a constant percentage above the good's cost. Markup-pricing is simple to understand, easy to administer using an unskilled workforce, and easy to justify to customers. For this reason, markup-pricing is exceptionally common, especially in the retail industry.

Firms that follow markup-pricing strategies will only increase prices when their costs rise. They will not look ahead and anticipate changes in the marketplace, nor will they adjust their prices to changes in demand. Because of this, some New Keynesian models have shown that markup-pricing strategies imply a significant amount of price inflexibility.

Firms are concerned about their relative prices. A firm's optimal price is often dependent upon the pricing strategies of its competitors. As a result, firms may be very reluctant to raise prices unless their competitors raise their prices as well, for fear of making their goods relatively more expensive. If firms could coordinate their changes in price, then prices would be perfectly flexible, but without a mechanism to ensure that some firms will not resist price increases in order to reduce their relative price and increase their market share, price are slow to adjust. This phenomenon is referred to as *coordination failure*, which was discussed previously in our discussion of the Keynesian model. Remember that Keynes argued that relative wage concerns led to coordination failure and wage inflexibility in the labor market.

Under what conditions will coordination failure lead to price inflexibility? Obviously, a market has to be imperfectly competitive so that firms are price setters. However, it also has to be the case that the demand curves firms face in this market have to be fairly price-elastic, meaning that consumers have to be responsive to changes in relative prices. If firm demand is highly elastic, then firms will lose a great deal of market share if there is an increase in their relative price. As a result, firms will be reluctant to change their price and there will be more price inflexibility in the industry. New Keynesians often refer to this as *real rigidity*, meaning rigidity in prices that stem from the market fundamentals of supply and demand in which these firms operate. More real rigidity means that prices will be slower to adjust and market disequilibriums will be more persistent. However, real rigidity does a better job of explaining why prices are slow to adjust upward than why they are slow to fall.

Models of Nominal and Real Wage Inflexibility

As opposed to models of price inflexibility in which business cycles originate in the goods market, other New Keynesian models have instead focused on Keynes' hypothesis that recessions originate in the labor market and are caused by nominal wage stickiness. These models have attempted to describe the microfoundations of how labor markets operate and explore in detail the reasons behind wage inflexibility.

Explicit wage contracts. Explicit wage contracts, such as union contracts, are an obvious source of nominal wage inflexibility. One reason for the existence of explicit wage contracts is that in industries with homogenous work forces and collective bargaining, wage renegotiations are very costly for both workers and firms because of the threat of strike. Explicit contracts are a simple method of reducing the frequency of these negotiations.

Stanley Fischer (1977) has shown that an important implication of explicit contracts is that if the timing of contract negotiations are staggered throughout an economy, the time it takes for wages to fully respond to a shock will be much longer than the length of the wage contracts themselves. Consider a simple, if unrealistic, example. Suppose that there exists an economy with two groups of workers. Each group of workers negotiates a two-year labor contract with their employers during alternate years. Now suppose that the money supply and price level double in this economy. Can the first group of workers up for renegotiation (call them group 1) afford to demand a doubling of their nominal wage? No, because if they double their wage, all of the workers in group 1 will be twice as expensive as the workers from group 2, meaning that many workers from group 1 will lose their jobs to workers in group 2. Instead, the obvious response is for group 1 to only partially adjust their nominal wages. Likewise, when it comes time for group 2 to negotiate, they will also be reluctant to double their nominal wage and become more expensive than group 1. As a result, each of these groups will see their nominal wages slowly leap-frog over each other until the economy-wide nominal wage doubles. An obvious analogy can be made to a prison chain gang, in which each worker has to walk a little slower when shackled to another prisoner than if he were alone. This wage adjustment process is likely to take an extended period of time and lead to persistent disequilibrium in the labor market.

Implicit wage contracts. When the direct monitoring of workers within a firm is difficult, individual job reviews of workers must be conducted on a regular basis. Because these reviews are costly, they are usually spaced at regular intervals, typically every six months or a year. Wages are usually held constant between reviews and, as a result, this review process implies a certain level of nominal wage inflexibility in labor markets.

Minimum wage laws. Minimum wage laws are legislated price floors on wages. When effective (meaning the legislated wage is above the equilibrium wage that would exist without the law), minimum wage laws create downward wage inflexibility. Of course, minimum wage laws are only really effective in certain subsectors of the labor market, namely the market for unskilled and low-experience workers. As a result, minimum wage laws, like explicit and implicit contracts, can only provide a partial explanation of nominal wage inflexibility by themselves.

Insider and outsider workers. The insight of insider-outsider models is that workers who are already working for a firm (insiders) might have interests that differ from those of the firms they work for, which is profit maximization. Specifically, when insiders participate in hiring and training potential new workers (outsiders), insiders want to avoid hiring outsiders who are willing to work for lower real wages and could threaten the insiders' future raises. On the other hand, insiders also do not want to hire outsiders who are going to make considerably more than they are making, which could threaten the insiders' self-esteem. As a result, insider-outsider models show how significant nominal and real wage inflexibility can be inherent in the bargaining process for new workers because of incentive problems in the hiring and training process.

Efficiency wages. The foundation of efficiency wage models rests on a seemingly contradictory idea: Firms want to pay workers wages that are higher than equilibrium and are reluctant to cut wages during downturns, even in the presence of an excess supply of workers. The reason is that firms realize that their workforce's productivity rises as real wages rise and falls as real wages fall. There are three reasons to think this is the case. First, workers are more likely to shirk their responsibilities at lower wages because it is not that costly to be fired from a low-paying job. As a result, higher wages are a way of monitoring worker effort, especially in jobs where direct monitoring of workers is difficult. Second, firms that pay higher wages are more likely to attract and maintain the most productive workers. Third, higher wages reduce worker turnover and reduce the training costs incurred by firms. Therefore, firms with heterogeneous workforces are very reluctant to reduce both nominal and real wages for fear of harming worker productivity and the firm's ability to compete. Notice that, like insider-outsider models, efficiency wage models imply both nominal and real wage rigidity.

These New Keynesian models of price inflexibility and wage inflexibility are not mutually exclusive. In fact, important interactions can exist between these different types of nominal rigidities. Consider the case where both prices and nominal wages are inflexible. In this case, real wages would then be roughly constant and move acyclically over the business cycle. Remember from our discussions in Chapters 4 and 7 that there is quite a bit of empirical evidence that suggests real wages in the United States do not fluctuate very much over the business cycle and are approximately acyclical. Thus, the interaction between price and nominal wage inflexibility might itself be an additional source of real wage inflexibility and play a large role in explaining the acyclical behavior of real wages. This could mean that a complete model of business cycles would include market failure in both the goods and labor markets simultaneously.

Models of Information and Risk

A significant amount of New Keynesian research has taken place along a much different line than the price and wage models just discussed. This third line of research focuses on the effects of imperfect information. In the real world, it is obvious that economic agents rarely have perfect information about the economy. This is especially true in financial markets where financial institutions typically have only partial information about the credit worthiness and character of the people and firms they lend money to. The most important implication of imperfect information is risk. In fact, distributing risk among those who are willing to assume different levels of it (and potentially receive the higher payoffs associated with higher risk) is a major function of financial markets.

New Keynesian models of risk recognize that the start of an economic downturn is characterized by an increase in the economic risk perceived by firms and banks. This increase in risk has a number of important macroeconomic implications that have been explored in various New

Keynesian models. First, and most important, risk reduces financial intermediation. During economic downturns, firms are forced to take on more debt because equity financing is more difficult and expensive when stock markets are declining. Because of this increased debt and the fact that the value of many of the firm's assets have fallen in value along with the stock market, the risk of bankruptcy for most firms rises. Banks respond to this higher bankruptcy and credit risk by *credit rationing*, or restricting their amount of lending to firms. Banks prefer credit rationing to raising interest rates because higher interest rates would only further increase the risk of bankruptcy among its borrowers. Credit rationing significantly reduces investment and magnifies the size of economic contractions. Thus, investment volatility during recessions in New Keynesian models is not driven by expectations that reduce the demand for credit, as in the Keynesian model, or reductions in the supply of credit cause by wrongheaded monetary policy, as in the Monetarist model; instead, contractions in investment during recessions are largely driven by banks reducing the supply of credit in response to financial risk.

Risk also decreases aggregate output in two other ways. Increases in risk increase the probability of not selling goods that have been produced during recessions. This discourages production and reduces aggregate supply. In addition, as noted by old Keynesians, the risk associated with recessions increases uncertainty about the profitability of future investment projects, which reduces investment demand and aggregate demand. Higher levels of uncertainty can also decrease aggregate supply if the capital stock depreciates and is not replaced through new investment.

Note that each of these factors associated with risk can negatively impact both aggregate demand and aggregate supply by decreasing the incentives to invest in capital and engage in production. As a result, increases in risk associated with the beginning of economic downturns can create the conditions in which a small economic contraction turns into a significant recession or depression. It is important to note that these amplifying effects of risk take place even within economies with completely flexible prices and wages.

Although the perception of risk in these models is subjective, changes in risk in New Keynesian models are very different from changes in expectations in the traditional Keynesian model. Here, changes in risk perception are based on rational responses to changes in the financial position of firms and banks, and they affect both the supply and the demand for credit as well as aggregate demand and aggregate supply. In the Keynesian model, expectations are governed by animal spirits, and changes in expectations are not necessarily rational reactions to changes in the fundamentals of an economy. Changes in expectations affect the economy by reducing the demand for credit and investment, which in turn reduces only aggregate demand.

These New Keynesian models, and many more not covered in the brief overview here, are closely related to a burgeoning area of micro-economic research that has focused on the economics of information. Some of the most important research on the economics of information deals with *moral hazard* and its effects on financial markets. Moral hazard exists when individuals are able to allocate some of the down-side risk of a project to others while keeping all of the up-side benefits of a project for themselves, thus encouraging these individuals to en-gage in riskier behavior than they otherwise would. Moral hazard is a serious problem for financial institutions, particularly banks. Because banks absorb much of the costs of bankruptcy without sharing any of the profits of successful ventures, borrowers from banks have a signif-icant incentive to engage in riskier activities than they otherwise would.

Moral hazard played a critical role in the two largest depressions of the twentieth century, the Great Depression and the East Asian Crisis. In Chapters 10 and 13, these depressions are discussed in detail. These depressions illustrate that unless moral hazard is kept in check by government regulation and vigilant bank managers, it can lead to lead to exceptionally risky behavior by borrowers. This can undermine the stability of financial institutions that, when subjected to a negative external shock, can quickly become bankrupt and fail. Failing banks lead to deposit withdrawals and drops in lending that can trigger a financial collapse and a depression. By focusing on the macroeconomic implications of imperfect information and risk, New Keynesian models have played a crucial role in improving our understanding of the causes of the Great Depression and the East Asian crisis.

NEW KEYNESIAN BUSINESS CYCLES

An all-encompassing description of business cycles in New Keynes-ian models is not easy because there are so many different New Key-nesian models. There is not one single cause of recessions that all of these models agree upon. Instead, these models highlight a number of market imperfections that, when considered together, explain how market failures and disequilibrium can persist over extended periods of time and create business cycles.

The "typical" New Keynesian recession, which is illustrated in Figure 8.1, begins with a decrease in aggregate demand. This fall in aggregate demand can be caused by a number of potential shocks. Aggregate demand could fall because of a change in expectations or risk percep-tions that reduces investment and consumption demand, similar to that

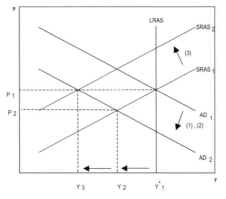

(1) A fall in AD caused by a decrease in investment and/or consumption, a decrease in the money supply, or credit rationing.

(2) Further declines in AD as higher risk reduces finanical intermediation, investment, and consumption.

(3) Fall in SRAS as capacity is reduced (lower employment and investment) and the risk of production increases.

End Result:
Output falls
Price level indeterminant

Figure 8.1   Recession Initiated by a Decrease in Aggregate Demand

argued by old Keynesians. Aggregate demand could also fall because of a contraction in the money supply, which reduces the supply of credit and investment, as argued by the Monetarists. Finally, and original to New Keynesian models, an increase in the default risk perceived by banks could lead to credit rationing that would reduce the supply of credit and investment.

New Keynesians also differ from previous theories in the propagation of recessions. New Keynesians provide a much more detailed analysis of the specifics of market failure and how market failure can magnify falls in output. First, inflexible prices can lead to persistent excess supply in the goods market, prompting firms to make additional cuts in production. Second, inflexible nominal and real wages can create excess supply in the labor market, leading to unemployment. Third, increases in risk can discourage production and also encourage banks to increase their credit rationing, which further restricts investment and consumption. Note that each of these three factors can not only magnify the initial fall in aggregate demand but can also decrease aggregate supply. This means that a recession that starts with a decrease in aggregate demand can sustain itself through subsequent decreases in both aggregate demand and aggregate supply. Thus, New Keynesian business cycles recognize that contractions propagate themselves through many sectors of the economy simultaneously and typically involve declines in both aggregate demand and aggregate supply through market failures in the labor, goods, and financial markets.

Demand-initiated recessions will only end after a number of things happen. First, investment and consumption will eventually rise as firms and households replace capital and consumer durables that have depreciated, increasing aggregate demand. As this happens, firms and

banks will reevaluate their risk appraisals, leading to both an increase
in the demand for credit and an increase in its supply. In addition, given
enough time, prices and wages will be able to fully adjust, which will
return the goods and labor markets to equilibrium and the aggregate
economy back to its natural rate of output. It is unclear how long this
entire process will take, but it could take a considerable length of time.

New Keynesians also accept the proposition that recessions can be
initiated by changes in aggregate supply, such as during the 1970s oil
price shocks, which reduce long-run aggregate supply and the natural
rate of output. However, once again, the propagation of a supply-initi-
ated recession is different from previous business cycles. An increase in
input prices would also lead to involuntary unemployment in the labor
market (because of inflexible wages) and higher risk and credit rationing in financial markets. This would, in turn, lead to a decrease in
aggregate demand and a decrease in short-run aggregate supply that is
larger than the amount that long-run aggregate supply initially fell by.
As a result, output in the short-run would actually fall below the new,
lower natural rate of output. Figure 8.2 illustrates a recession initiated
by a decrease in aggregate supply. After initially dropping significantly
(to Y_3), output will eventually rise to the new, but lower, natural rate of
output (Y_2^*) as wages and prices adjust and as firms and financial
institutions reduce their risk appraisals.

What should be the role of monetary and fiscal policy in offsetting
contractions to stabilize the economy? New Keynesians are much
more skeptical of discretionary stabilization policy than old Keynesians for a number of reasons. First, they believe that the use of
fiscal policy to offset shocks should not even be considered given the
long policy lags created by political realities. They are less skeptical

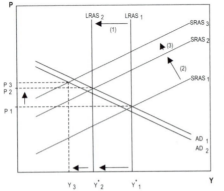

1) An increase in input prices (oil) reduces LRAS and the
natural rate of output.
2) This increase in input prices also reduces SRAS.
3) AD falls and SRAS continues to fall as credit rationing
occurs, capacity falls, and the risk of production
increases.

End Result:
Output falls
Price level rises

Figure 8.2 Recession Initiated by a Decrease in Aggregate Supply

about the effectiveness of monetary policy though similar, but shorter, policy and response lags exist. New Keynesians also believe in rational expectations and the Lucas Critique, meaning that they believe that policy changes can often have unpredictable effects on an economy depending upon the public's perceptions. Finally, New Keynesians believe that recessions usually take place because of market failures that lead to declines in both aggregate demand and aggregate supply. The use of monetary policy, which only works through aggregate demand, to "fix" a recession seems unlikely to many New Keynesians. For example, if banks are credit rationing, it might be impossible for the central bank to manipulate interest rates or expand the supply of credit available for new investment, severely limiting the impact of monetary policy.

As a result, most New Keynesians believe that policymakers should adopt some sort of policy rule. However, these rules tend to be broader than the simple money growth rules proposed by Monetarists like Friedman. The rules proposed by many New Keynesians adopt some combination of inflation and output targets. For example, Mankiw (1992) suggests that the Federal Reserve adopt a nominal GDP growth goal of 5 percent. If nominal GDP growth falls below 5 percent, because of either lower inflation or lower real output growth, the Fed would then increase the money supply until either inflation or real output growth rises.

EMPIRICAL EVIDENCE ON
NEW KEYNESIAN MODELS

Empirical research has focused on each of the three categories of New Keynesian models: price inflexibility, wage inflexibility, and imperfect information and risk. Because much of the empirical research on imperfect information and risk has dealt with reexamining the Great Depression, this line of empirical research will be discussed in Chapter 10. A few of the most important studies of price and wage inflexibility are briefly reviewed here.

Are nominal and real wages inflexible? In a review of U.S. industry-level data from the large contractions of 1893, 1929, and 1981, Christopher Hanes (2000) found that nominal wages were more rigid in industries with higher earnings, higher capital intensity, and higher market concentration. Each of these characteristics are highly correlated with heterogeneous work forces. Because heterogeneous work forces are more difficult for firms to monitor, the insider-outsider, implicit contracts, and efficiency wage models of wage determination are each plausible explanations of this nominal wage rigidity.

In previous discussions, numerous references have been made to studies that suggest that real wages have been mildly procyclical to acyclical across countries (see Table 4.1 from Basu and Taylor 1999). However, over shorter periods real wages have exhibited countercyclical (the 1930s) and procyclical (the 1970s and 1980s) behavior. One way to interpret this evidence is to say that a good business cycle model must be able to exhibit acyclical, procyclical, and countercyclical wage behavior depending upon different conditions. As discussed earlier, if both nominal wages, and prices are inflexible, real wages will be acyclical in New Keynesian models. However, if prices are more rigid than nominal wages then real wages will be slightly procyclical, and if nominal wages are more rigid than prices, then real wages will be slightly countercyclical. In other words, under different conditions, New Keynesian models can exhibit a wide range of real wage behavior just like that observed in the data.

In addition, New Keynesian models can exhibit different real wage behavior depending upon whether shocks to aggregate demand or aggregate supply are driving business cycles. Scott Sumner and Stephen Silver (1989) find that real wages tend to be countercyclical when prices are procyclical (which indicates that aggregate demand is moving) and real wages are procyclical when prices are countercyclical (which indicates aggregate supply is moving). Because New Keynesian models incorporate both aggregate demand and aggregate supply shocks in addition to nominal wage inflexibility, they are consistent with these different combinations of real wage and price cyclicality as well.

Are prices inflexible? In a study of magazine prices, Stephen Cecchetti (1986) found that the demand for magazines was elastic and that firms were very concerned about their relative price, implying a higher degree of real rigidity in the magazine industry. As a result, magazine firms averaged one price change every four years. His findings indicated that a magazine's real price fell by an average of 25 percent before a publishing firm would increase the price of a magazine.

In a broader survey of business executives, Alan Blinder (1991) reported that 55 percent of the 72 companies surveyed changed their price no more than once a year and that the average lags between a shock and a change in price was 3–4 months. Blinder found that delivery and service considerations, coordination failure, markup-pricing, implicit and explicit contracts, and menu costs were all rated as moderately important reasons for price inflexibility by more than 40 percent of business executives surveyed.

Daniel Levy, Mark Bergen, Shantanu Dutta, and Robert Venable (1997) looked at the cost of changing prices at supermarkets, which includes the costs of posting tags and signs or entering price information into computer systems. They find that these menu costs range between 0.5 percent and 1 percent of total revenues, which is a significant amount given the low profit margins in these stores. This suggests that menu costs might be a significant reason behind the reluctance of retailers to change prices.

Regarding the macroeconomic effects of this price inflexibility, Michael Kiley (2000) found that countries with higher mean inflation changed prices more often. For example, the United States averaged 4 percent inflation between 1948 and 1996, during which the average price changed every 3.5 years. On the other hand, Argentina averaged 58 percent inflation and the average price changed every year (which is still a remarkably low rate of change). These results make sense given that firms have more incentive to change prices more often when inflation is higher. Kiley also found that countries with higher mean inflation had less persistent deviations of output from their natural rate, presumably because they changed their prices more often. Likewise, Ball, Mankiw, and Romer (1988) found that the real effects of demand shifts were smaller both across countries and over time within a single country when average inflation was higher, not just when it was more variable. This suggests that these real effects are not simply the result of the public being fooled by unexpected demand shocks but are caused by price and wage inflexibility. In addition, numerous other studies have found that both expected (i.e., easily predictable) and unexpected changes in aggregate demand have real effects on output, with price changes lagging behind changes in output by 2–5 years. All of this research supports the proposition that price inflexibility exists and that it plays a central role in creating persistent fluctuations in aggregate output.

CONCLUSIONS

Business cycles are different in subtle ways. A complete model of business cycles has to incorporate both aggregate demand–driven and aggregate supply–driven business cycles. A complete model of business cycles has to be able to account for multiple shocks from different sectors of the economy, whether from goods markets, labor markets, or financial markets. A complete model of business cycles also has to be able to exhibit a wide variety of behaviors in certain key variables. Take, for example, real wages. As discussed in this chapter, over the long run real wages have been roughly acyclical. However, over shorter periods of time real wages have exhibited both countercyclical movements and procyclical movements.

Although the New Keynesian models discussed here are not yet a single, unified model of business cycles, taken as a whole they can explain this variety in behavior. By focusing on the microfoundations of market imperfections in goods markets (through price inflexibility), labor markets (through wage inflexibility), and in financial markets (through imperfect information and risk), New Keynesian models are consistent with both demand- and supply-driven contractions. New Keynesian models can also generate a wide variety of behavior in key variables. For example, once again consider the behavior of real wages in New Keynesian models. If both prices and nominal wages are inflexible, real wages will be acyclical. In the face of aggregate demand shocks, if nominal wages are more rigid than prices, then the real wage will be countercyclical, and if prices are more rigid than nominal wages (or if aggregate supply is shifting), then the real wage will be procyclical.

Of course, what is considered a strength by some is often considered a weakness by others. Critics of New Keynesian models charge that New Keynesian economics is not really a coherent school of thought but rather a hodge-podge of reasons for this or that market failure. To these critics, the fact that New Keynesian models can be consistent with any behavior in the real wage is an indictment of New Keynesian economics. How can you consider something a good model when it is always consistent with anything and everything you observe? A good model has to have empirically testable implications, and many economists feel that New Keynesian models currently fall short by this standard.

New Keynesian economists obviously have a considerable amount of work to do before they can provide a simple, specific, and complete model of business cycles. But by carefully focusing on the microfoundations of imperfect competition and market failure, they have advanced the discipline of economics considerably towards this goal. This is especially true regarding New Keynesian research on the role of financial markets during depressions, a topic that will be returned to in later chapters when the discussion turns to the causes of the Great Depression and other postwar international depressions.

SUGGESTED READINGS

Alan Blinder, "The Fall and Rise of Keynesian Economics" (1988): A discussion of why Keynesian thought has been so persuasive and persistent in macroeconomic theory. Included is a discussion of why Keynesian theory fell out of favor in the 1970s and 1980s and the reasons for its recent resurrection in the form of New Keynesian economics.

Bruce Greenwald and Joseph Stiglitz, "New and Old Keynesians" (1993): This paper describes the primary differences between old and new Keynesians. It also provides an excellent discussion of New Keynesian models of risk and imperfect information.

N. Gregory Mankiw, "The Reincarnation of Keynesian Economics" (1992): This paper, which was briefly summarized at the beginning of this chapter, presents an interesting and understandable discussion of the differences between new and old Keynesians.

David Romer, "The New Keynesian Synthesis" (1993): A broad overview of the past and future directions of New Keynesian research.

James Tobin, "Price Flexibility and Output Stability: An Old Keynesian View" (1993): A defense of old Keynesian economics against New Keynesian economics.

9

Macroeconomic Forecasting

INTRODUCTION

The jokes are almost as old as the profession itself. Q: Why did God create economists? A: To make weathermen look good. Did you hear that economists have forecast 8 of the last 2 recessions? Or how about the one-handed economist, who was popular because of his inability to say "On one hand, but on the other hand. . . ."

Economists themselves have been no less critical of their profession's ability to forecast the future. The economist John Kenneth Galbraith (*Wall Street Journal*, Jan. 22, 1993) claimed "There are two kinds of forecasters: those who don't know and those who don't know they don't know."

Because of the poor historical performance of economic forecasting, many firms have reassessed their need for extensive and personalized economic forecasts. In the 1950s and 1960s, many firms hired in-house economists to do their forecasting. Today, almost none of the Fortune 500 companies directly employ economists. For example, IBM had 26 economists on their staff in the early 1970s, but today they have zero. Instead, they avoid relying on forecasts altogether; or at the very least, they rely on one of a small number of commercial economic forecasting firms to provide general macroeconomic forecasts at a relatively small price.

Why has *economic forecasting*, or the methods of quantifying economic uncertainty, fallen upon such hard times? The primary reason is that the last 30 years have been filled with large, unanticipated shocks. Forecasters rely on the past as the basis for both their theories and their data.

When shocks occur that have never occurred before, the result is large forecasting errors. In the 1970s, higher oil prices increased the costs of production and decreased aggregate supply. This led to high levels of inflation and unemployment at the same time, an unprecedented event that forecasters could not have anticipated before the existence of OPEC. The 1981–1982 recession was caused by a large decrease in the money supply initiated by the Fed to reduce historically high inflation rates. This destabilizing action by the Fed was unparalleled in U.S. history and was largely unanticipated by forecasters. Finally, the remarkably long and resilient expansion of the 1990s, driven by strong productivity growth and a booming stock market (two of the most perplexing and unpredictable variables in modern economies) was also largely unanticipated by forecasters. Because of this, consensus forecasts of economic growth were an average of 1.4 percent too low for a remarkable five years straight between 1995 and 1999. Even the East Asian Crisis, which many predicted would depress the U.S. economy as well, failed to noticeably slow the surprisingly rapid rate of growth in the United States during this period.

Unique and unanticipated shocks, however, cannot fully explain the decline in economic forecasting. Economists' disagreements about what model to use in economic forecasting have played an important role as well. Economists disagree about whether models of market failure (such as Keynesian or New Keynesian models) or models of perfect competition (such as Classical, Monetarist, or Real Business Cycle models) are best to use as the basis of developing forecasts. In addition, a large and influential body of research on rational expectations suggests that without an understanding of how people adjust their expectations (which in any given circumstance may be impossible to accurately predict), any forecast of the future based on data from the past will be unreliable. This is the basis of the *Lucas Critique*, which by itself has done more to shake economists' faith in their ability to foresee the future than any forecasting mistake. Because of this loss of faith in forecasting by the profession, few top-notch academic researchers are currently engaged in work related to economic forecasting. Instead, the practice and advancement of forecasting has been largely left to a few commercial forecasting firms, leaving a sizeable disconnect between academia and the commercial world.

This chapter will review the four primary forecasting techniques used to predict future economic performance: macroeconomic indicators, econometric methods, structural modeling, and dynamic general equilibrium modeling. The advantages and disadvantages of each forecasting method will be discussed with an eye towards understanding what each of these techniques can add to our understanding of business cycles, both in the past and in the future.

MACROECONOMIC INDICATORS

Index of Leading Indicators

The oldest, and also the simplest, way to forecast business cycles is to identify a group of variables that are leading indicators of aggregate output and use these to predict turning points in the business cycle. Beginning in 1937, the Commerce Department began to report the Composite Index of Leading Indicators. Since that time, this index has undergone substantial revision and many variables have been added or removed over the years.

Table 9.1 reports the current variables that comprise the Composite Index of Leading Indicators. Notice that there are variables included in this index for proponents of every business cycle theory. Classical or Real Business Cycle economists who focus on fluctuations in aggregate supply get average weekly hours and vender delivery speed (slower speeds indicate that capacity constraints are becoming binding). Keynesians get consumer expectations, the stock market, new housing starts (a volatile component of investment), manufacturer orders, and unemployment claims. Monetarists get M2 as well as another measure of the tightness of monetary policy, the interest rate spread between long term T-bonds and the short-term federal funds rate (which is the overnight interest rate on interbank loans). A larger interest rate gap

TABLE 9.1   The Index of Leading Indicators and Its Components

Leading Composite Index

1. Average weekly hours of manufacturing production workers *(Average weekly hours)*
2. Average weekly initial claims for unemployment insurance, state programs-inverted scale *(Initial unemployment claims)*
3. Manufacturers' new orders for consumer goods and materials, in constant dollars *(Manufacturers' orders)*
4. Vendor performance *(percentage of companies receiving slower deliveries)*
5. Manufacturers' new orders for nondefense capital goods industries, in constant dollars *(Manufacturers' capital orders)*
6. New private-housing units authorized by local building permits *(Housing starts)*
7. Prices of 500 common stocks, index *(Stock market price indexes and dividend yields)*
8. Money supply (M2), in constant dollars *(Money supply)*
9. Interest rate spread, 10-year Treasury bonds less federal funds *(Interest rates)*
10. Consumer expectations, index *(Consumer attitude indexes)*

indicates that the Fed's policy is expansionary and is pushing down the short-term federal funds rate while at the same time increasing future expected inflation and increasing long-term interest rates. Thus, decisions regarding which macroeconomic variables to include in this index are not based upon one specific theory. Instead, the Index of Leading Indicators focuses on what works, meaning the variables that are the most reliable leading indicators of output.

Figure 9.1 presents data on both GDP growth and the Index of Leading Indicators. This figure illustrates that while the Index is a simple and intuitive way to forecast business cycles, there are two significant problems with its reliability. First and foremost is the problem of false signals. For example, in 1977 and 1987, the index fell and output growth did not. In addition, even when changes in the index correspond with changes in output, the index is much more volatile than GDP growth. There have been a number of times when the indicator has changed dramatically without any (or at least very much) change in growth. Some of the largest declines in the index, such as between 1975 and 1980, were associated with very short recessions. However, there was only a small decline before the severe recession of 1981–1982.

The second major problem with the Index of Leading Indicators is that it does not lead GDP growth by very much—one quarter at most. This is not enough time to make the Index very useful when formulating monetary and fiscal policy. Given the lags in monetary and especially fiscal policy, policymakers need much more than a one-quarter lead-time in order to take the appropriate actions to stabilize output.

Numerous empirical studies have been conducted investigating the forecasting effectiveness of the Composite Index of Leading Indicators.

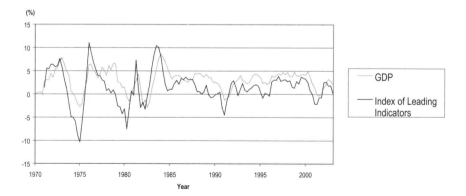

Figure 9.1 Real GDP Growth and the Index of Leading Indicators

Francis Diebold and Glenn Rudebusch (1999) review many of these studies and reach the general conclusion that the index is not a reliable indicator of business cycle turning points. Even when used in conjunction with other forecasting methods, the Composite Index of Leading Indicators does little to improve the accuracy of macroeconomic forecasts, especially in terms of identifying the peaks and troughs of business cycles.

Market-Based Indicators

Instead of relying on a composite of various macroeconomic indicators, many economists believe that market-based indicators of turning points in the business cycle are more reliable because they more accurately reflect the prevailing perceptions of those actively playing a role in future economic performance. The stock market is one such indicator, but as can be seen in Figure 9.2, stock market variability literally dwarfs the variability of output growth and is so filled with false signals that it cannot be a reliable indicator by itself.

Another more reliable market-based indicator is the yield curve. A *yield* is a measure of the yearly return on holding an asset, typically a bond. It is calculated by determining the interest rate that equates the present value of future payments received from the bond with the current price that the bond is selling at. One of the important determinants of the yield on various bonds is the risk of that bond. In order to

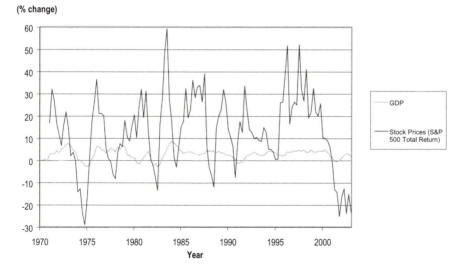

Figure 9.2 Real GDP Growth and Stock Prices

assume higher risk, a purchaser will demand a higher yield. The risk of a bond rises with the default risk of the firm issuing the bond. The risk of a bond also rises as the length of time until the bond's *maturity*, or the time at which the bond's principle is repaid, increases. Longer maturities mean more risk, both because the probability of default is larger over longer periods of time and also because the owner is exposed to more risk from large changes in market interest rates that could reduce the attractiveness of the bond on the secondary, or resale, market.

A widely accepted theory about how maturity affects the yields on bonds is the *expectations hypothesis*. This theory asserts the following relationship between long-term and short-term yields: The yield on a bond with n years to maturity should be equal to the average return from holding n number of 1-year bonds plus a premium to compensate the investor for the fact that the longer-maturity bond is riskier. Thus, the yield on a 5-year bond should be the average of the yields from holding five 1-year bonds plus an extra return to encourage the investor to accept the higher risk of holding a 5-year bond.

A *yield curve* is a representation of how the yields on comparable bonds change as their maturity changes. Yield curves are usually calculated using government bond yields (in the United States this means T-Bonds and T-Bills). According to the expectations hypothesis, the slope of the yield curve provides a clear indication about what the market expects to happen to short-term interest rates in the future. If short-term interest rates are expected to remain constant in the future, the yield curve should have a gradual upward slope because of the risk premium. If short-term interest rates are expected to rise in the future, then the yield curve should slope upwards very steeply. If short-term interest rates are expected to fall in the future, then the yield curve should be flat or downward sloping.

Figure 9.3 presents yield curves for the United States, Japan, Germany, and Britain. Notice how these yield curves are shaped quite differently. Based on an understanding of the expectations hypothesis, one can hypothesize what the markets were predicting would happen to future short-term interest rates in each of these economies. In the United States, markets were expecting short-term rates to be very constant or fall slightly for the next 10 years. Expected inflation definitely rose between 1998 and 1999, as evidenced by the shift up in the yield curve. Given the steepness of the curves in Germany and Japan, markets were expecting short-term interest rates to rise in the future, or at least to stay constant depending upon the size of the risk premium. In Germany the yield curve shifted higher, indicating that inflation expectations rose, while in Japan the opposite happened. In Britain, on the other hand, markets in 1998 and 1999 were expecting short-term

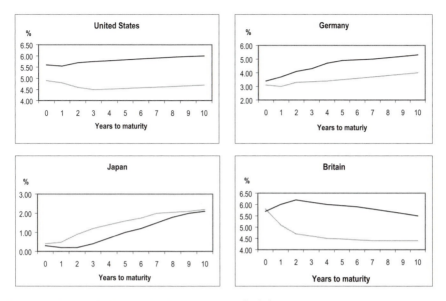

Figure 9.3 Yield Curves. Light line, 1998; dark line, 1999

interest rates to fall significantly in the future. Yield curves such as these, with a negative slope, are often referred to as an *inverted yield curve*.

What role can yield curves play in economic forecasting? There is a strong rationale for thinking that an inverted (or possibly flat) yield curve is a market-based signal of a future recession. The reason is that short-term interest rates are strongly procyclical in the empirical data. This is in part because investment demand and inflation are procyclical and in part because countercyclical monetary policy makes short-term interest rates procyclical. As a result, if an accurate measure of future short-term interest rates can be obtained, then a good indicator of future output growth has also been found. An expected decline in short-term interest in the future as evidenced by an inverted or flat yield curve likely indicates that markets are also expecting a decline in output growth.

Over the last 30 years, yield curves in the United States have been a reliable indicator of recessions. One good example is the 1981–1982 recession. By the end of 1980, short-term interest rates reached roughly 18 percent and the yield curve in the United States became significantly inverted. It became more so in 1981 when the Fed began cutting the money supply in order to reduce inflation, initiating a severe recession. Yield curves in the United States also became inverted in mid-1979 (before the 1980 recession) and mildly inverted in both mid-1989 and mid-2000 (before the relatively mild recessions of 1990–1991 and 2001–2002). Most important, yield curves have not provided false signals, meaning that there has not been a time when the yield curve became inverted but the economy did not soon slip into a recession.

A few studies have been conducted evaluating the forecasting power of yield curves. For example, Joseph Haubrich and Ann Dombrosky (1996) measured the slope of the yield curve by calculating the interest rate spread between the 10-year T-Bond and the 3-month T-Bill. They found that during the last 30 years there has been a strong correlation between this interest rate spread and GDP growth one year in the future. In fact, yield curve–based forecasts do better than other more complex forecasting methods. However, during the last 10 years the yield curve has not performed as well, raising questions about whether a longer period of time is needed to accurately assess its forecasting effectiveness. Arturo Estrella and Frederic Mishkin (1998) also found evidence that the slope of the yield curve outperforms a wide variety of other market- and nonmarket-based macroeconomic indicators such as the stock market, monetary aggregates, and the Index of Leading Indicators.

Thus, there are many reasons to believe that market-based leading indicators such as the yield curve may be important tools in accurately forecasting business cycle turning points. From an economist's point of view, they are certainly a more reliable measure of expectations than survey data, such as the Consumer Confidence Index, because they are market driven and not subjective. However, one big drawback of yield curves is that interpreting them is somewhat subjective. How flat does a yield curve have to be before it is clearly indicating a future recession? How steep does a yield curve have to be before it clearly signals an expansion? These are important questions that have not yet been fully addressed empirically.

Other market-based indicators may also be useful to forecasters. For example, in 1997 the U.S. government began to issue Treasury Inflation Protection Securities (TIPS), which are T-Bonds in which the principal and interest payments adjust with inflation. As a result, the yield on a TIPS bond is a real yield as opposed to the nominal yield received on a regular T-Bond. This means that the difference in yields between a TIPS bond and a regular T-Bond is a measure of the market's expected inflation rate, which should also be a good indicator of business cycle turning points given that inflation is typically procyclical (at least when aggregate demand shocks are driving changes in output). As a larger market develops for TIPS bonds over time, its implied measure of expected inflation could also become a useful tool in forecasting business cycles.

ECONOMETRIC TECHNIQUES

Econometrics refers to the use of statistical methods to address economic questions. Most econometric forecasting techniques are not based upon a specific macroeconomic theory. Instead, the objective is to examine a broad variety of macroeconomic data in order to determine reliable historical relationships and then extend these historical relationships into the future in order to generate a forecast.

The most common econometric technique used in forecasting is *ordinary least squares regression* (OLS). While the purpose of this discussion is not to examine the technical details of OLS regression, intuitively it works in the following manner. Assume that real GDP growth next period is a linear function of multiple current explanatory variables, X_{it}, and their marginal effect on GDP growth, β_{it}, as represented by the following equation:

$$GDP_{t+1} = \beta_{0t} + \beta_{1t}X_{1t} + \beta_{2t}X_{2t} \ldots + \beta_{kt}X_{kt} + \varepsilon_t \qquad (9.1)$$

Some of these explanatory variables are likely to be lagged variables, meaning that they may be from more than one or more periods in the past. The variable ε_t represents error in the hypothesized model that cannot be controlled for or is inherent in the determination of GDP growth. The objective of OLS is to choose the "best" values of each β_{it} using historical macroeconomic data, where best is defined as the values for each β_{it} that minimize the sum of the squared differences between the predicted and actual values of GDP. These errors are squared because it makes all of the errors positive and because it more heavily weights large errors than small errors when choosing the best β_{it}.

OLS regression is surprisingly flexible. While it only works well under fairly strict conditions, economists have developed a number of techniques that allow them to manipulate macroeconomic data so that these conditions are met. This includes circumstances when an explanatory variable has a nonlinear relationship with GDP growth.

Once an econometric model has been built, forecasting becomes straightforward. Forecasts of future values of GDP growth are generated by combining the current values of explanatory variables with the β_{it} coefficients that were estimated using historical data.

The advantages of econometric techniques are twofold. First, econometric methods are a relatively cheap and simple way of making economic forecasts, given the remarkable increases in computing power that have taken place recently. Some of the most popular econometric models are the Massachusetts Institute of Technology–Federal Reserve Board (MIT-FRB) model, the public National Bureau of Economic Research (NBER) model, and the commercial Data Resources, Inc. (DRI) model. Each of these models has more than 1,200 variables and more than 100 equations that are estimated simultaneously. Second, econometric methods generally do not rely on a single macroeconomic theory of output determination, which is important given that there is no agreement among economists on which model should be used. While theory does help the forecaster choose which explanatory variables should and should not be included in the regression, it does not specify a specific structural relationship between each explanatory variable and GDP. Instead, that relationship is determined empirically using historical data.

The things that make econometric models attractive, however, are the same things that limit their ability to accurately forecast business cycles, especially the turning points of business cycles. The fact that econometric forecasting relies little on economic theory is a big disadvantage in many economists' view, because theory tells you what should and should not be determining business cycles and, by implication, which variables should and should not be included in the econometric model. Without theory, econometric forecasting can turn into "data mining," where all sorts of data is entered into a computer in an attempt to find some correlation that can be used to predict GDP growth, even if there is no causation involved. An extreme example of this would be to use the length of ladies' hemlines to forecast stock market prices because there is a reported correlation between the two, even though there are no serious theories (only humorous ones) as to why there should be any relationship between them.

An additional problem with econometric techniques is that they are based on historical data, which means that the accuracy of their predictions relies on past conditions to continue to exist into the future. Many economists would ask how can forecasters believe that each β_{it} will remain constant in the future when different conditions that cannot be controlled for may not be the same? This is the basis of the Lucas Critique, originally discussed in Chapter 6. Basically, the Lucas Critique says that when policy changes, peoples' behaviors change as well. This changes the relationships (i.e., each β_{it}) that have historically existed between variables. Consider the following example. During World War II, the Fed and the U.S. Treasury reached an agreement that the Fed would peg interest rates at a low level during the war in order to aid the Treasury's financing of the war. Under this policy, why did people not change their expected nominal interest rate when government spending increased? Because they knew interest rates would remain unchanged. As a result, savings, investment, bond prices, and other variables sensitive to future interest rates would also remain unchanged. If you included data from this period in a forecast of future GDP growth, you would get much different values for each β_{it} than you would get if you used data from the postwar or prewar period alone.

Thus, changes in policy change expectations, which then change behavior. The Lucas Critique raised real questions in many economists' minds about the validity of using econometric techniques to forecast the future in a world where monetary policy, fiscal policy, and government regulations are constantly changing.

There have been studies, too numerous to mention here, that have evaluated the performance of the most popular econometric models in forecasting business cycles. One of the most comprehensive of these is Victor Zarnowitz (1992). He reports that econometric forecasts of real GDP growth generally have low median errors that have gotten smaller since the 1960s. However, there is a great deal of variability in these errors, which makes the average error of these forecasts quite large. These large errors almost always occur during business cycle turning points. For example, during the 1974–1975 and 1981–1982 recessions, econometric forecasts consistently and significantly over-predicted GDP growth. On the other hand, during the extended expansions that began in 1982 and 1991, GDP growth was consistently and significantly under-predicted. Steven McNees (1986) found that during the 1980–1985 period, a period of extreme output variability, the median error of real GDP growth forecasts was ±3.5 percent, a huge error given that average growth in the United States is 2 percent. The poor performance of econometric models during peaks and troughs (when accurate forecasting is most badly needed) is not at all surprising, given that these are the points in the business cycle when the past is the least accurate indicator of the future. Zarnowitz also concludes that econometric forecasts work well only for 2–4 quarters in the future, and past this their performance declines significantly. Once again, this is not surprising, given how quickly economic fundamentals can change and reduce the ability of past behavior to predict future behavior.

STRUCTURAL MODELS

Structural models are based on using a specific macroeconomic theory—and the relationships between variables that this theory implies—to forecast future economic performance. For example, Keynesian structural forecasts would involve using econometric techniques to estimate the parameters of the IS and LM equations in an economy. Given these equations, the expected values of policy variables such as government spending, taxes, and the money supply could then be used to determine the future value of aggregate output. Thus, structural modeling is really a synthesis between macroeconomic theory and the use of econometric techniques to match data to this theory.

Even more than econometric forecasting or macroeconomic indicators, structural modeling has almost completely fallen out of favor with most professional forecasters. The reasons are fairly obvious. First, structural forecasts are really conditional forecasts—conditional upon a specific theory. This is problematic, given that there is currently no generally accepted theory of business cycle determination. During the 1950s and 1960s, when Keynesian economics was generally accepted, Keynesian structural modeling was the most widely used forecasting method. However, the stagflation of the 1970s raised serious questions in most economists' minds about the simple Keynesian model of aggregate demand–driven business cycles. Keynesian structural modeling in the 1970s was plagued by huge and persistent forecasting errors, and also played an important role in justifying the inflationary monetary policies of the Fed during this time. In addition, the development of rational expectations and the Lucas Critique raised questions about the reliability of the estimated parameters in a structural model because these parameters can change as policy and expectations change. Finally, the fact that Keynesian structural models were not based on microeconomic foundations or the optimizing behavior of individuals raised serious questions in many minds. Many of the structural relationships between variables were simply assumed to exist, as opposed to being derived from a detailed microeconomic theory. Some structural forecasting still does take place, but it is largely used in academic research and not in the business community, where the large commercial forecasting models primarily rely on pure econometric methods.

DYNAMIC GENERAL EQUILIBRIUM MODELS

Dynamic general equilibrium (DGE) models are based on the assumption that microeconomic models of individual households, firms, and markets can be used to understand macroeconomic behavior. To do this and still allow these models to be manageable, DGE models assume *representational agents*, meaning individuals all have the same preferences and act alike in every way. When combined with the assumption of perfect competition, macroeconomic behavior becomes a simple summation of average microeconomic behavior. Real Business Cycle models, discussed in Chapter 7, are examples of DGE models. In Real Business Cycle models, representational agents operate in perfectly competitive markets where business cycle fluctuations are driven by productivity shocks to production.

DGE models can be used in simulation experiments to forecast the future path of an economy. If changes in exogenous variables such as technology or monetary or fiscal policy can be incorporated within a

DGE model, the behavior of the model economy can be observed. The critical idea behind the use of DGE modeling is that these models will more accurately predict changes in the real economy because only macroeconomic theory that is consistent with microfoundations can avoid the Lucas Critique and fully incorporate the fact that peoples' behaviors change as policy changes.

Like all forecasting methods, DGE modeling is fraught with difficulties. The biggest problem is that these models are extremely complex. They are so complex, in fact, that commercial researchers essentially ignore them, and they have been relegated to academic research. In addition, because of their complexity, the parameters in DGE models cannot be easily estimated. Instead, forecasters go through a process called *calibration*, in which they choose values for the parameters of the model so that it behaves in a way that is consistent with the long-run properties of the economy. Of course, once fixed parameters are chosen that govern key macroeconomic relationships, the Lucas Critique is once again applicable. This is a big problem, given that one of the principal rationales for DGE modeling is to avoid problems associated with the Lucas Critique.

DGE models are used quite frequently in academic research, especially in research related to policy analysis. The implications of changes in public policy, such as the economic implications of tax reform, can be interestingly investigated within these models. However, the assumption of representational agents severely limits their use in policy discussions with distributional implications, because the study of distributional issues requires that not everyone is exactly the same. Because of the problems associated with DGE models, their use in commercial forecasting will probably continue to be limited until economists are able to make these models more realistic and more user-friendly for non-academics.

CONCLUSIONS

The profession of macroeconomic forecasting is currently stuck in a long, protracted recession with no trough in sight. A few large commercial forecasters still exist, but the days when every Fortune 500 company had its own in-house forecasters are over. Maybe more important, interest in forecasting among the best academic research economists has waned, meaning future improvement will be slow. Much of this decline in the use of forecasting has been the result of its unreliable past performance. While econometric models and leading indicators do a good job predicting growth during stable economic periods, they are very poor predictors of turning points in the business cycle and generate large and persistent errors when there are major economic shocks such as the oil price shocks of the 1970s or the strong productivity growth of the 1990s. Yield curves might be more reliable indicators of business cycle turning points, but at this point interpreting yield curves is more of an art than a science. The use of yield curves in forecasting needs further study before it can completely gain forecasters' confidence. The same holds for dynamic general equilibrium models, which are attractive from a theoretical standpoint and widely used in academic research but have generated little excitement among commercial forecasters because of their complexity and unreliable performance.

The split between commercial and academic forecasting is a disturbing one, one that could signal deep problems for the discipline of economics. How can a discipline be taken seriously when its theoretical models are so widely ignored by those who operate in the real world? To understand why this does not have to necessarily be a bad thing, consider the following parable offered by Gregory Mankiw (1990). When scientists first tried to explain and predict the positioning of planets and stars in order to aid naval navigation, they developed a simple but mistaken theory referred to as the Ptolemaic system. Developed by the Egyptians, this theory assumed that the sun and planets revolved around the earth and that these bodies followed circular (not elliptical) paths. When the Copernican system was first introduced in the 1500s with its assumption that the Earth revolved around the sun in an elliptical orbit, it was widely rejected by ship captains, largely because its astronomical forecasts were not as accurate as those made using the old system. However, over time academics refined the more complex Copernican system, which eventually provided very accurate predictions. With work, getting the theory right eventually leads to getting the forecasting right. Economists hope that someday the study of macroeconomics can reach similar harmony between theory and practice.

SUGGESTED READINGS

Francis X. Diebold, "The Past, Present, and Future of Macroeconomic Forecasting" (1998): A nontechnical discussion of the historical evolution of macroeconomic forecasting and its track record. Included are the author's suggestions for future areas of research that are needed to improve the state of forecasting.

The Fair-Taylor Model: A Keynesian structural model that is periodically revised and has attempted to incorporate many New Keynesian features in an effort to respond to some of the criticisms of structural forecasting. This model can be downloaded and used to generate macroeconomic forecasts. Available at http://fairmodel.econ.yale.edu/main.

Joseph G. Haubrich and Ann M. Dombrosky, "Predicting Real Growth Using the Yield Curve" (1996): A brief and generally nontechnical review of the benefits of using the yield curve in macroeconomic forecasting.

Robert E. Lucas and Thomas J. Sargent, "After Keynesian Economics" (1978): A criticism of both econometric forecasting and Keynesian structural models of forecasting. The Lucas Critique and its role in the decline of macroeconomic forecasting is discussed in detail.

Part III

Business Cycles in the United States

10

The Great Depression

INTRODUCTION

The Great Depression is the most examined and analyzed economic event of all time. Even so, its sheer magnitude is still difficult to comprehend for those who did not live through it. Looking at figures and tables of data is a very poor substitute for experience, but this data still paints a sobering picture of a world that went remarkably bad. Table 10.1 reports macroeconomic data from the Great Depression. Real

TABLE 10.1   Key Macroeconomic Variables during the Great Depression

	Real GNP (in billions)	Unemployment Rate	Stock Prices	Bank Failures	Consumer Price Index
1928	$ 98.2	4.2%	153	498	100.0
1929	104.4	3.2	201	659	100.0
1930	95.1	8.7	161	1350	97.4
1931	89.5	15.9	100	2293	88.7
1932	76.4	23.6	36	1453	79.7
1933	74.2	24.9	79	4000	75.4
1934	80.8	21.7	78	57	78.0
1935	91.4	20.1	80	34	80.1
1936	100.9	16.9	112	44	80.9
1937	109.1	14.3	120	59	83.8
1938	103.2	19.0	80	54	82.3

Source: U.S. Department of Commerce, *Historical Statistics of the United States*; Board of Governors of the Federal Reserve System, *Banking and Monetary Statistics* (Washington, D.C.: National Capital Press, 1943).

income fell by 50 percent, which is ten times greater than any postwar contraction in output. Unemployment reached 25 percent, stock prices fell 85 percent, and 25 percent of all banks failed, in addition to high rates of personal bankruptcy.

One of the most important aspects of the Great Depression was that it was a worldwide phenomenon. Figure 10.1 reports industrial production in the four major economies of the time (United States, Germany, U.K., and France), and Table 10.2 reports unemployment rates in these same countries. While the Great Depression adversely affected every major economy, the United States experienced the steepest declines in production. Another important aspect of the Great Depression is that it was associated with international deflation. Figure 10.2 reports wholesale prices for three countries during the Great Depression. Between 1929 and 1932, prices fell by roughly 40 percent in the United States and by similar levels in Germany and Britain.

Many theories of business cycle behavior have been developed around providing a plausible explanation of the Great Depression. The most obvious example is the Keynesian model. Although many of Keynes' theories had been developed prior to the Great Depression, Keynes and his followers were quick to assert that their model not only explained the causes of the Great Depression but also provided policy recommendations for how best to deal with it. As discussed in Chapter 4, the Keynesian explanation of the Great Depression centered on a major decrease in aggregate demand caused by sharp falls in investment and consumption. These falls in investment and consumption were the result of a huge decline in expectations. This fall in aggregate demand had real effects on the economy because of wage inflexibility in the labor market. Keynes' policy solution for ending the Great Depression was to increase government spending in order to stimulate aggregate demand and move the economy back toward its potential level of output and full employment.

TABLE 10.2   Unemployment Rates in Four Countries before and during the Great Depression

Country	1921–29	1930–38	Average Rate	Difference	Ratio of difference to average
United States	7.9%	26%	17.0%	18.0%	1.07
United Kingdom	12.0	15	13.7	3.4	0.25
France	3.8	10	7.0	6.4	0.91
Germany	9.2	22	15.5	13.0	0.81

Source: Temin (1989)

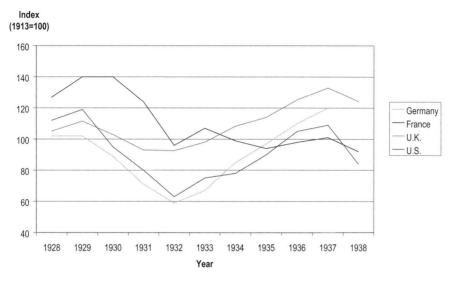

Figure 10.1 Industrial Production in Four Countries

The Monetarist theory of business cycles was also, in large part, developed around a hypothesis about what caused the Great Depression. Monetarists argued that the Great Depression was caused by a large decrease in the money supply that occurred because of the Federal Reserve's ignorance and incompetence. This decline in the money sup-

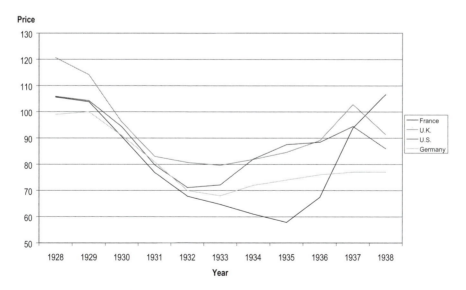

Figure 10.2 Wholesale Prices in Four Countries

ply reduced aggregate demand for two reasons. First, a lower money supply reduced aggregate spending in accordance with the Quantity Theory. Second, a decrease in the money supply reduced liquidity in the banking system, leading to banking failures and high real interest rates. The decline in financial intermediation that resulted led to further reductions in spending, investment, and aggregate demand. While this theory was developed well after the Great Depression, its policy recommendations for dealing with future contractions were simple: Constrain monetary policy and stabilize the money supply by legislating that central banks follow a simple money growth rule.

Other business cycle theories have fallen out of favor with many economists because of their inability to provide a plausible explanation of the Great Depression. Real Business Cycle models, with their emphasis on supply-driven business cycles, are viewed with skepticism by many economists because their explanation of the Depression is unconvincing. What was the source of the large decrease in aggregate supply that caused the Great Depression? If the Great Depression was caused by a fall in aggregate supply, why did prices fall instead of rise? Likewise, a big problem with the Rational Expectations model is that in this model, business cycles are caused by imperfect information and misperceptions about the state of the economy. What kind of mistaken expectations could cause output to fall by 50 percent and remain below its peak level for nearly eight years?

During the 1980s, economists once again began to reevaluate their hypotheses about what caused the Great Depression. Much of the new research that took place examined the Great Depression from a different perspective, one that viewed the Great Depression as not just an economic contraction but as an international financial crisis. This distinction is important because it places the focus on financial markets as playing a crucial role in propagating the Depression. Some of this new focus was inspired by the development of New Keynesian economics, specifically, the development of New Keynesian models that center on the macroeconomic effects of imperfect information and risk in financial markets.

This chapter will discuss this new approach to explaining the events of the Great Depression. Two economists in particular, Peter Temin (1989) and Ben Bernanke (1983, 1995), contributed to much of this recent research that focuses (though not exclusively) on the international financial aspects of the crash. Specifically, the role of the gold standard, which was reinstated after World War I, is closely examined and identified as a major culprit in setting the stage for a major international deflation. This deflation had important microeconomic implications for labor and financial markets that ultimately led to an economic collapse of unprecedented proportions.

THE GOLD STANDARD AFTER WORLD WAR I

Most countries dropped off the gold standard during World War I because of the constraints it imposed on monetary and fiscal policies—constraints that were superceded by the need to finance war efforts. However, most of the major economies reinstated the gold standard between 1925 and 1929. The main rationale for returning to the gold standard was a simple one: policymakers at the time had not thought through any feasible alternative. Until that point in history, countries had backed their currencies with gold and had maintained fixed exchange rates in order to facilitate international trade. The times when countries were not on the gold standard (primarily when they were engaged in war) were also periods when almost all international trade came to a halt. Most policymakers had not even considered a peacetime option to the gold standard and had assumed that abandoning the gold standard meant contracting international trade.

Temin (1989) asserts that the gold standard system that was reconstituted after World War I had four principal characteristics.

1. Countries fixed their currencies to gold and, as a result, fixed their exchange rates to each other.
2. Gold movements across countries were unconstrained. Gold flowed to countries with trade surpluses and flowed out of countries with trade deficits.
3. Asymmetries in the effects of running trade surpluses versus trade deficits were inherent in the system. A country experiencing a trade surplus could accumulate gold reserves without increasing the money supply, which is referred to as *sterilization*. This policy had no real downside risk. On the other hand, trade deficit countries were forced to reduce their money supplies as their gold reserves fell in order to avoid *devaluation*, or reducing their exchange rate. This meant that trade deficits led to deflation and a contraction in economic activity. As a result, countries had big incentives to bias their economic policy toward hoarding gold through running trade surpluses and avoid the negative effects of running trade deficits.
4. No organization or structure was in place to encourage international economic cooperation, to enforce international agreements, or to provide temporary financing to countries that were short of gold reserves.

It is important to understand how different the gold standard system is from floating exchange rates, such as what exists in the United States. When countries today let markets determine their exchange rate, they have the freedom to control their domestic money supplies and use monetary policy to stabilize domestic output. Under a gold standard system, countries controlled their exchange rate, but at the cost of giving up control of their money supplies. Because there was no way for a gold standard country to adjust its exchange rate in the face of large trade imbalances, a country experiencing a trade deficit was forced to contract its money supply instead. This would lead to a fall in aggregate demand and output, but in the long-run falling prices would make exports cheaper and improve the trade balance of the country.

Another difference between our current era and the interwar period is that today there are multiple layers of international organizations that provide help in financing and coordinating economic policies, such as the International Monetary Fund, the World Bank, and, to a lesser extent, the World Trade Organization. Before World War II, none of this international infrastructure existed. Many countries felt free to act as if they operated in a vacuum and not within an interconnected international economy. The result was that most countries attempted to run large trade surpluses at the expense of their trading partners. In addition, there was no safety net of emergency financing for countries that were running unsustainable trade deficits and losing gold reserves. Instead, they were forced to cut their money supplies and fend for themselves.

THE EVENTS OF THE GREAT DEPRESSION

1929–1931: The First Wave

In the aftermath of World War I, most countries resumed their commitment to the gold standard. The problem with this quick resurrection was that extreme economic inequities existed after the war was over. The British and German economies were much weaker after the war and immediately suffered from large trade deficits and gold outflows. On the other hand, the economies of the United States and France had suffered much less during the war and were relatively much stronger. Upon resumption of the gold standard, the United States and France began running trade surpluses and acquiring large gold stocks.

These trade imbalances led to falling money supplies and deflation worldwide because of the asymmetries inherent in the gold standard. The U.K. and Germany were forced to reduce their money supplies as gold flowed out of their countries. On the other hand, both the United States and France chose to sterilize their large gold inflows and not increase their money supplies because of worries about inflation. In fact, the United States actually reduced its money supply beginning in

1928 because of worries within the Fed about an inflated stock market. The end result was that by 1929 the United States and France had 60 percent of the world's gold but were still decreasing their money supplies. Coupled with the falling money supplies in much of the rest of Europe, the world economy began to experience significant deflation starting in 1929, before the Depression began (see Figure 10.2).

The obvious question is this: Couldn't the U.S. Federal Reserve understand what was going on with worldwide deflation and increase the money supply in order to avoid a worldwide recession? As Friedman and Schwartz (1963) make clear in their book *A Monetary History of the United States, 1867–1960*, Fed officials (and other central bankers at this time) were considerably less sophisticated than they are today. Their obsession with controlling inflation and maintaining the gold standard dominated all their thinking. The appropriate monetary policy under the gold standard was to sustain a trade surplus regardless of the worldwide economic situation. This policy of attempting to run trade surpluses at the expense of other countries is often referred to as a *beggar-thy-neighbor* policy. The problem with beggar-thy-neighbor policies is that every country in the world cannot run a trade surplus at the same time. The attempt to do so can lead to exactly what happened during the Great Depression: a contraction of world money supplies, world trade, and world incomes. Without any mechanism for coordinating international economic policy, other countries could not force the United States or any other country to reevaluate its deflationary policies and increase its money supply, even though the United States was quickly accumulating much of the world's gold and forcing the rest of the world to reduce their money supplies. As a result, the United States largely drove the world economy into deflation and depression by itself because of its unyielding commitment to the gold standard, low inflation, and trade surpluses.

Even though the decrease in the U.S. money supply that occurred during 1928–1929 was at least partially responsible for the October 1929 stock market crash, the Fed continued to reduce the money supply in order to protect against gold outflows and inflation during 1930 and into 1931. The stock market crash reduced consumption and investment by increasing uncertainty and reducing wealth. Coupled with the effects of the Hoover administration's fiscal policies, which involved cuts in government spending in order to balance the federal budget and higher import tariffs to protect the U.S. trade surplus, aggregate demand and prices continued to fall precipitously. However, this process was seen as a "cleansing" of economic excesses by many in the Federal Reserve and the federal government. For example, Andrew Mellon, Hoover's Secretary of the Treasury, urged markets to liquidate labor, liquidate stocks, liquidate the farmers, and liquidate real estate. . . . It will purge the rottenness out of the system. High costs of living and high living will come down. People will work harder, live a more moral life. Values will be adjusted, and enterprising people will pick up from less competent people. (Hoover 1952)

This is akin to arguing that the SARS outbreak in Asia during 2003 was not such a bad thing because it only affected the infirm and the elderly. Clearly, macroeconomic policy played a crucial role in creating the Great Depression—so great, in fact, that Peter Temin has referred to the Fed's monetary policy between 1929 and 1931 as "one of the biggest examples of misguided policy in history" (1989).

1931–1933: The Second Wave

The second, and most severe, phase of the Great Depression in the United States was characterized by banking panics and failures that effectively halted all financial intermediation and investment. Roughly 25 percent of all banks failed or suspended operations during this period. Bank depositors and stockholders lost an amount equal to 2.4 percent of GDP, a much larger loss than what occurred during the stock market crash in October 1929. As banks began to fail, the economy contracted rapidly. Industrial production fell by 43 percent between April 1931 and June 1932, and unemployment rose to 24 percent.

The monetary base was roughly constant between July 1929 and July 1931, but M1 fell by 28 percent as banks and the public began to hoard money and the money multiplier dropped dramatically. Finally, beginning in late 1931, the Fed reversed course (under threat from Congress) and began to rapidly increase the monetary base. By this time, it was too late. Despite a large increase in the monetary base, the money supply did not increase, primarily because money hoarding continued to be rampant. The currency-to-deposits ratio rose by 29 percent and the excess reserves-to-deposits ratio rose by 47 percent between June 1930 and February 1933. Together, these reduced the M1 multiplier by 35 percent, or roughly the amount of the fall in the level of M1. The money supply also began to fall when the United States began to experience huge gold outflows in 1931 because of speculation that it would abandon the gold standard. The U.K. abandoned the gold standard in 1931 (and, not coincidentally, rapidly recovered as gold flows, their money supply, and their trade balance immediately increased), leading many speculators to sell their dollars for gold in anticipation of the United States doing the same in the near future.

1933–1941: Recovery

The United States resisted abandoning the gold standard until 1933, when Roosevelt came to power and devalued the dollar. France and other European countries held onto the gold standard until 1936, while Germany held on throughout the decade (Germany is a special case because of the economic constraints placed on it by the allies after World War I—constraints that severely damaged the German economy and set the stage for Hitler's rise to power). Referring once again to Figure 10.1, no country other than Germany recovered from the Great Depression until it dropped off of the gold standard. Once it did, recovery was often quite strong. This is especially true in the U.K., which was the first to abandon the gold standard. Spain is also an interesting case study because it was never on the gold standard to begin with and suffered no banking panics and no depression. Bernanke (1995) found that beginning in 1931, non–gold standard countries had higher production, prices, money supplies, employment, interest rates, exports, imports, and stock prices than their counterparts that remained on the gold standard.

In the United States, the New Deal policies initiated by Roosevelt also helped to stabilize the economy. Increases in government spending and reductions in taxes stimulated aggregate demand and raised consumer confidence by creating the impression that the government was doing something to improve the economic situation. Bank holidays imposed by Roosevelt also slowed the bank runs and rampant speculation that were plaguing the U.S. financial system. However, these New Deal policies were not sufficient to end the Depression by themselves. These initiatives were simply much too small relative to the size of the contraction in output.

While the trough in U.S. GDP occurred in 1933, recovery from the Great Depression was painfully slow. Output had fallen so far below the natural rate that it would necessarily take a long time for it to recover. The recovery was also slowed by the large decline in the capital stock and the lost job skills and training that accompanied lost job opportunities. Output rose very gradually from 1933 to 1937, followed by a short recession from 1937 to 1938 (which was once again initiated by the Fed cutting the money supply in response to inflation fears). By 1940, unemployment was still at 14.6 percent. In fact, the United States did not return to the natural rate of output until 1941, when huge increases in defense spending (a 59 percent increase in government spending between 1940 and 1941) were triggered by Germany's invasion of France in May 1940. U.S. GDP increased by 17 percent between 1940 and 1941 and unemployment dropped below 10 percent for the first time since 1930.

WHY IS DEFLATION SO COSTLY?

There remains one missing piece to the puzzle of explaining what caused the Great Depression. Why was it that deflation, which was caused by falling money supplies and aggregate demands throughout the world, had such a huge impact on the real economy? In other words, why didn't the classical principle of money neutrality hold, where as long as markets were perfectly flexible then nominal policy shocks, such as those to the world's money supplies during the Great Depression, would not matter for real economy activity? New research has clarified exactly why deflation has such a large negative impact on an economy and turned the events of the early 1930s into not just another recession, but a depression. Two primary costs of deflation have received the most attention.

Deflation increases the real value of debt relative to the value of assets because the prices of nominal debt contracts are fixed. Most debt contracts are not *indexed*, meaning that they do not have contractual clauses that adjust the value of payments for changes in measured inflation. Because their price (or the principal to be repaid) is fixed, unexpected changes in the price level change the real value of debt. An unexpected decrease in the price level increases the real value of debt if the nominal value of this debt is fixed. This is a severe financial imposition on firms and households who tend to be borrowers, and while it might seem to be a good thing for banks to see the real value of their loan portfolio rise, the probability that these loans will be repaid has fallen significantly.

In the same way, consider how unexpected deflation affects the value of assets. The market prices of assets are not fixed and a decrease in the price level decreases the prices of these assets. This includes decreases in the value of assets a bank uses to generate income, such as stocks or bonds, and it also decreases the value of the assets firms and households used as collateral to back their bank loans, such as the prices of homes or land. Thus, firms and households will see the value of their assets fall and the real value of their debts rise as a result of a large and unexpected deflation. This means that many of these same firms and households will become bankrupt, leading to higher rates of default on loan payments and deterioration in the soundness of banks' balance sheets.

Irving Fischer (1933), one of the preeminent economists during the Great Depression, described this general process in what he referred to as the *Debt-Deflation theory*. A lower price level increases the real value of debt and decreases the value of collateral. As banks see the number of defaulted or delinquent loans in their portfolio rise, they panic and begin to sell assets. If a large number of banks do this, it further depresses asset prices and further weakens banks' financial positions.

Weak banks either fail or have to reduce the amount of new lending they undertake, both of which stifles investment and consumption, reduces aggregate demand, and reduces output.

Keynes (1931) himself recognized that nominal debt prices were fixed and that deflation weakened the financial position of banks, reducing the supply of credit supplied to firms. However, both Keynes and the Keynesians focused on the demand for credit, believing that low expectations were primarily responsible for low investment, regardless of the supply of credit that was available. As a result, the role of debt and financial stability receives little attention in *The General Theory* and from Keynesians.

Monetarists, on the other hand, agree with the Debt-Deflation theory that changes in the supply of credit drive business cycles. However, they believe that credit cycles are the result of vacillating monetary policy, not of the credit rationing of banks.

This Debt-Deflation theory appears to be an accurate description of what happened in the U.S. financial system during the Great Depression. U.S. banks, especially a large number of rural banks, had been weakened during the 1920s because of deflation in agricultural prices, which had dramatically increased farm foreclosures. During the generally prosperous 1920s, nearly 6,000 banks failed. When economy-wide deflation occurred in the 1930s, the debt-to-income ratio in the United States jumped from 9 percent in 1929 to 19.8 percent in 1932, and 45 percent of farms became delinquent in their loan payments. As a result, small, undiversified banks were left facing the fact that they had lent out money that could not be repaid. Coupled with the difficulty of borrowing funds elsewhere because of the tight money supply, these loan defaults led to an unprecedented number of bank failures. In addition, the initial failure of a small number of banks led to a loss of confidence among depositors, leading to bank runs across the country that further weakened banks' balance sheets. Consequently, between 1930 and 1933, roughly one-fourth of all banks in the United States failed or suspended payments.

While this debt-deflation theory of financial crises has been around since the Great Depression, New Keynesian economists such as Ben Bernanke (1983) gave it new life with their work on the macroeconomic effects of imperfect information and risk. Chapter 8 on New Keynesian economics discusses the microeconomic reasons behind why banks engage in *credit rationing*, or restricting the amount of new lending during recessions. During economic contractions, the risk of bankruptcy by firms and households increases because of increases in the real value of debt and also because of decreases in the value of collateral. Bernanke observed that even those banks that do not fail will become very reluctant to initiate new lending to existing customers because of this higher default risk. In addition, for the customers of banks that failed, getting a new loan from a new bank will be exceptionally difficult because of the loss of a long-term lending relationship. The typical method banks use to reduce lending, which is to raise the interest rate, may increase the probability of default on existing loans. As a result, surviving banks will credit ration during bad times, reducing financial intermediation and investment. Bernanke found a great deal of evidence that suggests that the costs of credit intermediation, meaning the costs of lending incurred by banks, dramatically increased during the Great Depression because of higher levels of debt, lower values of collateral, lower levels of bank deposits, and higher bankruptcy risk. He also found that both bank failures and increases in the costs of credit intermediation played significant roles in causing the steep declines in investment and industrial production during the Depression.

Thus, it appears that one key reason why deflation is so costly is that it increases the risk of default on loans. More defaults lead to failure for some banks and increases in the costs of financial intermediation for those banks that do not fail. This chokes off investment and decreases output, making financial markets a crucial component of a full explanation of why the Great Depression was so deep and so persistent.

Deflation increases real wages because of nominal wage inflexibility. One of the key tenets of Keynesian economics is that nominal wages are inflexible, particularly downward, so that a decrease in the price level increases real wages and generates unemployment in the labor market. One of the important contributions of New Keynesian economics has been to explain the microeconomic foundations behind this nominal wage inflexibility. In Chapter 8, a number of theories of why nominal wages are rigid were examined: implicit and explicit contracts, minimum wage laws, insider/outsider theories, and efficiency wage theories. Each of these models explains how wage rigidity and disequilibrium can persist within imperfectly competitive labor markets.

Bernanke (1995) investigated real wage behavior across countries during the Great Depression and reported that in gold standard countries such as the United States, real wages rose by an average of 11 percent in 1931 and 6.4 percent in 1932. This is in spite of the fact that nominal wages were falling in these countries–they were just not falling fast enough to restore equilibrium in the labor market. In the United States, real wages rose by roughly 3 percent during 1931, even though nominal wages fell nearly 13 percent and unemployment was over 20 percent. On the other hand, real wages in non–gold standard countries were either stagnant or falling, particularly from 1934 on. This is primarily because prices in these non–gold standard countries began to rise as they increased their money supplies in an effort to stimulate aggregate demand.

OTHER EXPLANATIONS OF THE GREAT DEPRESSION

The explanation of the Great Depression examined here, which focuses on the macroeconomic impact of deflation that resulted from naïve adherence to the gold standard, is not the only explanation of the Great Depression that has been proposed by economists. In fact, many other alternative explanations have been offered. Most of these alternatives are not mutually exclusive, however, meaning that an economic contraction the size of the Great Depression did not have just one cause. Multiple theories make sense if there are multiple causes. On the other hand, most other explanations are of secondary importance to the primary cause discussed in this chapter.

Keynesians believe that the Great Depression was caused by a decrease in expectations that reduced investment and consumption (i.e., a decrease in the IS curve), which in turn reduced aggregate demand and output because of wage inflexibility. While low expectations obviously played a role in the Depression, it is hard to see how a 50 percent fall in GDP could be initiated only by pessimistic expectations. If this were the case, why haven't we seen depressions comparable to the Great Depression since the 1930s? And what happened in 1929 that could explain such a large decline in confidence across countries? In addition, while Keynesians identified the role of inflexible nominal wages in driving involuntary unemployment in the labor market, they largely ignored other important factors that had a real impact on economic activity, such as the effects of nominal debt contracts and the role deflation played in weakening the financial system and reducing the supply of credit. Thus, the Keynesian explanation is only a partial one.

Monetarists focus on the role of money and the Federal Reserve's contractionary policies during the Great Depression. Friedman and other monetarists argue that a strict adherence to the gold standard led the Fed to contract the money supply, which had dire economic consequences. However, Monetarists believe that decreases in the money supply affect output by reducing the supply of credit, driving up real interest rates, and reducing spending. In their theory, bank failures were a symptom of the Depression, not a cause. These failures occurred only because of a shortage of liquidity that prohibited banks from meeting their deposit withdrawal demands.

Two problems exist with this Monetarist explanation. First, relying on the 250-year-old Quantity Theory, which assumes a direct relationship between the money supply and spending, seems suspect to many. Does monetary policy, through its ability to influence bank credit and spending, really have the power to reduce output by 50 percent by itself? Second, interest rates did not rise during the Great Depression as predicted by the Monetarists, but instead fell. This indicates that it may not have been tight monetary policy that was the cause of falling investment. More likely, it was credit rationing that restricted the supply of credit. This credit rationing was the eventual result of a large decline in the money supply that led to deflation. Deflation in turn led to higher real wages, higher loan default rates, and an increase in the costs of financial intermediation, precipitating credit rationing as well as bank failures and falling output. Thus, the proponents of the theory laid out in this chapter would say that the Monetarists were right about what started the Great Depression, but not about why monetary policy had real effects on the economy.

The explanation of the Great Depression most often mentioned by laymen is that it was caused by the stock market crash of 1929. While the stock market crash undoubtedly played a contributing role by increasing uncertainty and decreasing wealth, it is implausible to think that it was large enough, by itself, to explain an economic contraction the size of the Great Depression. The stock market has fluctuated wildly since the Great Depression (for example, the crash of 1987 was actually larger than the 1929 crash) but never with anywhere near such dire economic consequences.

Likewise, declines in the prices of rental space, raw materials, and food because of overproduction in the 1920s is often mentioned as a cause of the Depression. For example, the "dust bowl" conditions that existed in the West were largely the result of overproduction and overly intensive farming techniques. However, while these factors probably played some small role in the Depression, most of the decreases in the prices of rents, food, and raw materials were no greater than the overall deflation that occurred within the economy and had actually been occurring since well before the Depression began.

Finally, many Classical or supply-side economists intent on finding some supply-driven cause of the Great Depression have focused on the effects of the Smoot-Hawley export tariffs imposed at the beginning of the Great Depression. At the time, however, exports were only 7 percent of U.S. GDP, making it unlikely that these tariffs explained even a small fraction of the large contraction in output.

CONCLUSIONS

The main conclusion of the new research on the Great Depression reviewed here is that the Great Depression was primarily the result of a macroeconomic policy failure of unparalleled proportions. An un-flinching commitment to a flawed gold standard, where there were penalties for experiencing trade deficits and gold outflows but not for experiencing trade surpluses and gold inflows, provided the rationale for naïve policymakers to reduce money supplies, reduce aggregate demands, and reduce prices throughout the world's economies. This deflation had two devastating effects. First, in financial markets, defla-tion increased the real value of debt relative to the value of assets, increasing the bankruptcy risk of firms, households, and banks while also increasing the costs of credit intermediation within the banking industry. This led to credit rationing which placed a stranglehold on financial intermediation and investment. Thus, contrary to Keynesians and Monetarists, neither animal spirits no monetary policy is solely responsible for the large decline in investment. Second, in the labor market, deflation led to an increase in real wages because of nominal wage inflexibility. This led to unprecedented levels of involuntary unemployment. The end result was a historic economic contraction driven by labor and financial market imperfections. This same basic story holds throughout the world's economies that suffered from the Depression. However, it is especially true for the United States, which held much of the world's gold in 1929 but still stubbornly reduced its money supply until deflation, banking failures, and the Depression were so rampant that a reversal in monetary policy was completely ineffective.

Discussions of the Great Depression typically end by asking the following question: Could it happen again? Within developed countries such as the United States and Europe, it seems unlikely. Macroeconomic policy knowledge and responsiveness are much greater than they were during the Depression. Today it would be hard to imagine Federal Reserve policymakers decreasing the money supply during a recession in order to maintain a fixed exchange rate. At the same time, technolog-ical advances have made financial and labor markets much more flexi-ble and efficient than they were during the Depression. Finally, the U.S. economy as a whole, but particularly its financial markets, is much more diversified and is better able to withstand shocks than it was during the 1930s. For example, consider how well the U.S. economy withstood the September 11 terrorist attacks and the financial and stock market losses associated with it.

However, when this question is asked about a broader set of econo-mies throughout the world, the answer is a resounding yes. In fact, it has already happened. In Chapter 13 and Chapter 14, the East Asian crisis and the Argentinean economic crisis will be discussed. While many of the particulars are different, the basic explanation of what caused these crises will be disturbingly similar to the themes expounded upon in this chapter. Unfortunately, history does repeat itself, which is why continued research and investigation into the nature and causes of the Great Depression is so valuable.

SUGGESTED READINGS

Ben Bernanke, "Nonmonetary Effects of the Financial Crisis in the Propagation of the Great Depression" (1983): A review of the empirical regularities and differences between countries during the Great Depression, with an emphasis on the effects of the gold standard and deflation on the financial industry.

Christina D. Romer, "The Nation in Depression" (1993): A comprehensive review of the Great Depression in the United States.

Peter Temin, *Lessons from the Great Depression* (1989): A nontechnical review of the Great Depression on which much of the discussion in this chapter is based. This book's particular focus is on the international aspects of the Great Depression and contains interesting insight into cross-country differences in macroeconomic policy. Chapter 1 is particularly recommended.

11

Postwar Business Cycles in the United States

INTRODUCTION

When discussing the empirical regularities of business cycles in Chapter 2, the point was made that business cycles are not cyclical—meaning that they do not exhibit a regular pattern. To some extent, each business cycle is different. As a result, case studies of specific business cycle episodes in the United States is a potentially useful way to determine whether modern recessions and expansions share certain characteristics. A detailed review of postwar business cycles in the United States and a discussion of their common properties is the first objective of this chapter.

One of the questions often raised when discussing postwar business cycles in the United States is whether there has been any moderation in output fluctuations compared to earlier periods in history. Most economists would like to think so, because this would be a strong piece of circumstantial evidence that advances in business cycle theory are leading to more effective macroeconomic policies, which are having a beneficial impact on the economy. The second objective of this chapter is to examine the evidence on whether postwar business cycles are in fact more moderate than they were in the prewar era and why this might be the case.

POSTWAR BUSINESS CYCLE EPISODES

1945–1961: Not Waves but Ripples

Most economists and the public were worried about a return to Depression-era conditions once the war ended, in part because of large anticipated decreases in government spending and in part because of the huge increase in the labor force that would occur when soldiers returned from the war to find a large number of women now working outside of the home. While there was, in fact, a large and sharp decrease in GDP after the war, it was not nearly as severe as what had been feared. GDP fell by 19 percent in 1946 but only by 2.8 percent in 1947, leaving the economy at output levels that were still above the natural rate. Output did not fall by more because decreases in government spending were largely offset by huge increases in durable goods consumption (automobiles and appliances) and new housing, both of which were financed by household savings accumulated during the war. Unemployment also remained stable as many women returned to work in the home and many soldiers went to college under the GI Bill.

The 1946–1961 period was characterized by small, regular business cycles. The 1948–1949, 1953–1954, 1957–1958, and 1960–1961 recessions were all short and mild. A variety of factors contributed to each of these recessions, such as the increase and decrease in government spending before and after U.S. involvement in the Korean War (1950–1953) and a U.S. steel strike in 1959. Each of these recessions was also preceded by sharp but temporary decreases in the money supply that were the result of inflationary fears within the Federal Reserve (many of these fears at the beginning of the period were driven by the gradual expiration of wage and price controls imposed during the war). Thus, each of these recessions (and the following expansions) appears to have been aggregate demand driven. In fact, the Phillips curve and its prediction of a constant, negative relationship between unemployment and inflation was actually developed because of the observed stability of this relationship during the 1950s. In addition, the close relationship between aggregate output and the money supply over this period later played a role in the development of Monetarist thought during the 1960s.

While this was a relatively stable period economically, it was also a period of relatively slow economic growth. Real GDP growth during the 1950s averaged only 2.1 percent, which was low by historical standards. This was coupled with a slow but steady rise in unemployment, from an average of 3 percent in the early 1950s to an average of 4 percent in the late 1950s. At the same time, inflation was high by historical standards during the 1950s, fluctuating between 1.6 percent and 8.8 percent as measured by the GDP deflator. This suggests that, if anything, changes in aggregate supply during this period tended to be negative and might have been the consequence of increases in the minimum wage and labor unionization.

While monetary policy played a role in initiating each of the four recessions during this period, it does appear that the Federal Reserve was beginning to learn from the mistakes it made during the Great

Depression. In each case, the Fed quickly reversed itself when it became clear that it had overreacted, which is the primary reason why the recessions during this period were short. Other changes in the economy also helped to moderate business cycles. Primarily, Roosevelt's New Deal program created welfare insurance, unemployment insurance, social security insurance, and more progressive federal income taxation, each of which served as automatic stabilizers of consumption and aggregate demand during contractions. As a result, by the end of this period there was a feeling among economists, especially among Keynesians, that they were figuring out business cycles and could possibly eliminate them in the future if the proper policymakers were in power.

1961–1970: The Rise and Fall of Keynesian Economics

The expansion from 1961 to 1969 lasted 106 months and was the longest in U.S. history until the 1990s expansion, and output growth averaged 4.5 percent a year over this period. Once again, this expansion appeared to be largely aggregate demand driven, with investment and consumption growing at 8 percent and 9 percent, respectively, on average. Strong increases in the money supply, increases in government spending on the Vietnam War and Johnson's Great Society programs, and reductions in taxes on investment and income spurred aggregate demand growth over this period.

The 1961–1969 period represented the pinnacle of Keynesian influence. When Kennedy became president in 1961, he brought to Washington many of his Keynesian associates from Harvard. Once in power, they began to actively engage in Keynesian stabilization policy. Because government spending was largely constrained by military spending on the Vietnam War, these Keynesians relied on tax policy to manipulate aggregate demand. For example, tax cuts on investment were enacted in 1962 and income tax cuts were enacted in 1964, during periods when the U.S. economy appeared to be slowing.

In 1968, the Johnson administration enacted a temporary tax increase in an effort to slow down the economy at a time when output growth was clearly above its natural rate and inflation was rising. This temporary tax increase was a complete failure and shook economists' faith in the Keynesian model. The failure of this temporary tax increase to slow aggregate demand growth rested on the fact that it was only temporary. As a result, this tax increase did not really change households' incentives to spend. Instead, households anticipated future tax reductions and just paid for this tax increase out of their savings, leading to continued growth in aggregate demand. This temporary tax cut is an important episode in economic history because it clearly contradicted the predictions of the Keynesian model. For that reason, it is often referred to by proponents of Rational Expectations models as evidence in support of the Lucas Critique of stabilization policy.

By 1969, another unanticipated consequence of Keynesian stabilization policy was becoming evident: accelerating inflation. Inflation gradually rose throughout the 1960s, from 1.5 percent in 1964 to 3.6 percent in 1966 to 5 percent in 1969. Keynesian fiscal policy solutions aimed at reducing inflation failed, as government spending continued to rise throughout the period and the temporary tax reduction in 1968 failed to reduce aggregate demand. Consequently, the Federal Reserve was forced to cut money growth. The Fed first cut money growth in 1965, which would probably have driven the economy into a recession at that time if it had not been for the strong growth of government spending. Eventually, in 1969, the Fed once again reduced money growth and the economy slipped into a mild recession from 1969 to 1970. During this recession, unemployment increased to 5.8 percent. However, the reduction in the money supply was not large or sustained enough to rein in inflation and inflationary expectations. In fact, inflation actually rose slightly in 1970 to 5.5 percent. This was the beginning of *stagflation*, or a period of simultaneous increases in inflation and unemployment, which had never before been experienced in the United States.

1970–1980: Sustained Stagflation

The expansion that began in late 1970 was actually initiated by a negative shock—the collapse of the Penn Central Railroad. This bankruptcy shook financial markets, and the Fed responded by increasing the money supply in order to increase liquidity and stabilize the system. This monetary loosening also spurred economic activity. The resulting expansion, which lasted until 1973, was accompanied by rising inflation in spite of misguided attempts by the Nixon administration to place wage and price controls on the economy. These wage and price controls primarily created market distortions. Meanwhile, the Fed continued to increase the money supply at a robust pace throughout this period. While it is not clear exactly why the Fed continued to increase the money supply in the face of significant inflationary momentum, it appears that political pressures from the Nixon administration associated with the 1972 election played some role. One piece of evidence supporting this conclusion is the fact that the Fed immediately began reducing money growth as soon as the election was over.

Another important event during this period was the abandonment of the Bretton Woods system of fixed exchange rates. Under Bretton Woods, it was impossible for the United States to devalue its currency because every other currency was fixing its exchange rate to the dollar. As inflation rose in the United States, the dollar became overvalued and the United States began to experience significant gold outflows. In 1971, the United States suspended gold convertibility of the dollar, and by 1973 the dollar was allowed to float, removing another constraint on monetary policy and allowing further money growth.

By 1973, inflation had risen to 5.9 percent and real GDP growth had risen to 5.3 percent. In the fall of that year, however, the economy began to slow. This was partially because of slower money growth (post election). The main shock, though, was the OPEC oil embargo that was imposed in October 1973. This embargo increased the price of a barrel of oil from $3 to $12 and had a number of negative effects on the economy. It reduced real incomes, which decreased aggregate demand. More important, it reduced aggregate supply through two channels. First, it immediately made a large fraction of the existing technology and capital stocks too expensive to use. Second, it also increased the marginal cost of production across most industries because oil is a significant input into the production of almost every good produced in modern economies.

The 1973–1975 recession was the worst recession in the United States since the 1930s. Unemployment, from trough to peak, rose from 4.8 percent to 8.9 percent. At the same time, inflation rose from 7 percent to an unprecedented 12.1 percent in 1975. This stagflation completely ended economists' fascination with the Phillips curve and also left them more skeptical of Keynesian economics in general. In addition, Monetarism was also discredited by the fact that this recession was largely driven by supply factors and not by monetary factors. In fact, this period is best characterized as one in which all consensus of thought on business cycles broke down. Economists were left searching for alternative business cycle theories that were logically consistent but that could also explain stagflation.

In 1975, the oil embargo was loosened. Immediately, both the price of oil and inflation fell sharply. Aiding in the economic recovery, the Fed began to increase money growth in order to reduce the severity of the recession. The expansion that followed, which lasted until 1979, saw another buildup of inflation, from its trough of 6.4 percent in 1976 to 8.9 percent in 1979.

In hindsight, an obvious question can be raised about monetary policy throughout the 1970s: why did the Federal Reserve persist in increasing the money supply and inflation, even during times of relatively healthy output growth? While it is difficult to go back in time and read the minds of policymakers, especially those in what was then a more secretive Federal Reserve, the most plausible explanation of this prolonged policy mistake was that the Federal Reserve was wrong about the level of the natural rate of unemployment. The Fed's actions are consistent with a belief that the natural rate of unemployment was considerably lower than what it actually was, leading them to persistently increase the money supply even in the face of higher and higher inflation. This is exactly what Friedman predicted would happen to imperfectly informed policymakers in his 1969 address to the American Economic Association (see Chapter 5). Though unbeknownst to the Fed at the time, in hindsight it is clear that the natural rate of unemployment rose during the 1970s for a number of reasons. First, higher oil prices had reduced capacity and productivity. Second, government policies in the form of minimum wage laws, wage and price controls, and tax increases also reduced productivity and increased the costs of hiring labor. Third, a significant amount of structural unemployment was created by the struggling automobile and steel industries. Finally, a large increase in the labor supply took place as more women and baby boomers entered the labor force. As a result, while the Fed was consistently aiming for an unemployment rate of around 5 percent, it never fell below 6 percent throughout the entire decade. The result was increasing levels of inflation.

The 1970s ended on another down note. In the spring of 1979, the Iranian revolution led to another large jump in oil prices, from $14 to $29 a barrel. Coupled with slower money growth and credit controls imposed by the Carter administration (both aimed at slowing inflation) a recession occurred during 1980. However, both monetary policy and credit restrictions were quickly relaxed and the 1980 recession ended up being the shortest in U.S. history, lasting only 6 months. GDP fell only 2.3 percent, while unemployment only rose from 6 percent to 7.3 percent. Of course, the downside of experiencing such a small recession was that, once again, the Fed had failed to rein in accelerating inflation. Inflation rose from 7.3 percent in 1979 to 8.5 percent in 1980. Frustration began to grow inside the Federal Reserve over its inability to reduce inflation. With the election of Ronald Reagan in 1980, who campaigned against the "misery index" of high inflation and high unemployment that had existed during the Carter administration, the stage was set for a major policy correction.

1981–1991: A Policy Correction Followed by an Expansion

The shortest recession in U.S. history was quickly followed by one of the most severe recessions in U.S. history. The 1981–1982 recession was the deepest in the United States since the Depression, with unemployment peaking at 10.8 percent in 1982. The cause of this recession is well understood. Aided by political cover from the Reagan administration, the Federal Reserve, led by Chairman Paul Volcker, made a concerted effort to drive down inflation by decreasing money growth, even at the cost of postwar highs in unemployment. The Fed characterized their monetary policy during this period as a "Monetarist experiment," where they claimed to be reasserting control over the money supply and targeting monetary aggregates in an effort to reduce inflation. While Monetarists were upset by this characterization, primarily because money growth remained very volatile over this period, the decline in average money growth was large enough to drive inflation down from 9.9 percent to 3.6 percent in just under two years. The costs of driving down inflation were rising real interest rates and significant declines in investment and consumer durables spending.

The benefits of the Fed's policy correction were soon obvious. Inflation expectations and wages adjusted downward very rapidly in response to the credible commitment made by the Fed to lower inflation (a point not lost on Rational Expectations proponents). In fact, the Fed's disinflation was so successful that the Fed ended their Monetarist experiment and eased monetary policy in late 1982. Faster money growth and lower expected inflation provided the foundation for a protracted expansion that lasted for eight years, until 1990. The 1982–1990 expansion was driven by a number of factors. On the demand side, big budget deficits created by large increases in defense spending and income tax reductions, both pushed by the Reagan administration, stimulated aggregate demand. In addition, investment and consumer durable demand were quite strong over this period. On the supply side, the collapse of the OPEC oil cartel in 1986 dropped oil prices from $27 to $14, more than offsetting the price increase that occurred in 1979. Together, all of these factors lead to strong output growth (of roughly 3 percent), falling unemployment rates (below 5 percent by the end of the decade), and steady inflation (of roughly 3 percent).

One interesting event that took place during this period was the 1987 stock market crash. This crash was larger than the one that occurred in 1929, destroying roughly $1 trillion of wealth in 1987 dollars, or 20 percent of yearly output. However, a recession was avoided in large part because of the Fed's adept handling of the crash. The Federal Reserve's aggressive response, which was to immediately increase liquidity in the financial system but quickly remove it when it became apparent that there would be no major macroeconomic consequences from the crash, stabilized consumer expectations, investment, and consumer demand.

The expansion that began in 1982 lasted until 1990. At that time, a number of factors affecting both aggregate demand and aggregate supply turned negative. The major supply shock associated with the 1990–1991 recession was the Gulf War, which led to a brief but significant increase in the price of oil. In addition, a tax increase enacted in 1990 and new financial regulations that were imposed on banks may also have played some role in decreasing aggregate supply. In regard to aggregate demand, war worries and new financial regulations also reduced investment and durables consumption. At the same time, the Fed began to tighten money growth in early 1990 in response to inflation worries, possibly overreacting to a modest increase in the inflation rate at precisely the wrong moment. Finally, the world economy had also slipped into recession, decreasing U.S. exports and increasing the trade deficit.

1991–Present: A "New Economy"?

Following the Gulf War, consumer expectations and money growth rebounded strongly. Even though the 1991–2001 expansion, which is the longest in recorded U.S. history, was initiated by strong aggregate demand growth, it was remarkable increases in aggregate supply throughout this period that drove this unprecedented expansion. Strong increases in productivity from advances in information technology and strong investment led to falling unemployment, which reached a 25-year low of 4.5 percent in 1999. At the same time, inflation remained low and steady, once again violating the Phillips curve relationship. In fact, economic growth was so robust and inflation was so low throughout this period that economists began to question whether the U.S. economy was entering a new economic era—one with permanently higher productivity growth and faster improvements in standards of living without the threat of inflation. Much of this optimism has not been tempered by the stock market downturn of the early 2000s, the mild recession that took place in 2001, and a protracted period of slower than average growth that has followed.

Chapter 12 on the "New Economy" investigates the 1990s expansion in more detail and examines exactly what was driving these gains in productivity. In addition, the causes of the eight-month recession that occurred during 2001 is examined, including a discussion of whether the 2001 recession and its slow-growth aftermath is just a bump on the road to greater stability or a signal of something more significant for future business cycles.

ARE POSTWAR BUSINESS CYCLES DIFFERENT FROM THEIR PREWAR PREDECESSORS?

Quite a bit of circumstantial evidence suggests that modern business cycles have been less severe than those before World War II. For example, obviously nothing like the Great Depression has occurred during the postwar era. Likewise, the United States has not recently suffered from banking crises like those that occurred between 1890 and 1921, which shook financial systems and magnified the size of the contraction in output. Does a closer examination of business cycle data support the fact that business cycles have moderated? And if so, why has this occurred?

Comparing Postwar Business Cycles to Earlier Periods

Economists interested in comparing postwar fluctuations to those from earlier periods have faced a large hurdle in their investigations: the lack of reliable historical macroeconomic data. Until the 1920s (or even later for some data), almost no macroeconomic data was collected. As a result, economic historians have had to construct estimates of macroeconomic variables such as output, unemployment, and inflation by interpolating from the time series data that they did possess. Much of this was based on data on commodity prices and industrial data from manufacturing firms. While estimates could be constructed from this data, commodity and manufacturing data tends to be more volatile than aggregate output in general. As a result, estimates of aggregate output constructed using this data were also very volatile, probably more volatile than actual aggregate output would have been. It is not surprising then that studies that relied on commodity and manufacturing data to get their historical estimates of aggregate output found that business cycle fluctuations were much larger in the prewar era. Some of these early studies suggested that output fluctuations are 75 percent lower after World War II than before.

In a series of papers (surveyed in Romer [1999a]), Christina Romer reexamined historical business cycles using new and improved data. Using regression analysis on a much broader range of economic variables, Romer generated estimates of historical macroeconomic variables that were more reliable than those that were based only on commodity and manufacturing data. Table 11.1 reports her results for three periods: the prewar period (1886–1916), the interwar period (1920–1940), and the postwar period (1948–1997). A brief glance at this

TABLE 11.1 Standard Deviations of Percent Changes during Prewar, Interwar, and Postwar Periods

	Prewar 1886–1916	Interwar 1920–1940	Postwar 1948–1997
Industrial Production	6.2%	16.0%	5.0%
GNP	3.0	7.1	2.5
Commodity Output	5.2	9.0	4.9
Unemployment Rate	1.4	—	1.1

Source: Romer (1999)

table leads to a few important conclusions. First, the interwar period was extremely volatile. In fact, changes in output were roughly 2.5 times more volatile during the interwar period than either before or after this period. Even if the Great Depression had not occurred, the interwar period still would have been the most volatile economic period in U.S. history. In addition, while fluctuations in the postwar period are smaller than during the interwar period, there is not a dramatic difference between the postwar and prewar periods. Postwar fluctuations are only about 20 percent smaller than prewar periods. To break this down even further, Table 11.2 separates the postwar period into two sub-periods, 1948–1984 and 1985–1997. Interestingly, most of the stabilization in postwar business cycles has taken place only during the last 13 years of the postwar period included in this study. Output fluctuations during 1985–1997 were about half as large as those at the beginning of the postwar period (if the 1997–2002 period were included, this improvement would have been even larger). Hence, this seems to suggest that the United States has recently begun to experience a significant moderation in economic fluctuations. Oliver Blanchard and John Simon (2001) support this conclusion by finding evidence that suggests that output volatility has declined by one-third since World War II. However, it is difficult for anyone to say definitively whether this trend will continue. To do so on the basis of less than 20 years worth of observations (what amounts to less than two business cycles) is highly speculative at best.

While the magnitude of postwar business cycles might not be that much smaller than that of those before World War I, their frequency has changed. Table 11.3 reports the length of recessions and expansions in the prewar, interwar, and postwar periods. Once again, the interwar period is clearly unique and had much longer recessions and shorter expansions. Comparing the prewar and postwar periods, the lengths of recessions are not much different. In fact, average recessions are one month longer in the postwar period. However, postwar expansions have been considerably longer, almost 1.5 years longer on average, due

TABLE 11.2 Standard Deviations of Percent Changes during the Post-War Period

	1948–1984	1985–1997
Industrial Production	5.7%	2.2%
GNP	2.8	1.3
Commodity Output	5.3	3.6
Unemployment Rate	1.2	0.6

Source: Romer (1999)

TABLE 11.3   Length of Recessions and Expansions

Prewar 1886–1916			Interwar 1920–1940			Postwar 1948–1997		
Year of Peak	Mos. to Trough	Mos. From Trough to Next Peak	Year of Peak	Mos. to Trough	Mos. From Trough to Next Peak	Year of Peak	Mos. to Trough	Mos. From Trough to Next Peak
1887	5	66	1920	14	26	1948	11	45
1893	13	23	1923	14	32	1953	10	39
1896	12	39	1927	9	21	1957	8	24
1900	8	31	1929	34	61	1960	10	106
1903	8	40	1937	10	18	1969	11	36
1907	11	19	1939	3		1973	16	58
1910	16	37				1980	6	12
1914	6	17				1981	16	92
1916	8					1990	8	
Avg.	9.7	34.0	Avg.	14.0	31.6	Avg.	10.7	51.0

Source: Romer (1999)

in large part to the extended expansions of the 1960s, 1980s, and 1990s. Of course, the longer the expansion, the less frequent the recession. Diebold and Rudebusch (1999) have referred to this phenomenon as *duration stabilization.* They report evidence that only 20 percent of postwar time has been spent in recession, as compared to 40 percent of the time spent in recession during the prewar period. Thus, the most dramatic changes in postwar business cycles have not been in a moderation in the size of output fluctuations, but in the reduced frequency of recessions.

The Role of Macroeconomic Policy in Duration Stabilization

Why have recessions been less frequent during the postwar era, especially since 1980? A number of possible explanations have been suggested. Some have suggested that as the United States has gotten richer, it has become a more diverse economy in terms of the number of goods it produces. Diversification better protects an economy from negative shocks that might affect a small number of industries. U.S. financial markets and banks have also benefited from this economic development and diversification, making them more stable, which in turn have made investment and durable consumption demand less volatile. Also suggested has been the fact that the United States and numerous other developed countries have moved toward consuming more services and nondurables, as evidenced by the fact that services have risen from 39 percent of GDP in 1960 to 55 percent of GDP in

2001. Because the demand for nondurables and services are less volatile than the demand for durable manufactured goods, aggregate output should be more stable. In addition, government purchases have become a larger fraction of aggregate output and are also more stable than other components of aggregate output. Blanchard and Simon (2001) find evidence that changes in the behavior of inventories during the 1990s, possibly because of new management systems, have substantially contributed to output stability. Finally, some economists have argued that advances in communications and information technology have improved the quality of information and have stabilized business and consumer confidence, reducing its role in destabilizing aggregate demand.

However, the most often mentioned, and most analyzed, explanation for output and duration stabilization has been the increased use of macroeconomic stabilization policy in the U.S. economy during the postwar era. In the prewar period, macroeconomic policy did not really exist. There was no federal income tax, and government spending averaged only about 2 percent of GDP. In addition, the Federal Reserve did not exist until 1914 and at first was very weak, with decentralized control and little understanding of monetary policy. During the interwar period, things changed and the role of the federal government in the economy expanded. A federal income tax was adopted and government spending rose to its current level of slightly more than 20 percent of aggregate output during World War II.

To a large extent, the Great Depression and World War II set the stage for the expanded use of macroeconomic stabilization policy during the postwar period. As military expenditures began to shrink after the war, they were largely replaced by domestic spending programs aimed at providing an economic safety net. A number of automatic economic stabilizers were introduced into the U.S. economy immediately following World War II, such as unemployment insurance, bank deposit insurance, and welfare assistance. In terms of discretionary policy, the Federal Reserve was strengthened and power centralized within the Board of Governors in an effort to allow the Fed to better serve as a lender of last resort and also to allow better management of monetary policy. The Employment Act of 1946 was also passed, which legislated a role for the federal government in actively promoting growth and full employment. The final, and maybe most important, factor in the postwar rise of macroeconomic policy was the ascension of Keynesian economics. The Keynesians' role in providing a coherent argument for the use of discretionary macroeconomic policy to stabilize the economy cannot be understated.

Christina Romer and David Romer (1994) conducted research that attempted to quantify the costs and benefits of macroeconomic policy in the postwar era. First, they identified indicators of changes in monetary policy, fiscal policy, and automatic stabilization programs. They then used these policy indicators to predict how much output would have changed without any changes in macroeconomic policy. Their results indicated that monetary policy was the most important factor in explaining duration stabilization and in reducing output fluctuations. In fact, they report that a change in monetary policy toward faster money growth preceded the trough in output during every postwar recession. Their results also indicate that automatic stabilizers have played a significant role in business cycle stabilization, with discretionary fiscal policy playing only a small role. James Stock and Mark Watson (2002) provide similar evidence that suggests that monetary policy has been responsible for 25 percent of the decline in postwar output volatility. This is entirely consistent with the discussions of specific business cycle episodes conducted in the first part of this chapter, which also suggested that macroeconomic policy has been extremely important in preventing and moderating recessions. Other research on specific business cycle case studies has also found similar results. For example, Bernanke (1990) argues that the Fed's aggressive move to increase the money supply and liquidity following the 1987 stock market crash prevented a financial crisis and a contraction in output.

Of course, while macroeconomic policy has prevented some recessions, it has also clearly been the cause of other ones. In the words of MIT economist Rudy Dornbusch: "None of the U.S. expansions of the past 40 years died in bed of old age; every one was murdered by the Federal Reserve" (1997). The 1981–1982 recession is a clear case in point. In 1981, the Fed was forced to severely contract the money supply in order to reduce the accelerating inflation rates it helped create during the 1970s. This sharp decline in money growth led to the most severe economic contraction in the United States since the Great Depression. In fact, sharp declines in money growth have preceded six of the eight postwar recessions in the United States. Romer and Romer (1994) argue that output growth would not have been negative during the recessions of 1948–1949, 1969–1970, 1980, 1981–1982, and 1990–1991 if the Fed had not reduced money growth. Their results indicate that over the 11 years of these recessions, industrial production would have been constant if monetary policy had remained unchanged. Instead, industrial production fell during these recession years by 4 percent a year. In every one of these cases, worries about inflation were the primary cause of the Fed's contractionary monetary policy. Consistent with this, Blanchard and Simon (2001) find that a strong relationship exists between higher output volatility and higher inflation volatility during the postwar era. Thus, while macroeconomic policy has to some extent stabilized business cycles, an excessive focus on stimulating output has had the unintended consequence of increasing inflation rates. This in turn has led to policy corrections that have destabilized output, offsetting a large amount of the potential benefits of stabilization policy during the postwar era.

CONCLUSIONS

How do we characterize postwar business cycles in the United States? It is obvious that the rising importance of macroeconomic policy has played a crucial role in both moderating and creating business cycles. A brief review of business cycle episodes reveals that postwar expansions and recessions have largely been policy driven. The 1940s and 1950s were periods when growing concerns about a return to the Great Depression were followed by growing concerns about rising inflation, leading to unstable money growth and unstable aggregate demand. The 1960s saw the rise of a confident group of Keynesian policymakers who used macroeconomic policy to "fine-tune" the economy, but at the cost of ignoring the rising inflation that accompanied their overly expansionary policies. Macroeconomic policymakers faced their most crucial test in the 1970s; unfortunately, it was a test that they failed. In hindsight, it is clear that during the 1970s the Fed underestimated the natural rate of unemployment, which had risen because of negative shocks to aggregate supply, primarily from higher oil prices. Coupled with their misguided belief in the Phillips curve, political pressures, and higher levels of government spending that accompanied new social policies and the Vietnam War, the Fed consistently made the mistake of allowing money growth and inflation to expand too rapidly. Unprecedented inflation rates eventually forced the Fed to reduce aggregate demand and initiate economic contractions in order to reduce inflation, the most obvious example being the 1981–1982 recession. Although these "policy correction" recessions tend to be short, they are costly in terms of lost output. Thus, higher inflation has been the reason why the rise of macroeconomic policy in the postwar era has not led to greater moderation in postwar business cycles. Instead, stabilization policy has often given rise to policy-driven business cycles.

Overall, postwar business cycles have been more stable, primarily in terms of longer expansions and less frequent recessions. Although the 1990s and 2000s have been too short a period of time on which to base reliable predictions of the future, it appears that this trend toward output and duration stabilization has gotten much stronger during the last twenty years.

Some would argue that the relative stability of the U.S. economy in the 1980s and 1990s indicates that policymakers are learning from their past mistakes and are figuring out how to more effectively manage stabilization policy, better balancing the tradeoff between output stabilization and inflation. It does appear that Federal Reserve policymakers have been more cautious in their policy actions. For instance, the Federal Reserve changed their monetary stance only one time between 1994 and 1998, leading some to raise the following question: What is the difference between Alan Greenspan and a ham sandwich? Discretion is not just the better part of valor; it is also the better part of macroeconomic stabilization policy. Greenspan's successful term as Federal Reserve chairman seems to support this.

On the other hand, during good economic times—times when productivity and aggregate supply are expanding—it is a lot easier to make good macroeconomic policy decisions than during bad times. As mentioned earlier, Stock and Watson (2002) estimate that monetary policy is responsible for 25 percent of the postwar decline in output volatility. However, the other 75 percent is due to fewer external shocks (oil prices, etc.) and good luck. It is better to be lucky than good, and the Fed appears to have been both during the 1990s. However, who is to say that good economic luck will persist in the future? Many would argue that economists have been too fallible in the past to become arrogant about their ability to perfectly control business cycles and continue to believe that while stabilization policy might work well in theory, it often works poorly in practice. These critics advocate policy rules because of the many difficulties associated with enacting stabilization policy: policy lags, imperfect information about the natural rate of the economy, forecasting errors, rational expectations and the Lucas Critique, and political constraints. Only the next period of economic turmoil will tell whether economists and policymakers have learned the proper lessons about stabilization policy.

SUGGESTED READINGS

Susanto Basu and Alan M. Taylor, "Business Cycles in International Historical Perspective" (1999): A review of the long-run properties of business cycles, both in the United States and internationally. Basu and Taylor focus on the effects of international economic regimes on international business cycles—from the gold standard to the Bretton Woods system to the present day system of floating exchange rates.

Robert E. Hall, "Macro Theory and the Recession of 1990-1991" (1993): A discussion of the characteristics and causes of the 1990–1991 recession.

Robert E. Lucas, "Rules, Discretion, and the Role of the Economic Advisor" (1980): A discussion by the Nobel laureate on why he favors economic policy rules over discretion.

Christina D. Romer, "Changes in Business Cycles: Evidence and Explanations" (1999): A discussion of whether business cycles have changed during the post-postwar era. Part of the discussion here is based on this article.

12

A "New Economy"
in the United States?

INTRODUCTION

Perceptions about how well the economy is performing are even more volatile than the economy itself. This has never been more evident than recently. Three years ago, most discussions about the U.S. economy focused on the debate regarding whether there was a "New Economy" and whether the United States was entering a new era of greater prosperity characterized by permanently higher output growth and increased macroeconomic stability. Incredible advances in information and communication technology, remarkably strong productivity growth, a booming stock market, and outstanding real wage growth within both the richest and the poorest segments of the population fueled these exuberant forecasts. Now, things have changed. Economic discussions in the twenty-first century are characterized by phrases such as "double dip" recession, "jobless" recovery, deflation, and depression. These gloomy sentiments have been driven not only by the weak performance of the U.S. economy, but also by the increasingly turbulent political environment America faces abroad and the problems that this creates domestically.

This chapter has two primary objectives. First, the remarkably strong U.S. economy of the 1990s will be examined. The theoretical and empirical support for and against the proposition of a New Economy will be discussed, focusing on the role of information technology in creating a potentially fundamental change in the U.S. economy. The second objective of this chapter is to examine the relatively mild recession that lasted for eight months during 2001 and the lingering growth recession that followed it. Included will be a discussion of whether this recession is a temporary wobble in the progress towards greater economic prosperity and stability or portends serious problems in the future for the U.S. economy.

THE NEW ECONOMY: ECONOMIC EXPANSION, 1991–2001

Data on the Expansion of 1991–2001

The 1990s were a very good decade for the U.S. economy. After a short recession in 1990–1991, the United States experienced its longest peacetime economic expansion in history, beginning in March of 1991 and lasting until April of 2001, an amazing 121 consecutive months. Table 12.1 presents real GDP growth, unemployment rates, and inflation rates for the decades of the 1960s, 1970s, 1980s, and 1990s. Compared to the 1970s and 1980s, both unemployment and inflation were significantly lower in the 1990s and real output growth was just as strong. One of the more surprising aspects of the 1990s was that economic performance actually got stronger as the expansion went on. During the second half of the 1990s, there was a dramatic improvement in all three macroeconomic indicators compared to the two previous decades. In fact, the unemployment rate reached a 40-year low by 2000.

One of the most welcome occurrences of the 1990s was the remarkable growth in real wages. Real wages grew 1.3 percent a year between 1991 and 2001 (trough to trough), which is the highest real wage growth experienced in the United States since the 1950s and compares very favorably to the 0.2 percent average real wage growth between 1982 and 1991. Another key difference between the 1990s and the 1980s was that all workers across the income distribution shared in these wage gains roughly equally. During the 1980s, real wages actually declined among

TABLE 12.1 Macroeconomic Statistics by Decade

	1990s	Second Half (1995–1999)	1980s	1970s	1960s
Real GDP growth	3.2%	(4.0)%	3.0%	3.3%	4.4%
Unemployment Rate	5.8	(5.0)	7.3	6.2	4.8
Inflation Rate	2.9	(2.4)	5.1	7.4	2.5

Source: GDP growth figures are from the U.S. Department of Commerce, Bureau of Economic Analysis; unemployment rate and inflation rate are from the U.S. Department of Labor, Bureau of Labor Statistics.

the poorest members of the workforce; blue-collar workers saw their real wage decline by 3.5 percent between 1982 and 1991. During the 1990s, average real wages rose by a total of 14 percent from 1991 to 2001; while blue-collar wages rose 12 percent (Mandel 2001). These wage gains at the bottom were the result of intense competition among firms for unskilled workers as unemployment fell as low as 3.7 percent in 2000, which was clearly below the natural rate of unemployment.

Other measures of economic prosperity also indicate that the 1990s were a remarkable decade. Home buying and homeownership boomed. Between 1991 and 2001, homeownership among U.S. families rose from 64 percent to 68 percent, the highest level in U.S. history. There was also an education boom. The percentage of the workforce with some college education rose dramatically from 40 percent in 1991 to 57 percent in 2001. The U.S. stock market grew strongly at 11.1 percent a year (although, as measured by the S&P 500, stock market returns were actually slightly lower than returns during the 1982–1991 period of 12.8 percent), primarily fueled by spectacular increases in the stock prices of technology firms. One final measure of the strength of the U.S. economy was the size of capital flows into the United States. Between 1991 and 2001, the United States attracted $2.3 trillion dollars of net foreign investment, far and away more than any country in the world.

What Was Responsible for All of This Good News?

Macroeconomic evidence such as rising output growth coupled with falling inflation, historic growth in real wages, and postwar lows in unemployment suggest that the New Economy of the 1990s was driven by large increases in aggregate supply. A number of hypotheses have been offered as to why aggregate supply increased much more rapidly during the 1990s. Many have pointed to *globalization*, or the increased cultural and economic integration among individuals, markets, and nation-states. The argument is that globalization has resulted in increases in the volume of international trade, increases in international capital flows between countries, and increased competition that has spurred worldwide productivity (and, in fact, the 1990s outside of East Asia was a decade of strong growth for the world as a whole). Some have pointed to deregulation in the United States, especially deregulation of financial markets, as having increased economic efficiency and encouraged more capital flows. Others have argued that advances in management, such as better inventory control and better information systems, have allowed firms to more effectively respond to changing market conditions, increasing productivity and also reducing uncertainty and output volatility.

Still others have argued that monetary and fiscal policy played an important role by providing a remarkably stable macroeconomic environment during the 1990s in which to do business. Macroeconomic policy during the 1990s could be generally characterized as tight fiscal policy and loose monetary policy. The Clinton Administration placed a high priority on balancing the federal budget, which stood at $260 billion (almost 5 percent of GDP) in 1992. A tax increase in 1993, low growth in government spending throughout the decade (partially as a result of reductions in military spending made possible by the end of the Cold War), and remarkable increases in tax receipts generated by strong economic growth led to budget surpluses of upwards of $250 billion (or roughly 2 percent of GDP) by the end of the decade. Lower government borrowing helped drive down long-term interest rates and reduce the cost of financing investment, housing purchases, and consumer durables.

On the other hand, expansive monetary policy served to keep short-term interest rates low. The Fed's refusal to "lean against the wind" and slow the economy during the 1990s expansion, even though there were significant worries among many economists that its refusal to do so would eventually lead to inflation, provided enough short-term stimulus to offset any contractionary effects of tighter fiscal policy. Federal Reserve chairman Alan Greenspan was one of the first to realize that the 1990s expansion was aggregate supply-driven, meaning that the natural rate of output growth had risen and the Fed could allow faster growth without worrying about inflation. In hindsight, this one-two punch of fiscal discipline and accommodative monetary policy kept interest rates low and provided high levels of cheap financing for the U.S. economy.

However, the most commonly mentioned explanation for this extraordinary decade and the justification for the moniker the New Economy has been the remarkable advances in information technology (IT) that occurred during the 1990s. This "IT revolution," as it has been called, has led to extraordinary changes in the U.S. economy. Bradford De Long and Lawrence Summers (2001) estimate that the calculation speed of computers has increased by 56 percent a year over the last 40 years, leading to a 4 billion–fold increase in computational power over that same time. To consider one example of just how rapidly computer technology is expanding, over the last 15 years the speed of computer chips has doubled about every 18 months (this is often referred to as "Moore's Law," named after Intel co-founder George Moore). One result of all of this new computational power has been a dramatic decline in the price of sharing and obtaining information. The real cost of information processing and communication is estimated to have fallen by roughly 10 percent–20 percent a year over the last 10 years.

Cheaper and faster transfer of information has been a driving force behind many of the explanations of the 1990s expansion discussed previously. For example, IT has been a major factor in increasing globalization and also in the development of better management systems. However, the IT revolution has increased aggregate supply in additional ways. Computer technologies have allowed for more automation and standardization of manufacturing processes, especially in the production of computers themselves. Furthermore, IT has increasingly become a tool in the process of experimentation, playing an integral role in generating new technologies that lead to additional advances in productivity. IT also reduces the cost of education and of technology transfer. Finally, some of the by-products of the IT revolution, such as the Internet, give firms access to new or larger markets that were previously unavailable, allowing firms to take advantage of economies of scale and increase their productivity.

Many studies have attempted to quantify the productivity benefits of the IT revolution. One method of measuring productivity, often referred to as growth accounting (see Chapter 7 for a more detailed description), involves taking output growth and subtracting out capital and labor growth, weighting each based on their share of aggregate income. What is left over is the growth in output that cannot be explained by growth in inputs. This measure of the change in total productivity is referred to as *multifactor productivity* (also known as the *Solow residual*). Many studies have recently undertaken such growth accounting exercises. Table 12.2 presents results from a study by Stephen Oliner and Daniel Sichel (2000). They focus on three periods: 1974–1990, 1991–1995, and 1995–1999. According to their calculations, IT has played two important roles during the 1990s in increasing output growth compared to earlier

TABLE 12.2   Contributions to Growth in the U.S. Economy: Capital, Labor, and Multifactor Productivity

	1974–1990	*1991–1995*	*1996–1999*
Output Growth	3.06%	2.75%	4.82%
Total Capital	1.35	1.01	1.85
IT Captial	0.49	0.57	1.10
Total Labor	1.38	1.26	1.81
MFP	0.33	0.48	1.16
Computer and Semiconductor Sector	0.20	0.28	0.65

Source: Oliner and Sichel (2000)

periods. First, the amounts that firms have invested in information technology and communications capital has increased quite dramatically. For example, increases in IT capital account for all of the increase in the contribution of capital to growth between the 1974–1990 and the 1996–1999 periods. Second, better computer and semiconductor technologies have increased the efficiency of computer production. These efficiency benefits show up in the data as higher multifactor productivity growth. Oliner and Sichel estimate that improved computer production accounts for roughly 50 percent of the increase in multifactor productivity growth between the 1974–1990 period and the 1996–1999 period. Together, when the effects of both higher capital growth and higher multifactor productivity growth are considered, Oliner and Sichel's results indicate that changes in IT directly account for roughly 60 percent of the increase in growth during the New Economy period. This ignores many of the indirect productivity benefits of information technology that are more difficult to measure, such as increased market size and competition.

These results, and others like them, can be criticized on a number of levels. The most common criticism has to do with the nature of growth accounting itself. Multifactor productivity is not a direct but an implied measure of productivity. Everything other than input growth that contributes to output growth, including things economists do not well understand or cannot easily measure, is lumped together under the name multifactor productivity. This includes things such as unmeasured changes in the quality of labor or capital, errors in data collection, changes in worker effort, changes in government policy, and other structural changes in the economy. As a result, many would argue that the fact that IT is highly correlated with multifactor productivity and output growth does not in any way prove that IT is the cause of these changes in economic performance.

On the other hand, clearly dramatic changes occurred during the 1990s that increased aggregate supply, and a great deal of circumstantial evidence supports the conclusion that IT played a major role in these changes. Martin Bailey (2002) reports industry-level data that indicates that IT-intensive industries increased their productivity by more during the 1990s than less IT-intensive industries. In case studies of eight major industries, the McKinsey Global Institute (2001) concluded that the primary cause of higher productivity growth was increased competition that directly resulted from better IT. This is especially true in the retail sector, which Wal-Mart has come to dominate because of its size and high productivity, both of which owe a great deal to new management systems that rely heavily on new IT. Obviously, things went right with the U.S. economy during the 1990s, and at this point the most reliable evidence points to IT as the primary source of these improvements.

Will This Revolution Last?

There are always reasons to be skeptical of any assertion that good economic times will last forever. Based on his idea of creative destruction (see Chapter 3), Joseph Schumpeter argued that economies inherently go through long cycles of booms and busts that are driven by changes in technology. New technologies increase productivity, often quite dramatically, but not at first because of the costs of switching to this new technology. After this transition has occurred, productivity can grow very rapidly, but eventually the growth benefits of a new technology wanes as diminishing marginal returns set it. Technological revolutions only last until the next technology coup; then some new technology comes along that initially reduces productivity because of switching costs but eventually increases productivity growth once the technology has been fully adopted.

There is empirical support for this idea that the 1990s were a good, but not unprecedentedly good, period of time. Refer once again to Table 12.1, which reports macroeconomic data by decade. Noticeably absent from our previous discussion of this table was a comparison between the 1990s and the 1960s. The New Economy of the last half of the 1990s looks a lot like the old economy of the 1960s. The 1960s were a period of remarkable advances in petrochemicals, electronics, aviation, and pharmaceuticals. However, the boom times of the 1960s were followed by the volatile 1970s, a decade characterized by painful periods of stagflation.

Robert Gordon (2000), taking a Schumpeterian view of economic progress, argues that the impact of the IT revolution is much more limited than past technological revolutions, for a number of reasons. First, according to Gordon, most of the increases in productivity that took place during the 1990s were in computer hardware, which directly affects only 12 percent of the economy. In the other 88 percent of the economy, productivity growth actually decelerated. Gordon argues that this is because jobs that could be automated by computers were automated long ago. As a result, future advances in productivity from IT appear limited within most industries.

Second, because computer hardware is a relatively minor part of any production process, diminishing returns to new computer technologies set in very quickly. As a result, doubling the megahertz of a computer does not make that computer twice as productive. For example, consider the time spent by a student writing a paper. Faster computer speeds and the invention of word-processing software reduced the amount of time spent writing papers quite dramatically at first. Today, however, faster computers and new software lead to little reduction in the time spent on writing a paper. The primary constraints are human ones: how fast a student can think and communicate (or type) ideas. Better computer hardware cannot eliminate these restrictions.

Finally, it can be argued that many of the technologies most closely associated with the IT revolution, such as the Internet and cellular phones, have not significantly altered production. Instead, they are better thought of as entertainment media, more akin to the television than the combustible engine. Many of the markets created by the Internet are duplicative, meaning they exist in similar forms elsewhere, such as the Web services provided by previously existing retailers (the primary exception to this is eBay). Their main advantage is not one of productive efficiency but of convenience for the consumer. This does not mean that these communication technologies are worthless; it only means that most of the benefits come in the form of utility to consumers and not higher productivity to firms. As a result, compared to other technological revolutions such as electricity, the combustible engine, chemicals and plastics, and plumbing sanitation, IT has not changed things as much as those who are myopic to the history of technology might think.

Other more optimistic economists argue that the IT revolution has not yet run out of steam and will continue to generate higher productivity for the foreseeable future. For example, Bradford De Long (2002) argues that based on IT's rapidly increasing share in GDP, the most reliable estimates indicate that the U.S. economy should experience strong productivity growth for at least the next decade before diminishing returns to IT begin to slow growth. Likewise, Martin Bailey (2002) argues that as long as the U.S. government continues to do the things that they are doing—opening markets to international trade, increasing competition, improving education, providing prudent government regulation, and maintaining budgetary and monetary restraint—all evidence points to strong productivity growth for the foreseeable future. The recession of 2001 has not changed the minds of these optimists. In fact, they are quick to point out that productivity growth has continued to be remarkably robust throughout this slowdown, averaging more than 2 percent since the recession started.

THE 2001 RECESSION AND THE POST-RECESSION SLOWDOWN

A Brief Description of the Slowdown

The best way to characterize the 2001 recession is to note just how difficult it was for the National Bureau of Economic Research (NBER) to determine exactly when this recession began and when it ended. The movements into and out of recession were so gradual as to be almost imperceptible. What is more obvious, however, is that the 2000–2003 period has been one of persistent below-average growth. As seen in Figure 12.1, growth has been below 2 percent for 8 of the 11 quarters between the third quarter of 2000 and the first quarter of 2003

The NBER dates the beginning of the 2001 recession to March, which is actually before the September 11 terrorist attacks. Even though GDP growth has been positive (but low) since the fourth quarter of 2001, it wasn't until July of 2003 that the NBER chose November 2001 as the ending date of the recession. In other words, the NBER did not recognize that this recession began until it ended, and it took 20 months for the NBER to recognize officially that it was over, because the recovery has been so weak.

Six basic facts about the 2001 recession and its slow-growth aftermath are important.

The size of the recession itself was exceptionally small and its length exceptionally short. Output fell by only –0.6 percent during this recession, as compared to the 2 percent by which output usually falls during an average recession. Lasting only eight months, it barely reached the minimum six consecutive months needed to qualify as a recession under the NBER's working definition.

A significant decline in stock prices preceded this recession. Stock prices peaked during early 2000 and fell consistently until their trough in early 2003. As measured by the S&P 500 index, stock prices fell by roughly 40 percent from their highs. Most severely hit was the technology sector, which had played a big role in the bull market of the 1990s. Technology stocks are best represented by the NASDAQ stock index, which has fallen from its high point by 80 percent.

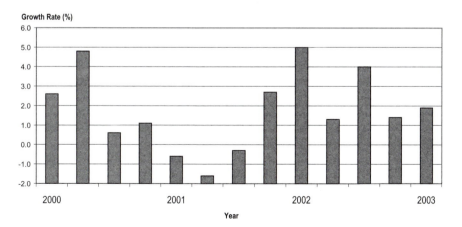

Figure 12.1 Real GDP Growth in the United States

Fixed business investment has experienced a sharp decline. Figure 12.2 presents quarterly fixed business investment, or the non-housing component of private investment. Fixed business investment fell by an average of −5.6 percent a year during 2001 and 2002, with quarterly growth rates as low as −14.5 percent in the second quarter of 2001. The largest factor in this decline has been sharp reductions in technology equipment investment, which had played a major role in the strong rates of overall investment growth during the 1990s.

There has been a "jobless recovery." It is unusual for unemployment and output to be moving in the same direction, but this is what has happened since 2001. Many economists have characterized the 2002–2003 period as the weakest post-recession job market in postwar history. Figure 12.3 presents the unemployment rate in the United States. Unemployment stood at a 25-year low in 2000 and increased only from 4 percent to 5.6 percent by the end of 2001. However, not only did unemployment not fall after the recession, but it actually crept upward slightly until mid-2003, when it slowly began to creep downward. By the end of 2003, the U.S. economy had lost nearly 2.3 million jobs from its peak employment levels.

International political turmoil and corporate scandals have affected the business environment. The 9/11 terrorist attacks, wars and unpredictable reconstruction efforts in Iraq and Afghanistan, and a building conflict with South Korea, coupled with shocking corporate scandals involving Enron, WorldCom, Arthur Anderson accounting, and numerous major stockbrokers, have all increased uncertainty and reduced consumer confidence. These destabilizing events have played a large role in the 30 percent fall in the Consumer Confidence Index between 2000 and mid-2003. Economic uncertainty is likely one important reason behind the slow post-recession growth of investment and employment, as

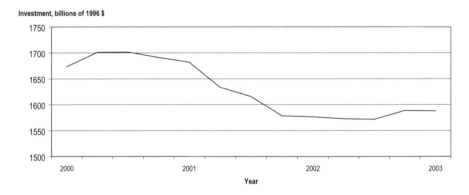

Figure 12.2 Fixed Business Investment in the United States

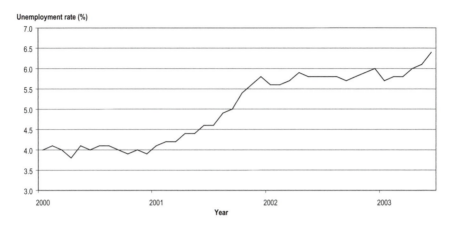

Figure 12.3 Unemployment Rate in the United States

many firms seem unwilling to expand their capacity in the midst of this turbulence.

Things would have been worse without timely and aggressive monetary and fiscal policy. Federal tax reductions were passed soon after George W. Bush took office in 2001. Coupled with increased government spending, particularly military spending on wars and reconstruction in Iraq and Afghanistan and higher spending on domestic security, fiscal policy has been quite expansionary during the early 2000s. A $250 billion surplus in 1999 has turned into what was a $374 billion deficit in 2003 and is expected to be a $480 deficit in 2004.

At the same time, the Federal Reserve has been very proactive, allowing M2 to grow at an average annual rate of roughly 12 percent and reducing the Federal Funds Rate (the interest rates on overnight loans between banks) dramatically from 6.5 percent in late 2000 to 1 percent by mid-2003. This, coupled with continued low inflation of between 1 percent and 2 percent, has reduced nominal interest rates to 40-year lows. The interest rate on the 3-month T-bill fell to nearly 1 percent and the 10-year T-Bonds fell below 4 percent in 2003. Low interest rates have spurred the housing market and consumer spending. In addition, low interest rates have encouraged an unprecedented amount of mortgage refinancing, which has effectively increased the disposable income of households and further stabilized consumer spending.

One thing that should be clear after considering these six basic facts: the 2001 recession and the following growth recession have been driven by weak aggregate demand. This recession appears to be consistent with a Keynesian-style recession, in which falling expectations and a falling stock market have reduced wealth and investment, dampening aggregate demand. On the other hand, aggregate supply growth (in spite of spikes in the price of oil) has been robust. In fact, labor productivity growth has remained remarkably solid throughout this period, growing in an exceptional rate of 4.8 percent in 2002. Coupled with expansionary stabilization policy, these productivity gains have largely offset the declines in aggregate demand and has prevented this recession from being worse.

How Long Will the Slowdown Last?

There are two ways to view this 2001–2003 growth recession. The "glass is half full" view is that things could have been much worse given the dramatic and destabilizing events of the early 2000s. Consider the events that have impacted the U.S. economy since 2001. First, the terrorist attacks of 9/11 occurred, which struck directly at the heart of the nation's financial system. Markets re-opened only a week later and stayed open as nearly $1 trillion in wealth disappeared. The financial system continued to operate, and no significant financial panics or failures occurred despite these financial losses, which were on top of stock market losses that had been accumulating since 2000. Production and consumption dropped dramatically during September, but many of these declines were offset by a strong bounce-back in production and consumption in October. Productivity growth was inhibited as firms were forced to devote more resources to security improvements. Oil prices increased after 9/11 and in the lead-up to the wars in Afghanistan and Iraq. Corporate scandals at Enron and MCI in 2002 led to two of the largest bankruptcies in U.S. history, while other bankruptcies took place among major retailers and airlines. And yet overall productivity growth continued to remain strong, allowing output to grow, albeit slowly, despite rising unemployment. To support this optimistic view, growth in the third quarter of 2003 was a remarkable 8.2 percent, the highest rate of quarterly growth in 20 years, and was driven by strong growth in corporate investment and profits.

The "glass is half empty" view of the U.S. economy is that given the Keynesian nature of this slowdown, the inability of macroeconomic policy to decisively end it is troubling. Despite the aggressive use of monetary and fiscal policy, the economy has continued to limp along, and analysts have used phrases like "double-dip" recession to describe persistently weak employment and output growth. The continued weakness in the U.S. economy is most evident in the labor market. While growth was a remarkable 8.2 percent in the third quarter of 2003, only 1,000 jobs were created during that same time. Unemployment remained at 5.7 percent, and there is evidence of an increasing pool of discouraged workers that are dropping out of the labor market and are not being counted in these unemployment statistics. In fact, 23 percent of all of those unemployed during the third quarter of 2003 had been unemployed for more than 6 months, the highest proportion in 20 years.

Disturbingly, the future use of monetary policy to stimulate the economy out of its doldrums appears to be limited, given that interest rates cannot be driven much lower without approaching their floor of 0 percent. As discussed in Chapter 4, a key component of Keynesian theory is that of a *liquidity trap*. A liquidity trap for monetary policy occurs when interest rates get so low that holding bonds becomes unattractive because interest rates are likely to increase, which will reduce the value of any bonds being held. Likewise, low interest rates reduce the opportunity cost of holding money, making bank accounts and other interest-bearing assets unattractive. As a result, any change in the money supply when interest rates are extremely low is likely to be hoarded, severely limiting the influence monetary policy can have on investment, consumption, and aggregate demand.

Many economic pessimists look at the U.S. economy of the 2000s and see the Japanese economy of the 1990s. Chapter 15 of this book presents a detailed analysis of the Great Recession of the 1990s in Japan. Briefly, after a decade of remarkable output and investment growth, a stock market crash in Japan signaled the beginning of a period of prolonged recession. Questionable business practices in the previous decade (Enron?) exaggerated the economic success of an economy that was structurally weak. Deflation (which has been worrying many economic observers of the United States) further weakened the balance sheets of already shaky firms, and in a process consistent with the Debt-Deflation theory (see Chapter 10) raised bad loans to such a level that risk-laden Japanese banks were pushed to the brink of failure. These banks responded by credit rationing their lending, which placed a severe drag on the Japanese economy. Because the central bank was caught in a liquidity trap, traditional monetary policy that relied on interest rate manipulation proved powerless to stimulate the Japanese economy.

While the U.S. economy and U.S. economic policy are more efficient and flexible than their counterparts in Japan, the most important difference between the United States and Japan rests in the fact that the U.S. financial system, particularly its banks, appears to be fundamentally strong. The events surrounding 9/11 seemed to prove this. However, Japanese and other East Asian banks were thought to be strong during the 1980s and early 1990s. Sustained deflation and skyrocketing levels of bad loans have a way of turning good banks into bad banks and of making an economy that appears to be structurally strong become fundamentally weak.

CONCLUSIONS

Which is the aberration, the remarkable growth of the 1990s or the slowdown of the 2000s? Your answer to this question will largely be determined by what you believe was the driving force behind the New Economy of the 1990s. The optimists believe that the IT revolution has had and will continue to have a strong impact on productivity and output growth for the foreseeable future. The slowdown of the 2000s will purge the excesses of the 1990s (such as an overvalued stock market) and set the stage for a resumption of prosperity based on the sound fundamentals of the U.S. economy. In the words of Martin Bailey (2002), the U.S. economy is now prepared to catch its "second wind."

> The enthusiasm for information technology and for the shares of high technology companies went too far. Growth became unsustainably rapid and a corresponding slowdown inevitable. But the excessive optimism of the 1990s should not give way to excessive pessimism now. Many of the drivers of faster productivity growth in the 1990s, both those linked to information technology and those unrelated to it, remain in place.

Most economists tend to agree with Bailey. Yield curves are currently steep, indicating that the market is expecting an economic recovery in the near future, and forecasters are predicting productivity growth of between 2 percent and 2.5 percent and output growth of roughly 3 percent over the next several years.

The pessimists believe that the New Economy was primarily a bubble economy built on over-enthusiasm, over-investment, over-building, and over-spending. The 2000s are when the bill has come due, and there is no reason to expect an exceptionally strong recovery, especially since the recession itself was so mild that many of the excesses have yet to be fully driven from the economy. For example, the stock market continues to look overvalued to many observers based on price-to-earnings ratios that remain high relative to historical levels. Robert Gordon (2000) summarizes many of the concerns of the pessimists:

> The New Economy has meant little to the 88 percent of the economy outside of durable manufacturing; in that part of the economy, trend growth in multifactor productivity has actually *decelerated*, despite a massive investment boom in computers and related equipment. The fundamental limitation on the contribution to productivity of computers in general and the Internet in particular occurs because of the tension between rapid exponential growth in computer speed and memory on the one hand and the fixed endowment of human time. Most of the initial applications of mainframe and personal computers have encountered the rapid onset of diminishing returns. Much of the use of the Internet repre-

sents a substitution from one type of entertainment or information-gathering for another.

In other words, the New Economy is the old economy and is still subject to unsustainable expansions, recessions, and, potentially, depressions. Only time will tell if the optimists or the pessimists are right, and the answer will undoubtedly influence the way economists think about business cycles in the future.

SUGGESTED READINGS

Martin Neil Bailey, "The New Economy: Post Mortem or Second Wind?" (2002): An argument that the New Economy in the United States will continue for the foreseeable future, by the chairman of the Council of Economic Advisors during the Clinton Administration.

Bradford De Long and Lawrence J. Summers, "The 'New Economy': Background, Historical Perspective, Questions, and Speculations" (2001): A historical review of the IT revolution and speculation about its future impact on the U.S. economy. Included is a discussion of the implications of the stock market crash and the difficulties in developing public policies that will foster this revolution.

Robert J. Gordon, "Does the 'New Economy' Measure Up to the Great Inventions of the Past?" (2000): A discussion of whether the IT revolution will spur a new industrial revolution. Gordon criticizes the work of Oliner and Sichel and argues that IT is unlikely to live up to the benefits of great inventions from the past.

Stephen D. Oliner and Daniel E. Sichel, "The Resurgence of Growth in the Late 1990s: Is Information Technology the Story?" (2000): A review of the empirical evidence in support of the assertion that an IT revolution has taken place in the United States and a discussion of its future impact on productivity and output growth.

Part IV

Modern International Recessions and Depressions

13

The East Asian Crisis

INTRODUCTION

Between 1997 and 1999, an exceptionally large and virulent economic crisis swept through a large number of East Asian economies; economies that for the previous 35 years had experienced sustained growth at unprecedented levels. Table 13.1 reports GDP growth rates for East Asian economies from 1991 to 1999. During 1991–1996, with the exception of the Philippines, all of these countries averaged more than 5 percent growth a year, with 10 percent growth common for Singapore and China. Growth rates in the 1970s and 1980s were even higher than this throughout East Asia, commonly reaching 10 percent. Even in 1996, when output growth had noticeably slowed across most of these countries, growth appeared to be fundamentally sound. In fact, in November of 1996, just eight months before the onset of the economic crisis, the International Monetary Fund (IMF) reported in the *World Outlook* that

> (East Asia's) sound fundamentals bode well for sustained growth. . . . (The IMF's endorsement) was rooted in the region's strong macroeconomic fundamentals; in (East Asia's) tradition of, and commitment to, efficient allocation of investment; and in the widespread belief that the external environment will continue to be supportive.

Unfortunately, many of these East Asian countries saw real wages fall by a third, unemployment triple, and aggregate income fall by more than 10 percent between 1997 and 1999. This East Asian crisis was the largest and most significant economic crisis to strike the world since the Great Depression. Hardest hit during this crisis were those that were

TABLE 13.1   GDP Growth in East Asia

	1991	1992	1993	1994	1995	1996	1997	1998	1999
Thailand	8.2%	8.1%	8.4%	8.9%	8.8%	5.5%	−0.4%	−10.4%	4.2%
Indonesia	7.0	6.5	6.5	15.9	8.2	8.0	4.6	−13.2	0.2
Malaysia	8.5	7.8	8.4	9.2	9.5	8.6	7.8	−7.5	5.4
Korea	9.1	5.1	5.8	8.6	8.9	7.1	5.4	−6.7	10.7
Philippines	−0.6	0.3	2.1	4.4	4.8	5.8	9.6	−0.5	3.2
Singapore	7.3	6.3	10.4	10.1	8.8	7.3	8.4	0.4	5.4
Hong Kong	5.0	6.2	6.2	5.5	3.9	5.0	5.0	−5.1	2.9
Taiwan	7.6	6.8	6.3	6.5	6.0	5.7	6.8	4.7	5.5
China	9.2	14.2	12.1	12.7	10.6	9.5	8.8	7.8	7.1

Source: International Financial Statistics of the IMF. Data for 1998 and 1999 are from the IMF's December 1997 World Economic Outlook.

the most vulnerable: the poor, the young, and women. For example, one-fourth of the South Korean population and 22 million throughout the region fell into poverty during the crisis.

What shocked economic observers was not so much the size of the crisis but the fact that it happened in East Asia. How could a depression strike countries that had so long been held up as examples for other, less-developed countries? The East Asian crisis highlighted a very important fact that prior to the crisis had not received much attention from economists in their closed-economy models of business cycles: globalization has the power to change countries dramatically, both for the better and for the worse. *Globalization* is the term often used to refer to the increasing cultural and economic integration among individuals, markets, and nation states. Globalization has been driven by advancements in information technology and falling communication costs. Economically, it has resulted in not only increases in the volume of international trade but also in large increases in international financing and capital flows across countries. The fact that these East Asian countries were some of the most globally integrated economies in the world plays a major role in explaining why these countries grew so fast during the 1980s and 1990s and also why they crashed so hard in 1997. The primary goal of this chapter is to explain what economists have learned from the East Asian crisis and how globalization affects both the propagation of business cycles and the public policies governments should follow to prevent future crises.

INTERNATIONAL CURRENCY CRISES
IN RECENT HISTORY

In order to put the East Asian crisis in some perspective, it is important to understand a few basic facts about some of the other major international financial crises that have occurred in the postwar era outside of the United States

Throughout the 1960–1980 period, a series of currency crises occurred under the Bretton Woods (1944–1971) and subsequent Smithsonian (1971–1972) international financial agreements. The principal objectives of the Bretton Woods agreement were twofold. Its primary goal was to coordinate international economic policy in order to avoid potential recurrences of the Great Depression, when countries followed "beggar-thy-neighbor" policies that raised tariffs and contracted money supplies in an effort to create large trade surpluses at the expense of their trading partners. These policies contracted aggregate demand worldwide and initiated the Depression. To achieve its goal, Bretton Woods established a system of fixed but adjustable exchange rates throughout the world. The IMF was given the responsibility of evaluating and approving applications for devaluation by a member country that was experiencing an unsustainable disequilibrium in its balance of payment account. This process of evaluation was aimed at preventing competitive devaluations by which a country might manipulate exchange rates in an attempt to make its exports cheaper. Second, Bretton Woods encouraged liberalization and deregulation of world trading institutions, which had suffered a complete breakdown during World War II. The IMF was made available to provide temporary financing to countries experiencing balance of payment problems in return for promises of economic reform.

Most of the crises that occurred under Bretton Woods and in its immediate aftermath resulted when countries attempted to maintain a fixed exchange rate that, because of high domestic inflation or other domestic fiscal policies, was much higher than would exist if the exchange rate were allowed to float. Overvalued exchange rates helped these countries attract foreign investment and also reduced the price of imports. To maintain an overvalued exchange rate, countries were forced to sell their foreign-denominated reserves and buy their own currency in an attempt to defend this exchange rate. Eventually, investors and speculators observed declining foreign reserves and recognized that the government could not defend its exchange rate much longer. Speculators began to flee the domestic currency, selling all assets denominated in the domestic currency. This put further downward pressure on the exchange rate until either (1) the country devalued (usually by an amount significantly larger than would have been necessary to pacify markets before the crisis occurred), and/or (2) the country received a loan from the IMF of sufficient size to convince markets that the country could defend its existing exchange rate and that no future devaluation would be necessary. Usually, both of these events occurred simultaneously.

What are the root causes of this type of currency crisis? In most cases, it is governments that adopt poor macroeconomic policies that make the fixed exchange rate they are trying to maintain overvalued and indefensible. For example, the currency crises that struck Latin America in the early 1980s were all the result of large levels of international debt that led to large government budget deficits. These deficits were eventually financed by increases in the money supply, leading to high rates of inflation (in some cases, such as Argentina, larger than 5,000 percent a year) and significant downward pressure on exchange rates. Another example of a crisis that followed this basic script was the Mexican Peso crisis of 1994.

As mentioned above, crises of this sort usually end with an intervention by the IMF and the provision of a bailout package. These bailouts come with strings attached, usually with the condition that the country in question first devalue and then defend its new exchange rate and also with the imposition of changes in the poor macroeconomic policies that the country was previously following. In the case of these Latin American countries, reforms usually consisted of *austerity conditions*, or the imposition of severe budget cuts and new taxes aimed at cutting large budget deficits in order to reduce future pressures to increase the money supply and inflation. Typically, after accepting these bailout conditions and adopting reforms, the worst of these currency crises was over. Thus, intervention by the IMF usually signaled the trough of the crisis, though it often took years for these countries to return to their natural rates of output.

The European Monetary System (EMS), which predated the European Monetary Union and was a system of fixed exchange rates among European Union countries, was subjected to a currency crisis in 1992. This crisis was different from previous crises in Latin America. In this case, the root cause of the crisis was not necessarily bad monetary and fiscal policy, but the fact that different countries in the EMS had different fiscal and monetary policies. Specifically, Britain maintained a looser monetary policy and smaller government budget deficits than the rest of Europe. As a result, it had lower domestic interest rates, which eventually led investors and speculators to flee the pound (much of this speculation was fueled by the hedge fund manager George Soros). Unwilling to tighten monetary policy and increase interest rates, Britain was forced to abandon the EMS and devalued the pound. However, this devaluation did not lead to a domestic economic crisis in Britain. After the pound was allowed to float, the currency crisis was essentially over and, in fact, output growth in Europe immediately recovered.

THE FUNDAMENTALS OF THE
EAST ASIAN CRISIS

How did the East Asian Crisis differ from the currency crises just described? There are two fundamental differences. First, it is clear that the East Asian crisis was not the result of bad monetary and fiscal policy, at least not in the traditional sense of high budget deficits and inflation. None of the East Asian countries that experienced a crisis was running sizeable budget deficits (in fact, some were running budget surpluses prior to the crisis) and none was experiencing high levels of inflation. The solid macroeconomic performance of these East Asian countries is in direct contrast with that of the Latin American crisis countries during the 1980s and 1990s.

Second, the worst of previous currency crises was over when the country gave up its exchange rate peg and devalued, with or without the help of the IMF. In almost every case, domestic growth and unemployment began to immediately, if slowly, rebound. However, devaluations in East Asia did not end the crisis, and the first devaluation essentially signaled the beginning of the spread of the crisis throughout East Asia. As a result, the East Asian crisis was more than just a currency crisis primarily centered in international financial markets; instead, it was a full-blown economic crisis that had persistent effects on all markets within these economies. It is the magnitude and persistence of the East Asian crisis, coupled with the fact that typical policy prescriptions did not work, that makes the East Asian situation so important to study and understand.

Why these two differences from previous crises? The East Asian crisis is really better thought of as two distinct crises that occurred simultaneously. The first crisis that these countries were experiencing was a currency crisis that was caused by maintaining exchange rates that were pegged to the dollar and became overvalued. The results were large current account deficits and, beginning in early 1997, a speculative attack on pegged exchange rates throughout East Asia. Thailand was the first to devalue, in July of 1997, followed by Malaysia, Indonesia, and the Philippines. Korea suffered only mild depreciations until October 1997.

In each case, however, the currency crisis and eventual devaluation signaled only the beginning of the economic crisis within each country, not the end. At the same time that currency crises were breaking out in these countries, a second, and less immediately obvious, series of crises was erupting. This second crisis was a banking system crisis. Banks throughout the region were heavily leveraged in short-term debt denominated in foreign currencies and heavily invested in highly speculative assets. As a result, even before the events of 1997, the banking systems in many East Asian countries were on the brink of collapse. The devaluations that alleviated the currency crisis made the banking system crisis even worse, leading to a downward spiral that spread to all sectors of the economy. This is the primary plot line of the East Asian Crisis: the countries in East Asia that experienced both a currency crisis and a banking system crisis tumbled into a full-blown economic crisis, while countries that had sounder banks experienced only a currency crisis and were able to avoid the worst of the economic crisis. To understand this process more fully, it is important to describe in more detail the situation that existed in early 1997 in East Asia regarding each of these twin crises.

The Currency Crisis in East Asia

In early 1997, a large number of East Asian countries were maintaining pegged (or floating within a small range) exchange rates with the U.S. dollar in order to attract foreign investment. Because of the appreciation of the dollar versus the yen in 1995, these pegged exchange rates became overvalued relative to Japan and the rest of the world. This appreciation of the dollar against the yen was due in large part to the strong U.S. economy and the weak Japanese economy (although fundamentals were probably not sufficient alone to explain the size of this appreciation). In April 1995, the dollar was trading at 100 yen, but it rose precipitously to 150 yen per dollar by early 1997. Because of this large appreciation, each of these East Asian countries began to run significant current account deficits. Other contributing factors to these deficits were the weak demand for imports in Japan and Europe, gluts in the computer chip and electronics markets, and high domestic interest rates. Those countries that experienced the largest increase in their current account deficits were those countries whose currencies were pegged most rigidly to the appreciating dollar: Thailand, Malaysia, and the Philippines. The end result was that these countries were poised to experience a good old-fashioned currency crisis. However, none of these countries' exchange rates were so overvalued that a speculative attack seemed imminent to most observers, at least not until right before the first series of speculative attacks on Thailand during July 1997.

Table 13.2 reports the current account deficits for selected East Asian countries. Other than Taiwan and Singapore, these countries were running significant current account deficits. A common rule of thumb is that any country that has a current account deficit of more than 5 percent of its GDP is in danger of having a rapid capital flow reversal. By this standard, Korea, Indonesia, Malaysia, the Philippines, and Thailand were all in danger of suffering a currency crisis during either

TABLE 13.2   Current Account Balance as a Percentage of GDP

	1991	1992	1993	1994	1995	1996	1997
Thailand	−8.01%	−6.23%	−5.68%	−6.38%	−8.35%	−8.51%	−2.35%
Indonesia	−4.40	−2.46	−0.82	−1.54	−4.27	−3.30	−3.62
Malaysia	−14.01	−3.39	−10.11	−6.60	−8.85	−3.37	−3.50
Korea	−3.16	−1.70	−0.16	−1.45	−1.91	−4.82	−1.90
Philippines	−2.46	−3.17	−6.69	−3.74	−5.06	−4.67	−6.07
Singapore	12.36	12.38	8.48	18.12	17.93	16.26	13.90
Hong Kong	6.58	5.26	8.14	1.98	−2.97	−2.43	−3.75
Taiwan	6.97	4.03	3.52	3.12	3.05	4.67	3.23
China	3.07	1.09	−2.19	1.16	0.03	0.52	3.61

Source: International Financial Statistics of the IMF.

1995 or 1996, with Thailand, the Philippines, and Malaysia having experienced sizeable current account deficits for more than 10 years. These large deficits were sustainable only as long as these economies continued to grow at high rates, but at the lower rates of growth that began in 1996, these deficits were no longer manageable. Those countries with smaller current account deficits or surpluses, such as China, Hong Kong, Singapore, and Taiwan, did not suffer large depreciations as the crisis spread throughout the region.

Therefore, at least on the surface, the East Asian countries that slipped into crisis during 1997 appeared to be suffering from currency crises akin to the currency crises suffered in Latin America in the early 1980s. However, a key difference between the East Asian and Latin American crises is that the Latin American crises were clearly the result of bad macroeconomic policy. This is not the case in East Asia, where all countries were maintaining fairly stable or declining rates of inflation of less than 10 percent, while maintaining roughly balanced budgets. The problem here was a naïve adherence throughout the region to maintaining fixed exchange rates even when these exchange rates reached unsustainable levels.

Even though the source of this currency crisis in East Asia was different, the solution to a currency crisis remains the same: devalue your currency enough to restore a sustainable equilibrium to your balance of payments. In addition, countries typically adopt austerity conditions and tighten fiscal policies (higher taxes and lower government spending to reduce the budget deficit) and monetary policy in order to increase domestic interest rates and reduce the outflow of foreign investment. However, another series of hidden crises were also occurring simultaneously within these economies that made these devaluations disastrous.

The Banking System Crisis in East Asia

East Asian economies have traditionally relied on banks as the primary source of financial intermediation within their economies. For example, banks provide two-thirds of corporate finance in Indonesia (Corsetti, Pesenti, and Roubini 1998). In Thailand, this share is 75 percent. In Korea, 50 percent of corporate financing is done directly through banks, 87 percent of corporate bonds are guaranteed by banks, and only 7 percent of corporate financing is in equity. These statistics on corporate finance are very different from those found in other developed countries. For example, in the United States only one-third of corporate finance comes from banks (and this number is falling).

Beginning in the mid-1980s, East Asian countries, as well as other countries throughout the world, began a process of rapid bank liberalization and deregulation. This financial liberalization has included (1) abolishing credit controls, (2) deregulating interest rates, (3) opening entry into banking markets, (4) reducing banking regulations, (5) allowing for the private ownership of banks, and (6) allowing the free movement of funds across international borders. A recent survey by John Williamson and Molly Mahar (1998) of 34 rich and poor countries indicated that in 1973, 24 of these countries were classified as having repressed capital flows while only 2 had liberal capital markets. In 1996, no countries were classified as having repressed capital flows, while 18 were classified as having liberal capital markets.

The experience of the United States, however, illustrates that financial deregulation can potentially be both good and bad. While rapid deregulation in the early 1980s increased the efficiency of the U.S. financial system as a whole, it also led to an increase in speculative behavior by financial institutions that contributed to a crisis among savings and loan banks. The bailout of the savings and loan industry eventually cost U.S. taxpayers roughly $250 billion. Deregulation in East Asia, especially in Thailand, Korea, Malaysia, and Indonesia, was far more rapid and greatly exceeded that which went on in the United States.

In addition, a great deal of financial innovation took place throughout Asia in the 1980s, much of it driven by new information technologies and globalization. Better information communication greatly increased the potential size of financial markets by allowing banks easier access to international capital, which in turn allowed banks to take advantage of economies of scale in their operations. *Securitization*, or the transformation of non-marketable assets (such as mortgages) into marketable assets (such as bonds) played a critical role in the development of better secondary, or resale, financial markets throughout the region. Finally, the development of *offshore banking* (international banking conglomerates that are chartered in countries with little or no financial regulation) and hedge funds (discussed later in this chapter) greatly increased the volume of foreign investment that was available to Asian economies.

Four key factors stemming from financial liberalization and financial development in East Asia contributed to an increase in bank riskiness and eventually to the crises in East Asian financial institutions. The interaction of these factors eventually served to magnify the effects of currency crises into full-blown economic crises.

The flip side of running large current account deficits is that these same East Asian countries were also running large capital account surpluses. In other words, before the crisis these countries were attracting large levels of foreign investment in order to fund their current account deficits. Much of this was foreign-denominated debt, meaning that it was debt that had to be paid back in a foreign currency, usually dollars. The primary reason why Asian countries chose to peg their exchange rates to the dollar in the first place was to attract foreign investment. Foreign investment in East Asian countries ranged between 5 percent and 14 percent of GDP before the crisis (Corsetti, Pesenti, and Roubini 1998). Speculative bubbles in many financial markets, including a real estate bubble in Malaysia, fueled some of these inflows of foreign capital. Most of this foreign investment was filtered through East Asian banks, but it also arrived through Asian corporations that were borrowing heavily from abroad.

Much of the foreign debt that these banks accumulated was short-term, meaning that these banks relied heavily on periodic rollovers of their debt in order to finance their lending activities. Short-term debt is often referred to as "hot money" because of its tendency to be quickly passed around. Table 13.3 presents the ratio of short-term debt to foreign reserves of the central bank. If this ratio is small it implies that the central bank of a country could cover the short-term financing needs of its banks in the event that foreign creditors become unwilling to rollover their short-term debt. Not surprisingly, three of the four countries that were hit the hardest during the crisis were countries in which this ratio was the largest, namely Thailand, Indonesia, and Korea. To put these numbers in perspective, consider these facts: (1) Indonesia alone had more than $200B worth of short-term borrowing; (2) short-term borrowing in 1996 alone was $93B in Indonesia, Malaysia, Korea, and Thailand, up from $41B in 1994 (these short-term inflows turned into a $12B outflow in these countries in 1997); (3) in Korea, 56 percent of the foreign-denominated debt (which was 37 percent of Korea's total debt) was in short-term liabilities (Krueger 2000). The implication of all of this hot money was that when the speculative crisis hit, large amounts of foreign capital quickly and easily left these highly leveraged countries.

In addition to a foreign borrowing boom, a domestic lending boom was also taking place within these countries. Domestic lending by banks grew

TABLE 13.3　Short-Term Debt as a Percentage of Foreign Reserves

	1991	1992	1993	1994	1995	1996
Thailand	7.31%	72.34%	92.49%	99.48%	114.21%	99.69%
Indonesia	154.62	172.81	159.70	160.36	189.42	176.59
Malaysia	19.05	21.12	25.51	24.34	30.60	40.98
Korea	81.75	69.62	60.31	54.06	171.45	203.23
Philippines	152.31	119.37	107.68	95.00	82.85	79.45
Singapore	2.67	2.35	2.04	1.75	1.78	2.60
Hong Kong	21.78	18.38	17.09	16.49	14.16	22.35
Taiwan	20.21	21.00	23.64	21.76	21.64	21.31
China	24.68	66.76	68.33	33.04	29.62	23.74

Source: International Financial Statistics of the IMF.

between 17 percent and 30 percent a year between 1991 and 1996 in East Asian countries (Corsetti, Pesenti, and Roubini 1998). Because a large source of the funds banks used for these loans were from foreign creditors, banks in the region found themselves holding large amounts of debt denominated in foreign currencies, but holding assets primarily denominated in domestic currencies. Table 13.4 reports the ratio of foreign liabilities to foreign assets for banks and non-bank financial institutions, where the largest ratios existed in the crisis countries of Thailand, Indonesia, and Korea. The result of these binges of lending and borrowing was that banks in the region were left with huge exposures to exchange rate risk. A depreciation of their domestic currency (and an appreciation of the dollar) would reduce the value of their domestic-denominated assets and increase the value of their foreign-denominated liabilities.

The fourth and final piece of the banking systems crisis was the poor quality and riskiness of the investment projects that the lending boom financed. Well

TABLE 13.4　Ratio of Foreign Liabilities to Foreign Assets

	1993	1994	1995	1996	1997
Thailand	6.93	7.73	7.81	11.03	8.12
Indonesia	2.95	4.01	4.26	4.24	5.43
Malaysia	0.83	1.40	1.44	1.48	2.22
Korea	2.98	2.97	3.31	3.75	2.51
Philippines	1.14	0.97	1.10	1.72	1.71
Singapore	1.51	1.62	1.66	1.62	1.38
Hong Kong	1.42	1.43	1.56	1.65	1.59
Taiwan	n/a	n/a	0.61	0.61	0.62
China	0.99	0.94	1.17	1.20	1.36

Source: Bank of International Settlements (BIS) as reported by Corsetti, Pesenti, and Roubini (1998).

before the crisis of 1997, there was a great deal of worry about not only the quantity but also the quality of the loans that were being made within East Asian banking systems. As discussed in Chapter 8, New Keynesian economists have focused on the macroeconomic effects of imperfect information and risk. Especially important is the effect of risk on financial intermediation, particularly in regards to *moral hazard*. To reiterate, moral hazard exists when individuals are able to allocate some of the down-side risk of a project to others while keeping all of its up-side benefits for themselves, thus encouraging individuals to participate in riskier projects than they otherwise would. Higher levels of moral hazard existed in three areas of Asian economies well before the crises of 1997.

First, moral hazard was rampant within the operations of East Asian banks. Because of financial deregulation in many of these countries, banks found themselves subjected to little or no restriction regarding the types of loans they could make or the types of debt they could acquire. Because of low capital adequacy requirements, undercapitalized banks had little to lose by gambling on riskier and riskier assets, such as overvalued stocks and real estate.

One way to measure the riskiness of bank lending is to look at the number of non-performing loans (NPLs) as a percentage of total lending, which is reported in Table 13.5. With the exception of China, the countries with the highest percentage of NPLs in 1996 suffered the worst crises: Thailand (13 percent), Korea (8 percent), Indonesia (13 percent), and Malaysia (10 percent). To put these numbers in some perspective, the rate of NPLs in the United States is less than 1 percent of total loans. Default rates on bank loans in East Asia had been rising well before the speculative crises of 1997 and, in fact, a large number of Korean and Thai banks were technically bankrupt even before the currency crisis began.

TABLE 13.5   Non-Performing Loans as a Percentage of Total Lending

	End of 1996	End of 1997
Thailand	13%	36%
Indonesia	13	15
Malaysia	10	15
Korea	8	30
Philippines	14	7
Singapore	4	4
Hong Kong	3	1
Taiwan	4	n/a
China	14	n/a

Source: Column 1, Bank of International Settlements Annual Report, as reported by Corsetti, Pesenti, and Roubini (1998). Column 2, Peregrine (1997).

Second, moral hazard also existed at the national and international level. Many banks, particularly in Thailand, Indonesia, and Korea, engaged in excessive borrowing of foreign funds and excessive domestic lending based on the belief that their government would bail them out in the event of an economic downturn, which was a plausible assumption given the extent of government involvement and subsidization in these financial industries. Even though explicit deposit insurance did not exist, the governments of Korea, Thailand, Taiwan, and Malaysia effectively guaranteed all deposits, given that none of their domestic banks had ever been allowed to fail. If things became exceptionally bad, banks could also reasonably believe that they would be indirectly bailed out by the IMF when their government appealed for a loan. Hence, many banks felt protected from the exchange rate risk to which they exposed themselves when they borrowed short in foreign currencies and lent long in their domestic currency.

Finally, moral hazard was also evident at the corporate level. Corporations are much more highly subsidized and market power is much more concentrated in East Asian economies than in other developed economies. Many outsiders have referred to the domination of most sectors of East Asian economies by a few large and interrelated conglomerates by the term "crony capitalism." The end result has been little competition in many markets and low returns on capital for these conglomerates. The best example of this is South Korea, a country with an exceptionally high degree of industrial concentration, primarily within 30 large conglomerates referred to as *Chaebols*. In 1997, as many as 7 of the 30 largest Chaebols were insolvent (meaning their debt was greater than their assets) and the return on invested capital was less than the cost of capital in 20 of these Chaebols (Krueger 2000).

By 1998, 31 percent of Korean, 45 percent of Indonesian, and 18 percent of Malaysian and Filipino corporations were insolvent, up from their 1994 levels of 16 percent in Korea and 8 percent in Indonesia, Malaysia, and the Philippines (Pomerleano 1998). This suggests that despite many of these East Asian countries' excessively high rates of investment, much of this money was not being channeled into productive projects. Together, little competition, easy capital, and the belief that many of these conglomerates were too big for the government to allow them to fail created incentives for these corporations to adopt exceptionally risky projects in the absence of government regulation.

The Interaction between the Twin Crises and the Role of IMF Policies

How did these currency crises and financial crises interact to create the massive and far-reaching economic crisis that swept through East

Asia between 1997 and 1999? Consider the typical policy response of a country that is experiencing a large capital outflow because of an overvalued exchange rate, which is to devalue their currency. As discussed in Part II, in the event of a currency crisis alone this depreciation usually ends the crisis as long as the country follows appropriate fiscal and monetary policies so that no future devaluations will be necessary. However, in those East Asian countries that were also experiencing a banking system crisis, a devaluation of their exchange rate was only the beginning of their troubles because this devaluation adversely affected the balance sheets of highly leveraged banks and corporations. East Asian banks and corporations saw the real value of their foreign-denominated debt rise and the real value of their domestic-denominated assets fall as their exchange rates fell. For example, in Indonesia the exchange rate depreciated by 75 percent, meaning that foreign-denominated debt quadrupled in value at the same time that domestic-denominated assets fell by three-fourths. As a result, many banks and corporations very quickly became insolvent. The crisis in Thailand began in July and by December 8 the government had announced the closing of 56 of the 58 largest banks in the country. This insolvency led many banks to sell off as many assets as they could, further depressing asset prices in financial markets worldwide and reducing the amount of collateral for any future loans.

In this regard, the similarities between the East Asian crisis and the Great Depression are obvious. According to the Debt-Deflation theory of financial panics (Chapter 10), the falling price of assets caused by deflation during the Great Depression or depreciation during the East Asian crisis reduced the value of assets but increased the real value of debt because debt prices are fixed at the time of the loan (in the case of depreciation, these changes in the value of debt and assets are in terms of dollars). As a result, firms saw their assets fall in value and the real value of their debt rise, leading to severe financial difficulties, which in turn reduced the financial health of banks that had made extensive loans to these firms. The result was either bank failure or, at best, credit rationing, meaning that banks would significantly reduce the amount of new lending they would undertake in order to minimize their exposure to more risk. Thus, deflation and currency depreciation work in similar ways within countries that are as exposed to international capital flows and exchange rate risk as the banks in East Asia were during the 1990s.

Depreciation also led to unprecedented capital flight because it significantly reduced the return on East Asian assets and raised concerns about the stability of East Asian financial systems. Capital outflows averaged 11 percent of GDP for Indonesia, Malaysia, Korea, the Philippines, and Thailand. This capital flight magnified the financial difficulties of already shaky East Asian banks. Precipitous drops in investment and growth followed, which in many investors' eyes validated the initial foreign exchange speculation that started this whole process. Thus, the crisis spread from currency markets to the rest of the economy through a highly leveraged banking system.

The two crises that many of these East Asian crisis countries were facing simultaneously put them in an unenviable bind, a bind in which any policies they could enact to deal with one crisis would make the other crisis worse, and vice versa. Many domestic governments in these countries seemed to understand the conundrum they were in from the beginning of the crisis, as evidenced by their reluctance to follow the conventional policy reaction to a currency crisis, which is to devalue in conjunction with tightening monetary and fiscal policy in order to increase domestic interest rates and reattract foreign investment. Not only did these governments initially attempt to resist devaluation by trading large amounts of their foreign reserves at unfavorable terms, but they also resisted tightening monetary and fiscal policy because they realized that higher interest rates would only further weaken their already fragile banking systems. Of course, the opposite policy—to loosen monetary and fiscal policy in an attempt to reduce domestic interest rates, stabilize bank portfolios, and spur economic growth—would only have led to more capital flight and further exacerbated the currency crisis.

Unfortunately, it is not clear that the IMF completely understood that two distinct crises were occurring in East Asia. The IMF bailout programs negotiated throughout Asia typically focused on three general reforms as a condition for short-term financing. First, countries were asked to close insolvent banks and recapitalize other domestic banks, with those funds at least partially coming from an IMF loan and partially through reductions in government spending. Unfortunately, without the protection of deposit insurance, these IMF orchestrated closures frightened depositors throughout East Asia and initiated large deposit outflows that compounded the banking crisis. Second, countries were asked to reduce their reliance on short-term debt, mainly through bankruptcy reform and "sunshine" regulations that required better dissemination and measurement of banking information. While this is a laudable long-term goal, it did little to help an already devastated banking system. Third, the IMF asked these countries that already had low inflation and balanced budgets to further tighten monetary and fiscal policies. The thinking, which appears to have taken place almost reflexively, was that the standard policy solutions to a currency crisis—devaluation (which these countries had already experienced) and higher domestic interest rates—should be followed in East Asia as well, ignoring the condition of East Asian banking systems. This is the reason that the IMF's involvement in the crisis triggered a worsening of banking conditions throughout the region.

How Can Variations in the Magnitude of the Crisis across Countries Be Explained?

While there was quite a bit of variation in the size of the contractions in each of these East Asian economies, one simple observation explains most of this variation: The countries with the most fragile banking systems were also the countries that experienced the largest falls in output growth. The countries with the riskiest banks were those that were the most severely affected by the currency crisis: Thailand, Indonesia, Korea, and to a lesser extent Malaysia. Additional factors, however, played a role as well. Many of these countries were also suffering through a variety of political problems, including elections and labor unrest in Korea, the collapse of a government in Thailand, the revocation of an election and the eventual removal of President Suharto in Indonesia, and the rantings of Prime Minister Mahathir in Malaysia (which will be discussed later).

The best example of the importance of banking system stability is the Philippines. By almost every measure, the Philippines had the worst macroeconomic fundamentals in the region, with the lowest growth rates, the highest inflation and unemployment rates, and the largest current account and budget deficits. However, GDP growth rose strongly in 1997 to 9.6 percent, only fell to –0.5 percent in 1998, then rose again to 3.2 percent in 1999. As can be seen in Table 13.5, the Philippines was the only country that actually lowered the level of NPLs between 1996 and 1997 and, in fact, had been steadily improving in this category since the mid-1990s. Likewise, Singapore, Taiwan, and Hong Kong had relatively low levels of NPLs and also avoided the worst of the crisis. The reason is that, relative to the rest of the region, these countries had the most stringent financial regulations.

The one exception to this relationship between banking stability and the size of the economic crisis is China, which was able to avoid much of the economic crisis despite a weak banking system because of a stringent series of capital controls (including a nonconvertible currency) that placed restrictions on the amount of capital that could leave and enter the country. These capital controls also limited the amount of foreign investment that flowed into the country before the crisis occurred.

ARE FOREIGN INVESTORS TO BLAME?

Many feel that someone has to receive the blame for what happened in East Asia. Was it international financiers, who attempted to use the force of their wealth to make billions at the expense of poor nations? This hypothesis that the investment managers of large foreign investment funds were responsible for the East Asian crisis dates to the very beginning of the crisis. After his country was forced to devalue in the face of a speculative attack that his central bank did not have enough foreign reserves to prevent, Malaysian Prime Minister Mahathir Mohamad immediately blamed the crisis on foreign financiers such as George Soros. The fact that he also blamed the crisis on Jewish speculators and claimed that IMF policies were part of a Western conspiracy to recolonize Asia did not lend his claims any credibility. Large international hedge funds, like the Quantum Fund managed by Soros, became easily identifiable symbols of what many claim is wrong with the financial liberalization and globalization that has taken place within world financial markets since the 1980s.

In brief, *hedge funds* are large investment funds financed by very large investors or banks, typically requiring minimum deposits of $100 million or more. Hedge funds engage in highly risky behavior and attempt to make large returns by speculating on changes in asset prices, either positive or negative. Often these assets are currencies. Because hedge funds can move large amounts of capital within very short periods of time, hedge funds have often been accused of trying to influence markets to their advantage. For example, George Soros is widely credited for having sparked the European Monetary System crisis almost singlehandedly, by heavily betting on the pound's depreciation while widely publicizing his belief that the pound was overvalued.

Hedge funds, however, are just a small part of the big picture, which is the incredible amount of liberalization in the laws that govern capital movements between countries. One implication of more open and highly developed financial markets is that large amounts of investment now flow more freely into all regions of the world, both rich and poor. As previously discussed, the unprecedented flow of foreign funds into East Asia directly fueled the unprecedented investment rates that these countries were able to maintain until 1997. Of course, the problem with financial liberalization is that while it improves the flow of funds to regions of the world that need them the most, it also, in the words of Alan Greenspan, improves "the transmission of financial disturbances far more effectively than ever before" (Greenspan 1998). While it is easier for capital to flow in, it is also easier for capital to flow out. As discussed earlier, this is exactly what happened in East Asia during the crisis.

However, an outflow of capital does not necessarily mean that foreign investors are causing the crisis. Since the mid-1980s, Argentina, Venezuela, South Africa, and Sri Lanka were all closed to short-term capital flows at the time they suffered economic crises. Foreign investors who left East Asia were in large part properly responding to poor fundamentals in these economies, particularly in regard to overvalued exchange rates and unstable banking systems. Consistent with this view, Kenneth Froot, Paul O'Connell, and Mark Seasholes (1999) found that foreign investors did not begin to pull out large amounts of capital before the crisis, only during and after. Their study suggests that the correlation between what different foreign investors do is now higher than ever before because of the better dissemination of information. This creates a "herd" mentality among fund managers that increases the changes of panic and capital flight. The East Asian crisis has shown that these mass exoduses can be exceptionally costly.

Thus, while foreign investment and globalization may make the symptoms worse, they almost certainly do not cause the disease. To significantly reduce foreign investment and to deliberalize financial markets in a haphazard way would almost assuredly be a situation in which the cure is worse than the disease. Roman Ranciere, Aaron Tornell, and Frank Westermann (2003) find that across 52 developing countries, those that most actively liberalized their financial markets grew 2 percent a year faster than those that did not liberalize. Of this 2 percent, growth in bank credit alone accounted for 1 percent of this higher growth. Because of compounding, these small differences in growth rates from financial liberalization can lead to huge increases in standards of living. Remember the case of Korea, where even after the East Asian economic crisis GDP was still 50 percent higher in 1999 than 1990. Much of this sizeable growth was fed by large inflows of capital. If the region is to completely recover from the East Asian crisis, capital inflows will continue to be a big part of the economic recovery, provided that these funds are used in an efficient manner. This does not mean, however, that East Asia should not rethink its approach to financial liberalization and development, which brings us to the real culprit of the crisis.

REFORMING DOMESTIC INSTITUTIONS

While East Asian countries have benefited from globalization and the increased capital inflows that have taken place since the 1980s, their experience also proves that you can have too much of a good thing, especially if it comes too quickly. Commonly there were huge inflows of short-term foreign debt without proper consideration for how the risk associated with this debt could be hedged or whether this project to be financed had any merit. It is now clear that deregulation during the 1980s took place indiscriminately in those East Asian countries that suffered banking crises. Too often deregulation meant no regulation. As a result, moral hazard ran rampant throughout East Asian banking systems, and borrowers were often gambling with the house's money, eventually leading to disastrous results.

While many of these East Asian governments seemed to be operating effectively from a macroeconomic perspective—maintaining high growth, low inflation, and small budget deficits—at a more microeconomic level they were not fulfilling their fundamental responsibilities of monitoring the marketplace. Financial markets do not fit the definition of perfectly competitive markets because of the existence of imperfect information. Even the most ardent free traders realize the importance of government regulation when it comes to financial systems because of the existence of moral hazard. Unfortunately, in the face of domestic political pressures from the business sector or from other pressures exerted by Wall Street—often via Washington and the IMF (see the next chapter)—these governments closed their eyes to the behavior of their domestic banks, with disastrous consequences.

The best way for these countries to avoid future financial crises is to strengthen their financial institutions and corporate finance in recognition of the market failures that accompany imperfect information. This does not mean throwing the baby out with the bath water by eliminating foreign capital inflows altogether in an effort to prohibit unpredictable capital outflows in the future. The better approach is to be smarter about what kinds of foreign investment a country tries to attract and about what kinds of projects to finance with this foreign investment. To do this, governments have to follow five basic guidelines.

Governments need to encourage more long-term investment, not just hot money, or short-term investment denominated in foreign currencies. This can be done in part by allowing more foreign direct investment, meaning more foreign ownership of domestic businesses and banks. More foreign ownership of banks would be especially beneficial because most international banks have more experience in hedging exchange rate risk, have more diverse portfolios, and are usually subject to a more extensive set of regulations, either in the form of international capital regulations or from their country of origin. However, this recommendation is made with the caveat that proper regulation of these foreign banks must exist to ensure that lending to domestic businesses continues and that these banks do not simply become conduits through which deposits can be funneled to hot-money destinations throughout the world.

In addition, Asian equity markets need encouragement to become more developed. Changing tax codes to provide incentives to corporations to rely more on equity and less on debt is an excellent way to more evenly share the risks of financial intermediation (for example, consider how well the U.S. financial system has withstood the wild fluctuations in its stock market during 2000–2002).

Governments need to ensure that banks and corporations do a better job of protecting themselves against exchange rate risk. As mentioned before, having more foreign ownership of banks may help, but it also means more government regulation regarding the levels of foreign-denominated debt that a bank can assume. Most important, it means abandoning exchange rates that are fixed to a single currency. Too often, pegging to a single currency such as the dollar is destabilizing, if that currency becomes out of line with the rest of the world. Even at the cost of foreign investment inflows, East Asian governments need to maintain more flexible exchange rate policies, either target zones (floating exchange rates within a range) or exchange rates that are fixed not to a single currency but to a bundle of regional currencies.

Governments need to regulate the lending practices of banks more closely. This means imposing better accounting and disclosure standards along with providing more resources for independent regulators to take prompt corrective actions when there is noncompliance. This also means increasing capital requirements on banks so that the owners of banks have more to lose when loans go bad. Most important, however, it means placing limits on the amounts that banks can lend to specific firms and industries, often referred to as "connected lending." Weakening the *Chaebols* and their "too-big-to-fail" attitudes, introducing more diversity in lending, and creating more competition among banks will ensure that only the best projects will be funded, which in turn will reduce the overall riskiness of the banking system.

Governments need to learn to say no. By continuously bailing out or promising to support banks that have undertaken risky lending and borrowing activities, these governments have created moral hazard and have left the impression among many bankers that there is no downside risk to their behavior. The only way to avoid this in the future is to refuse to bail out any more poorly run banks and corporations, even if this means paying off depositors and incurring a large one-time payout (banks that are having short-term problems not caused by mismanagement are another matter). This is something that the IMF should encourage by providing more financing to governments attempting to do just this, especially if these bailouts are taking place before, and not after, a crisis occurs.

Governments need to move more slowly when deregulating financial markets. Tempted by big economic payoffs, financial liberalization has often taken place recklessly, especially within poorer countries. This is true of East Asia, where the poorer countries like Malaysia, Indonesia, and Thailand have liberalized the most rapidly, often pushed to do so by the IMF's request. The world community needs to be satisfied with slow but positive movement. The IMF and developed countries also need to provide short-term financing to countries before crises strike to encourage liberalization at a more thoughtful pace.

Since the conclusion of the East Asian crisis in 1999, economies throughout East Asia have rebounded dramatically. Growth in East Asia averaged 7 percent in 2000, 3 percent in 2001, and 5 percent in 2002, and these growth levels are expected to continue for the foreseeable future. Not surprisingly, the economies that have recovered the most strongly were the economies that took financial reform most seriously. The best example of this is South Korea. Beginning in 1999, South Korea worked with creditors to reschedule its foreign debt. At the same time, South Korea set aside an amount equal to 15 percent of its GDP to buy bad loans and close bad banks. It addition, it merged some stronger banks and sold others to foreigners, opening up South Korean financial markets to international competition. It placed new restrictions on connected lending and set higher loan safety standards. South Korea worked to shore up its Chaebols, while at the same time opening domestic markets to international firms in an effort to increase competition. Finally, South Korea abandoned its rigid peg to the U.S. dollar. As a result, Korea grew 6 percent in 2002 and is expected to grow at faster than 5 percent through 2004. However, challenges remain. Like its neighbors, South Korean markets still remain relatively closed to international trade, which dampens competition and affects competitiveness.

Korean reforms stand in direct contrast with Indonesia. Despite having the weakest banking system in the region, Indonesia has done little to deal with its nonperforming loan problem since the crisis ended. Credit rationing remains strong, and both investment rates and foreign investment in Indonesia remain well below their 1997 levels. Other East Asian countries fall somewhere between Korea and Indonesia in terms of both the extent of the reforms enacted and their economic success since the crises ended.

CONCLUSIONS

In 1998 alone, $200 billion of foreign investment left East Asia. Scaling appropriately, what would happen to the U.S. economy if $1 trillion of investment left the United States in a few months? How many U.S. loans would look bad? How many U.S. banks would fail? The events of September 11, 2001 provide a conditional answer. While only minimal capital flight occurred, roughly a trillion dollars of wealth disappeared in the United States as markets fell following the terrorist attacks. The economy slowed but banking systems stayed sound, for a number of reasons. The reliance on equity financing and not just debt financing, the reliance on long-term and not just short-term debt, the existence of a large number of small but diversified banks, and strong banking regulations restricting connected lending have all played an important role in maintaining the stability of the U.S. financial system.

The East Asian crisis has highlighted the importance of strong financial markets in withstanding economic fluctuations. However, this should not be surprising. As discussed in Chapter 10, new research on the Great Depression leads to the conclusion that the Depression was initially a financial crisis precipitated by a naïve but strict adherence to fixed exchange rates under the gold standard. Balance of payment imbalances led to deflation (as opposed to depreciation in the case of East Asia), which had a devastating effect on the labor market but, more important, on a fragile financial system. Recent New Keynesian research has also highlighted the importance of imperfect information, credit rationing, moral hazard, and the financial implications of deflation in generating business cycles, bringing the role of financial institutions to the forefront of business cycle theory.

Given what is now known about depressions and the critical role financial institutions play in them, the relevant question is not "Why in East Asia?" but "Why didn't economists see this crisis coming?" The only excuse is that the modern era of globalization only really began in 1989 with the fall of the Berlin Wall. Many of globalization's implications, whether it be for business cycles or international politics, have simply not yet been fully understood, given the speed in which they have taken place.

While globalization and financial liberalization have made it possible for poor countries to develop at rates that 30 years ago would have been thought to be impossible, it has also brought with it great costs, especially in countries where governments are not vigilant. One of the unforeseen implications of globalization is that business cycles are likely to increasingly take on an international flavor as countries become more interconnected. For instance, the East Asian crisis sparked intense speculation in Argentina that triggered an economic crisis there (see Chapter 14). In addition, speculative panics threatened Russia and Brazil, and the effects there played a role in the collapse of a major U.S. hedge fund, Long Term Capital Management, which shook U.S. financial markets. It is up to economists to make sure that the costly lessons from East Asia are learned properly. To do this, economists must further develop small, open-economy models of business cycles that capture this interconnectedness and that incorporate exchange rate fluctuations that have real effects on the financial sector and output. It is imperative that both economists and developing economy governments focus their full attention on these issues in order to avoid future crises and provide more stable standards of living for future generations.

SUGGESTED READINGS

Giancarlo Corsetti, Paolo Pesenti, and Nouriel Roubini, "What Caused the Asian Currency and Financial Crisis? Parts I and II" (1998): A complete review of the data and timeline of the East Asian crisis.

Frederic S. Mishkin, "Financial Policies and the Prevention of Financial Crises in Emerging Market Countries" (2001): An excellent review of the policy failures that precipitated the East Asian crisis and specific proposed reforms to prevent future crises.

Joseph E. Stiglitz, *Globalization and Its Discontents* (2002): Chapter 4 of this book provides a review of the East Asian crisis, focusing on a critique of IMF policies adopted during the crisis.

14

Argentina and the Role of the International Monetary Fund

INTRODUCTION

The East Asian crisis did not end when East Asian countries slowly began to grow again. Unfortunately, this crisis has had long-lasting effects in many different areas across the globe. One of these places is Argentina. Argentina's economy began to contract during the East Asian crisis, in part because of speculative crises that originated in East Asia but spread to Russia, Brazil, and eventually Argentina. As events played themselves out (events that in many ways are eerily similar to those in East Asia, but in a few crucial ways different), Argentina's recession turned into a full-blown economic crisis when it defaulted on all of its external debt in December 2001. By the end of 2002, Argentina was experiencing GDP growth of –15 percent a year, unemployment of 30 percent, and inflation of 30 percent. This chapter will investigate the events that led to the Argentinean crisis, paying particular attention to the ways that it is both similar and different from the East Asian crisis.

The role of the International Monetary Fund (IMF) in managing this and other economic crises will also be examined in this chapter. Is the IMF to blame (as many critics charge) for crises like those in Argentina or East Asia, either because of its own stupidity, through its role as an agent for globalization and the interests of the rich, or through its role in funding moral hazard? This chapter investigates the culpability of the IMF and evaluates its success in mediating (or magnifying) economic crises.

A DESCRIPTION OF THE ARGENTINEAN CRISIS

The Argentinean crisis has followed the same broad outline of the East Asian crisis, which is that of a twin crisis—both a currency crisis and a banking crisis, which occurred simultaneously. Beginning in 1991, Argentina fixed its exchange rate to the dollar, which over time led to an overvalued exchange rate and a current account deficit. Eventually, speculation against the Argentinean peso initiated a currency crisis, leading to a larger devaluation than would have been necessary had the exchange rate been floating all along. Meanwhile, in the financial sector, banks had borrowed large amounts of foreign-denominated debt and used this money to make risky domestic loans. As a result, when the exchange rate was devalued, the value of bank debts greatly increased relative to the value of bank assets. As financial institutions collapsed, financial intermediation stopped, and the Argentinean economy fell into a severe and protracted contraction. However, while the general outline of the Argentinean crisis is similar to that of the East Asian crisis, the particulars differ in important ways that have significant implications for understanding the causes of economic depressions.

The Currency Crisis in Argentina

Until the 1990s, Argentina had suffered through a history of poor economic performance, large budget deficits, and hyperinflations. In 1991, Argentina undertook a novel approach to committing itself to more stable monetary policies: a *currency board*. A currency board is a monetary system in which each Argentinean peso would be backed on a one-to-one basis with reserves of U.S. dollars. As a result, under a currency board Argentina committed itself to maintaining a fixed exchange rate of one with the dollar. Why would a country so severely tie the hands of monetary policy by using such a system? Too often, budget problems led short-sighted policymakers in Argentia to print up currency in order to pay budget shortfalls, creating hyperinflations of more than 5,000 percent a year. A currency board is a way to anchor monetary policy and make a commitment to low inflation. Even though the United States is not Argentina's largest trading partner, the dollar was chosen as the anchor because of its role as the predominant international currency. Pegging the peso to the dollar allowed Argentina to attract large amounts of foreign investment throughout the early 1990s, although much of it was short-term, dollar-denominated debt known as "hot money."

Initially, the currency board worked remarkably well. During the first 11 years of the currency board, Argentina grew at 3.4 percent a year and maintained low inflation. Compare this to the preceding 11 years, when growth averaged –1 percent and inflation was very high. However, beginning in the mid-1990s, four events caused the Argentinean peso to become greatly overvalued, which gradually undermined the whole system. First, just as happened in East Asia, the large appreciation of the dollar in the mid-1990s caused the peso to appreciate as well. Second, the Brazilian currency (the real) plummeted during 1999 because of speculators' fears that spread from East Asia to Brazil, eventually forcing devaluation of the real and making Brazilian goods considerably cheaper than Argentinean goods. Third, Argentina began to run large budget deficits because of a bloated public sector. Between 1993 and 1998, the ratio of public debt to GDP rose from 29 percent to 41 percent at a time when Argentina was growing at 4.4 percent a year. These large deficits drove up domestic interest rates to over 10 percent and caused the peso to appreciate (in this area the Argentinean crisis differed significantly from East Asian crisis: macroeconomic policy in the form of reckless fiscal policy played a crucial role in the Argentinean crisis). Finally, the low productivity of the Argentinean economy and slower growth beginning in 1995 meant that these increases in the exchange rate could not be justified based on fundamentals, but instead were the result of a balance of payment disequilibrium that could not be sustained forever.

Because of these four factors, the peso had become significantly overvalued by the end of 1999, especially relative to other currencies in the region (such as the real). This overvaluation led to large current account deficits that were paid for with large amounts of foreign borrowing. Argentina's external debt/GDP ratio rose to more than 50 percent, which is much too high for a relatively poor and inefficient economy. To make matters worse, much of this debt was denominated in foreign currencies, meaning it typically had to be paid back in dollars, not pesos. Argentina's foreign-dominated debt to exports ratio was greater than 5, meaning that their foreign-denominated debt was five times greater than the exports that could earn dollars to pay off this debt. Obviously, everything considered, it seemed obvious to many observers that Argentina was poised to experience a significant loss of investors' confidence and a currency crisis.

The Banking System Crisis in Argentina

As a result of its high level of indebtedness and falling growth, the Argentinean government was forced to default on $155 billion (B) of government debt in December 2001, the largest government default ever. This default immediately led to a massive capital flight of hot money, the collapse of the currency board, a currency crisis, and a 50 percent depreciation of the Argentinean peso.

A 50 percent depreciation meant that the value of dollar-denominated debt doubled in terms of pesos, while the value of peso-denominated

assets fell by one-half in terms of dollars. This obviously had devastating consequences for banks, especially the weak Argentinean banks
that were laden with foreign debt. Most unfortunately, many Argentin-
eans had realized that its financial system was in danger of a collapse
after observing what happened during the East Asian crisis, but policymakers did not get serious about reform quickly enough. Argentinean
banks suffered from all of the same problems that East Asian banks
suffered from: little government regulation, moral hazard and poor
quality loans, and heavy borrowing in short-term foreign-denominated
debt. In an effort to avoid total collapse, Argentinean banks immediately suspended withdrawals and imposed capital controls, some
of which, as of this writing, have still not been removed. Almost all
financial intermediation and investment in Argentina stopped, which
played a significant role in the country's –15 percent GDP growth in
2002.

IMF Policies in Argentina

What has been the role of the IMF in the Argentinean crisis? The IMF
has long been involved in Argentina. In fact, during the 1990s the
IMF held up Argentina, particularly its currency board system, as a
poster-child for successful IMF-led reforms. As conditions began to
deteriorate, the IMF initially lent Argentina $40B in 2000 before the
government defaulted and the actual crisis struck. Attached to this loan
were *structural adjustment conditions*, meaning required market reforms
aimed at increasing productivity and efficiency in an economy, such as
deregulating markets, improving legal systems, and banking reform. In
addition, *austerity conditions* were imposed, meaning that the IMF asked
Argentina to cut its money supply, cut its government spending, and
raise taxes in order to reduce inflation rates and budget deficits. It was
expected that these lower inflation rates and budget deficits would
stabilize the exchange rate and reattract foreign investment so that the
Argentinean economy would begin to grow again. However, this contractionary monetary and fiscal policy only led to further declines in
income and more capital flight.

In 2001, more than $10B of the IMF's original $40B was frozen because
of the IMF's dissatisfaction with the pace of structural and fiscal reform
in Argentina, particularly with its inability to rein in government
spending and ballooning budget deficits. In November of 2002, Argentina once again defaulted, this time on a World Bank loan. The impasse
with the IMF and World Bank temporarily ended in 2003 (primarily
because the IMF backed down under the urging of the United States
and Europe), and much of the debt payments were rescheduled. However, Argentina still owes roughly $16B to the IMF (nearly 15 percent of

the IMF's total lending) and $88B to foreign creditors. As a result, the brinksmanship between these groups will continue until Argentina significantly reforms. Unfortunately, Argentina's large budget deficits and the problems created by its insolvent financial systems continue, and no serious effort at reform is foreseeable in the near future.

Things have been slightly better in Argentina recently. In 2003, unemployment fell to 16 percent and the economy grew at a remarkable 7 percent; it is expected to grow at the same rate in 2004. However, 50 percent of the population remains in poverty. Argentina would have to maintain a 7 percent growth rate until 2005 just to get back to its 1998 level of GDP. Given the outstanding debt issues and shakiness of its banking system, Argentina's continued recovery is in no way assured.

TO WHAT EXTENT IS THE IMF TO BLAME FOR THESE CRISES?

Probably no other institution has been more widely criticized as a result of the Argentinean and East Asian crises than the IMF. Its impotence in quickly ending these crises has attracted a great deal of blame from many sources. The IMF has been harshly criticized from the right, from the left, and from the center of the political spectrum.

Criticisms from the Right

Complaints from the right have generally fallen into two categories. The first complaint is that the IMF costs the taxpayers of developed countries money; money that is eventually wasted by corrupt governments. With regard to the costs to taxpayers, the funds that countries like the United States provide to the IMF, referred to as *subscriptions*, are only loans to the IMF that earn interest payments. Not one penny of the U.S. subscription (which is currently a little more than $35B, or 18.25 percent of the IMF's total subscription of $193B) has ever been lost. Worries regarding corruption have mainly stemmed from the IMF's program in Russia in the 1990s, where billions of dollars were wasted or stolen by corrupt Russian officials. This is money that Russia will still eventually have to repay to the IMF. However, other than the Russian fiasco, there is little evidence that the funds provided through IMF bailouts have been wasted because of excessive levels of corruption (although the World Bank's funding programs may be a different story). Thus, on the whole, this criticism holds little weight, especially regarding Argentina or East Asia.

The second criticism from the right pertains to the IMF's role in funding moral hazard. In order for investors and bankers to behave responsibly and efficiently, they must incorporate all of the relevant risks and returns into their decisions to fund projects. Far too often investors and bankers incorporate all of the possible positive returns into their analysis but disregard many of the relevant risks based on the assumption that their governments, aided by IMF financing, will bail them out if economic conditions deteriorate. In a sense, the IMF provides free insurance to investors and bankers during a crisis, which encourages riskier behavior.

To deal with this, many on the right have called for disbanding the IMF in order to eliminate this potential source of moral hazard. However, many others feel that the IMF does have an important role in helping governments that are otherwise well managed to survive short-term macroeconomic problems. There is a large literature that indicates that IMF involvement in a country does, on balance, improve existing conditions and help smooth some of the economic cycles that appear to be inherent in the process of development. As discussed in Chapter 10, before World War II the world economy had none of the international infrastructure that exists today. The result was that during the Great Depression many countries acted as if they operated in a vacuum, with no regard for how their economic policies affected their trading partners. In addition, the absence of a safety net in the form of emergency financing allowed preventable recessions to build into depressions. History has shown us that for a country in crisis the proper outside help, both financially and intellectually, is exceptionally important in avoiding a sustained economic depression.

The preferable solution to the problem of moral hazard is not to simply disband the IMF but, in fact, for member countries who largely set the boundaries of IMF policy to give the IMF more power—the power to say no more often by making the IMF more independent in its policy decisions. In other words, the best solution would be for the IMF to function more as a world central bank and lender of last resort. The IMF would continue to provide financing to good governments, but by being more independent the IMF would have more power to say no to investors and bankers who have taken unacceptable risks, to say no to poorly governed countries, and to say no to developed countries that apply pressure on the IMF to conduct bailouts or to place new conditions on bailouts that further their own self-interested political or economic interests.

Criticisms from the Left

Many on the left have complained about the IMF encroaching on the sovereign rights of poor nations. While the protesters who violently disrupted the annual IMF/World Bank conference in Seattle in 1999 had a disparate collection of complaints, the objection voiced most often was that the IMF takes advantage of countries in crisis situations in order to force capitalism, financial liberalization, and globalization on the poor at the behest of rich countries.

The conditions the IMF places on its loans, specifically structural adjustment conditions, have recently come under close scrutiny. In the mid-1980s, on average, fewer than three structural adjustment conditions were associated with an IMF loan. Now, the average loan comes with more than twelve attached. While many of these conditions are things most economists can agree upon as being beneficial, such as stricter banking standards, many of the conditions are much more controversial. For example, 140 structural adjustment conditions were placed on Indonesia during the East Asian crisis, regulating things like the price of gas and the manner of selling plywood. The IMF asked the central bank of Korea to declare price stability as its only goal when choosing its monetary policy and to ignore output stabilization, even though monetary policy and inflation played no role in the East Asian crisis. It also required changes in Korean labor laws to make layoffs easier and mandated more openness to international trade in the Korean auto market (which was, not surprisingly, pushed hard by Japanese and American representatives to the IMF). In addition, the IMF placed requirements on fighting government and financial corruption that the IMF has no history or expertise in administering. Not surprisingly, many of these conditions fostered broad resentment among East Asians, not necessarily because these conditions were harmful but because they were dictated to them from the outside.

It is clear that the IMF has suffered from "mission push" in the last decade as it has tried to expand its authority into areas outside of its original mission, which was to provide macroeconomic advice and short-term financing to countries in economic difficulties. However, much of this mission push is the responsibility of the United States and other developed countries that, for economic or political reasons, have prodded the IMF into imposing structural reform conditions that fall outside the scope of traditional macroeconomic policy. Goldstein (2000) reports results from an IMF survey in which IMF staffers themselves consider only 30–40 percent of the structural adjustment conditions imposed during crises critical to a recovery. In addition, as the number of structural adjustment programs has increased, compliance rates with these programs have decreased as countries either have a hard time meeting all of the conditions or devalue individual conditions as the total number increases. Taken together, these facts support the view that the IMF has increasingly overstepped its mandate.

However, just because the IMF has become overly ambitious does not mean that the IMF should not impose structural adjustment conditions in the future. Certain conditions must always be attached to future IMF lending, for three reasons. First, the IMF needs to attach conditions that improve the chances that its loans will be repaid. The IMF is not set up to be a grant organization, and it has a right to improve the chances that loans will be repaid. Promises of structural adjustment are the only real source of collateral that the IMF has at its disposal.

Second, the IMF cannot act preemptively within a country. Crises afford the IMF its only opportunity to facilitate change within a country that, while beneficial in the long run, would otherwise be politically unpopular in the short run. It is important to note, however, that the IMF cannot force any country to accept any structural adjustment condition. Because participation with the IMF is entirely voluntary, all bailouts must be negotiated between the IMF and the crisis country. Often countries agree to structural adjustment conditions with the IMF because they believe in their effectiveness and because the IMF provides convenient political cover and an easy scapegoat on which to lay the responsibility for difficult actions.

Third, there is evidence that structural adjustment programs, if enacted, are beneficial. Anne Krueger (1998) and Sebastian Edwards (1998) find evidence that countries with structural adjustment programs were more likely than countries without them to improve across a variety of economic measures.

Therefore, attaching structural adjustment conditions to future financing must continue, but it must also change. The IMF has to refocus its mission and reconsider what it believes to be its most important objectives. IMF policymakers should ask themselves the following: "If this policy is not enacted, is it important enough to stop the Fund's financing?" Failure to answer "yes" should drop this condition from any future lending. The IMF's objectives should all fall within four categories: reform of fiscal policy, reform of monetary policy, reform of the financial sector, and exchange rate management. By prioritizing its objectives in this way, the IMF will introduce more realism into its conditions, be more likely to obtain some consensus as to what is and is not important, and improve compliance. An additional advantage of a more parsimonious approach is that it will provide the IMF with a better justification for refusing future financing to those countries that fail to comply with structural adjustment conditions. Thus, granting the IMF the ability to say no to mission creep is an important step not only toward placating some of the worries of the left regarding superfluous conditionality, but also toward reducing easy lending and moral hazard, pleasing the IMF's critics on the right.

The IMF will only be able to avoid mission creep in the future, however, if its principal financiers and policymakers, namely G7 countries such as the United States, meddle less and allow the IMF to operate more independently. Developed countries often push for bailouts of countries where their own banks and corporations have economic interests. By forcing their own self-interested objectives into IMF conditionality while at the same time complaining about an overreaching IMF, developing countries are being more than hypocritical—they are reducing the effectiveness of the IMF and the chances of useful help for countries in crisis.

When the Bush administration took office, it promised to do its part to make the IMF a more reluctant lender. To this point, this tougher stance has not made the IMF more effective, primarily because the situation has become even more difficult since the terrorist attacks of September 11, 2001. Two important countries in this war on terrorism, Pakistan and Turkey, are current recipients of IMF funding and have failed repeatedly in the past to fulfill a number of the structural adjustment conditions in their programs. The IMF has been reluctant to get tough with these countries in light of their increasing geopolitical importance. As things stand, the IMF's situation is best described by Paul Volcker, former chairman of the Federal Reserve: "When the Fund consults with a poor and weak country, the country gets in line. When it consults with a big and strong country, the Fund gets in line. When the big countries are in conflict, the Fund gets out of the line of fire" (Volcker and Gyohten 1992).

Criticisms from the Center

Many critics attack the IMF not from an ideological standpoint, but on more pragmatic grounds, asserting that the culture and policy approach of the IMF needs to be reformed.

In discussions of the Argentinean and East Asian crises, the typical IMF bailout program was explained. This program consists of structural adjustment conditions (market reforms aimed at increasing productivity) and austerity conditions (cutting money supplies, cutting government spending, and raising taxes in order to reduce budget deficits in an effort to prevent further devaluation of the exchange rate). In addition, even for countries not in crisis, the IMF advises rapid financial liberalization and fixed exchange rates to help attract foreign investment. For example, the IMF encouraged its model student, Argentina, to commit to a currency board that fixed exchange rates and encouraged foreign investment.

Paul Krugman (1999) has referred to the IMF's rationale for advocating fixed exchange rates and austerity conditions in response to a crisis as "the confidence game." In order to stem the tide of capital outflows, the IMF asks policymakers to contract monetary and fiscal policy during a crisis. The theory is that higher domestic interest rates will boost the exchange rate and assuage the confidence of foreign investors. However, this comes at the cost of a more severe economic recession in the crisis country. In other words, the confidence game refers to abandoning the typical Keynesian policies that developed countries like the United States follow during economic recessions, which is to stimulate aggregate demand by loosening monetary and fiscal policy. Instead, the IMF asks poorer crisis countries to do the exact opposite of stabilization policy in an effort to maintain foreign capital inflows (this abandonment of Keynesian policies is ironic given that Keynes was the chief architect of the IMF). It is not surprising, then, that financial and economic conditions worsened immediately after the IMF's involvement in East Asia and Argentina. Most disturbingly, these contractionary policies never did achieve their intended result, which was to restore investors' confidence. This should not be surprising, given that deeper depressions are never confidence building.

The impression the IMF leaves with many of the citizens in these crisis countries is that the IMF worries about the prejudices of investors to the exclusion of everything else. Because the IMF tends to focus on restoring capital flows, it often ignores domestic political considerations, failing to build more support for its programs within the crisis country. This reinforces the impression that the IMF is simply a tool of international financiers and not overly concerned about the fate of those who are suffering as a result of the crisis. Most important, IMF austerity policies increase the risk of social and political turmoil, which could truly have devastating long-term effects on politically unstable countries.

Joseph Stiglitz (2002), former chief economist and vice president of the World Bank between 1997 and 2000, has been a very harsh critic of the behavior of the IMF. Other noted economists such as Jeffery Sachs (1997) have joined him in his criticisms. Their complaints fall into three primary categories. First, according to Stiglitz and Sachs, the IMF is decidedly autocratic and spends too little time debating alternatives. Instead, policy is often determined in a secretive, top-down process where arrogant chiefs of the IMF make important decisions without being familiar with the particulars of the crisis country and with no participation from anyone outside the IMF who might have more specific expertise. This is the reason why IMF programs across countries are often very similar even when the fundamentals in each country are very different. (For example, consider the IMF's almost reflexive request that East Asian countries cut budget deficits and raise interest rates, even when it was clear that fiscal policy was not to blame for the East Asian crisis.)

Second, the IMF has been criticized for not being able to attract top economic talent. As a result, the claim is that most of the economists at the IMF are older and not as familiar with current economic theories, too often falling back on "tried and true" policy measures that may or may not be applicable.

Finally, Stiglitz claims that IMF policymakers are inherently biased toward the economic interests of the developed nations by which they are appointed. As a result, they blindly push for market-based reforms before the proper social and economic infrastructure is in place, which is needed for markets to work efficiently.

One clear problem with IMF policies is that the IMF does not encourage gradual reforms before crises occur. The IMF has substantial resources that can provide crucial help to all developing countries, especially in the areas of financial and legal reform. However, the IMF does not foster a consistent dialogue with these countries, only focusing on a country when a crisis is looming and then pushing for reform all at once. This, in part, explains why too often countries have rapidly liberalized their financial markets without the proper legal and regulatory frameworks in place. As mentioned before, the IMF cannot act preemptively within a country. But by forging a closer and more consistent relationship with developing countries, the IMF can be more persuasive in encouraging reforms during good times and not just during bad times. This is especially true for economies like Argentina, where a crisis was obviously brewing over a period of several years. Argentina did not receive enough proactive encouragement for reform from the IMF, however, until it was too late.

The IMF does appear to be paying attention to some of its critics. In recent months the IMF has increasingly talked about refocusing its objectives and reducing the amount of conditionality in its programs. The IMF also claims to be reorganizing under a more informal structure so as to invite more diverse opinions and create more consensus. While the IMF continues to preach financial liberalization, it will do so more slowly and more cautiously in the future. In addition, the IMF acknowledges that it must be more sensitive toward building domestic political support for its programs and it must also develop newer "early warning" techniques aimed at crisis prevention. Finally, the IMF is currently discussing plans to allow countries to declare bankruptcy and restructure their debt under the IMF's guidance, as opposed to receiving periodic bailouts. It is still too early to judge the effectiveness of these reforms.

CONCLUSIONS

Is the IMF to blame for the Argentinean crisis? The IMF encouraged Argentina's commitment to the currency board, which, coupled with appreciation of the dollar and the depreciation of the Brazilian real, played a crucial role in the crisis. By advocating the currency board system before the crisis, then advocating austerity conditions without any concern for its destabilizing effects, the IMF is at least partially to blame for making the crisis worse. But it was the things that Argentina could control—its inefficient industries, its large budget deficits, and its risky financial systems—that were ultimately responsible for Argentina's depression. Regarding these factors, the IMF had been criticizing Argentina's economic policies well before the crisis, although maybe not loudly enough to encourage fundamental reform.

While the IMF did not create the crisis in Argentina, it did not do enough to calm it. The IMF points to the strong growth of East Asian economies since their crises as evidence of its success, but the fact remains that the IMF has done a lot of backtracking from the policies it proposed in the early days of the East Asian and Argentinean crises. Four specific reforms discussed in this chapter should help the organization deal with the next series of economic crises.

The IMF needs to change its focus from a reactive institution that responds only to crises to a preemptive institution that works closely in cooperation with poor countries before crises hit. The objective here is to encourage more gradual reform and financial liberalization. IMF involvement is especially important when it comes to providing expertise and financing to developing economies that are reforming unstable banking systems, setting up legal systems (such as bankruptcy laws and accounting transparency), and encouraging equity market development. The IMF needs to stop pushing for immediate liberalization without the appropriate regulations and market incentives first being in place.

The IMF needs new and more flexible thinking instead of reflexively imposing the same structural reform and austerity policies in crisis after crisis. While most structural reforms the IMF advocates are good long-term objectives, crisis countries may never get there without more emphasis on short-term stabilization. The original purpose of the IMF was to help provide Keynesian stabilization policy for the world economy. The IMF needs to return to this original mission by encouraging expansionary monetary and fiscal policy at measured levels during crises and not just reflexively pushing austerity conditions to reattract foreign investment. The IMF cannot restore the confidence of foreign investors by first running the economy into the ground. Once the IMF has helped to stabilize an economy and restore confidence, structural reforms will have a better foundation on which to take place, especially in countries that are threatened with political and social turmoil. In addition, by better balancing unpopular structural adjustment policies with popular stabilization policies, the IMF will be better able to build domestic political support for its programs. Reforming the culture of the IMF by encouraging more open discussion and attracting more diversity of opinion should help in this more creative and balanced approach to bailouts.

New thinking is also needed regarding fixed exchange rates. The IMF has pushed for fixed exchange rates because of its belief in the necessity of an anchor for monetary policy and its belief in the need to attract large amounts of foreign investment. Too often, however, countries find that their fixed exchange rates (often fixed to the dollar) become out of line with a wide range of other exchange rates. Overvalued exchange rates lead to large current account deficits and speculative attacks. Countries spend billions of dollars defending these overvalued exchange rates, taking on billions of dollars of debt from the IMF. In the end, they often have accomplished nothing more than providing a sure bet for speculators and a short respite for foreign investors to flee the country before devaluation takes place. In addition, fixed exchange rates encourage banks to engage in risky behavior and not protect against the risk of a speculative crisis and devaluation. This is the basic scenario that played itself out in both Argentina and East Asia. The obvious solution is to avoid rigid exchange rate pegs and advocate more flexible exchange rate policies, either target zones (floating exchange rates within a range) or exchange rates that are fixed to a bundle of regional currencies and not to a single currency.

The IMF has to say no more often. If the IMF is serious about reducing moral hazard, it needs to say no to providing free insurance to careless bankers and investors in search of a bailout. It also needs to say no to crisis governments that do not meet the structural adjustment conditions of their bailout packages, especially if these conditions are pared down to only those that are essential for economic improvement. Finally, if the IMF is serious about reducing mission creep and avoiding the appearance of forcing market-based reforms onto poor countries in crisis, it also needs to say no to developed countries that pressure the IMF to tie numerous, self-interested conditions to its bailout programs.

Instead of weakening the IMF, these reforms call for the IMF to be given more power by granting it more independence to say no, by granting it more flexibility to have open debate, and by making it more proactively involved with developing countries before crises strike. The IMF is in the inherently difficult position of balancing the desire to provide short-term stability with the problem of financing long-term moral hazard and of balancing reform with political reality. With more power and independence, the IMF would be better able to strike a balance between these objectives. They need to do this quickly, however, as the Argentinean crisis threatens to spread to its neighbors throughout Latin American, especially in Uruguay and Brazil. No one, especially the IMF, wants to see this twin crisis scenario occur once again.

SUGGESTED READINGS

Martin Feldstein, "Argentina's Fall: Lessons from the Latest Financial Crisis" (2002): A brief but insightful summary of the Argentinean crises.

Paul Krugman, *The Return of Depression Economics* (1999): A thoroughly readable and engaging description of economic depressions and policymakers' often inept response to them.

Joseph E. Stiglitz, *Globalization and its Discontents* (2002): An oftentimes scathing indictment of the IMF and its policies from a Nobel Prize winner in economics and one-time chief economist of the World Bank.

15

The Great Recession in Japan

INTRODUCTION

Japan is currently in the midst of the longest period of below-average growth experienced by any developed country since World War II. Figure 15.1 presents GDP growth and unemployment in Japan since 1980. After a decade of very strong growth in the 1980s, beginning in 1991 the Japanese economy averaged roughly zero growth over the next 12 years, and unemployment more than doubled, to postwar highs. If the Japanese economy had instead grown at a reasonable 2 percent a year over these 12 years, Japan would be 25 percent richer today than it is. To put this in perspective, by growing at 0 percent instead of 2 percent, Japan has lost what is equivalent to the entire GDP of Italy.

This Great Recession has actually been composed of two closely spaced recessions, the first lasting from 1992 to 1995 and the second beginning in 1997, with no definitive end in sight. As illustrated in Figure 15.2, this recession has been accompanied by a significant decrease in inflation since the early 1990s and deflation since 1998—the first deflation experienced in an OECD country since the Great Depression. This deflation had the unprecedented effect of driving nominal interest rates to, and even slightly below, zero. In addition, the Japanese stock market fell by 75 percent and commercial property values were down 80 percent from their prerecessionary highs in 1990. Most disturbingly for the future prospects of recovery, Japanese banks are currently holding billions of dollars of bad loans, and their financial industry teeters on the brink of collapse.

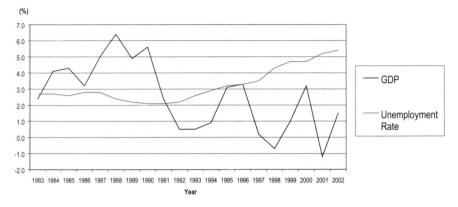

Figure 15.1 Real GDP Growth and Unemployment Rates in Japan

It has not always been like this. In fact, not long ago the worry among
U.S. and European policymakers was that the Japanese economy was
becoming too strong, not too weak. In late 1989, highly respected
economist Lawrence Summers (future U.S. Treasury Secretary and president of Harvard University) said the following: "An Asian economic
bloc with Japan at its apex . . . is clearly in the making. This all raises
the possibility that the majority of American people who now feel that
Japan is a greater threat to the United States than the Soviet Union are

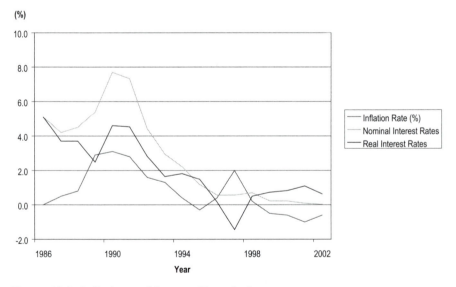

Figure 15.2 Inflation and Interest Rates in Japan

right" (Summers 1989). Summers was in no way alone in this opinion. Japan was the most amazing growth miracle of the twentieth century, averaging 5 percent per-capita GDP growth a year and more than quadrupling standards of living between 1960 and 1990. In a little over two decades, Japan went from an agriculture-based economy to the world's largest exporter of steel and automobiles. Based on the assumption that this remarkable economic growth would continue indefinitely, many anticipated a day when Japan would dominate the United States and Europe.

The predicted rise to preeminent economic superpower has not happened. In this chapter, the reasons for the lengthy Japanese slowdown will be investigated. This examination begins with a discussion of Japan and the unique institutions that characterize its economy. Included is an explanation of Japan's dual economy, with a small export-oriented sector but essentially closed domestic markets, its heavily regulated and concentrated industries, its low consumption and high savings rates, its large but weak banking system, and its slow-moving bureaucratic government. Next, the role that each of these factors has played in the Japanese recession is examined. We will see that there are striking similarities between the Great Depression of the 1930s, the East Asian Crisis of 1997–1999, and the Great Recession in Japan, specifically regarding the real consequences of deflation on the stability of banking systems and how weak banking systems can magnify the size of economic contractions. Finally, the failure of stabilization policy in Japan, both monetary and fiscal, to stimulate the Japanese economy and to end the recession is examined. One conclusion of this chapter is that macroeconomic theory, particularly Keynesian and New Keynesian business cycle theory, explains what is happening in Japan quite well. The study of the Great Recession in Japan lends credence to the argument that economists are making advances in their understanding of business cycles.

A BRIEF DESCRIPTION OF THE JAPANESE ECONOMY

Japan's economy is structured differently than other developed economies, including other economies in Asia. The key differences fall into three broad categories.

Japan's Dual Economy

Japan has a reputation as an export-oriented economy, but in reality only about 15 percent of its firms produce exports. This export sector is highly efficient because of intense international competition and is composed of the companies that most consumers outside of Japan are familiar with. However, the other 85 percent of Japanese firms, which are primarily devoted to the production of goods and services for domestic consumption, are highly protected from international trade. The government closely regulates prices and other market conditions in this domestic sector, and market power is concentrated within a small number of very large firms. As a result, there is a significant productivity difference between Japan's competitive export sector and its inefficient domestic sector.

Another reason productivity in Japan has been falling is that the Japanese population has been aging rapidly because of falling birthrates and restrictive immigration barriers. As a result, Japan's labor force has been contracting since 1995 and will continue to do so for the foreseeable future.

Together, inefficient domestic markets and a shirking labor force have encouraged Japanese firms to move their operations outside of Japan in order to increase productivity. For example, Japanese car manufacturers now produce more cars abroad than they do at home (Katz 2000). Another implication of this market inefficiency is that goods and services are considerably more expensive in Japan than they are anywhere else in the world. For example, the average American household spends 10 percent of its income on food, as compared to 20 percent for the average Japanese household. In fact, many goods produced by Japanese companies are sold cheaper in the United States than in Japan itself. The result is that Japan has become the most expensive country in the world in which to live. Tokyo and Osaka, Japan's two largest cities, are the two most expensive cities in the world, with cost-of-living indicators roughly 35 percent higher than in New York.

Japan's Investment-Driven Economy

The development strategy Japan adopted after World War II focused on building manufacturing industries that could produce goods to be exported abroad. The idea behind this strategy, referred to as *export promotion*, was that it would allow Japan access to larger international markets, which would in turn allow Japan to take advantage of economies of scale and increase its productive efficiency. To do this, however, huge amounts of funds had to be funneled to Japanese corporations in order to finance their capital purchases. The primary economic objective of the Japanese government during the postwar era has been to use public policy as a tool to facilitate cheap financing for Japanese industry. The government has done this directly by providing subsidies and loans to corporations. It has also done this indirectly through two channels. First, Japanese tax policies encouraged household savings by relying heavily on consumption taxes. Second, the dual-economy structure of the economy increased the prices of domestic consumption goods, which in turn discouraged consumption and encouraged savings. Together with Japan's rapidly aging population, these factors explain why Japan has consistently saved nearly 20 percent of its GDP. This is a much higher rate than the 3 percent savings rate in the United States. This high level of savings in Japan has not only led to low interest rates and high investment, but to private consumption that is about 10 percent lower, as a share of GDP, than it is in the United States.

Japan's Banking Conglomerates

Bond and stock markets in Japan are relatively small. Banking in Japan, as in most Asian economies, is a much more important source of financial intermediation than in other developed economies. Just like in other areas of the economy, the Japanese government has played a major role in the development of the Japanese banking system by using financial regulations and subsidies as a tool to encourage households to hold their savings in banks. In the United States, households hold only about 10 percent of their assets in currency or bank deposits. In Japan, this number is an astounding 54 percent, which is the primary reason that Japan had 8 of the 10 largest banks in the world during the early 1990s (Yamaguchi 2002).

Japanese firms rely heavily on banks for their financing. In Japan, 39 percent of corporate financing comes from bank loans, with only 33 percent coming in the form of equity financing. It is the opposite in the United States, where banks account for 12 percent of corporate financing and equity 66 percent. In spite of their size and influence (or maybe because of it), Japanese banks are protected from international competition and are inefficient. In addition, because there are no rules separating the operations of banks from the firms they lend money to, most Japanese banks have very close financial ties with large corporations. These corporate/banking conglomerates are referred to as *Keiretsu* (these Keiretsu are similar to the Chaebols in South Korea, which were discussed in Chapter 13). The rationale for these Japanese conglomerates is that, in theory, closer relationships between firms and banks should allow each to make better-informed lending and investment decisions. In practice, however, it has often led to "crony capitalism," where loans are made not on the basis of profit but on the basis of relationships. It has also encouraged a "too-big-to-fail" mentality that has greatly increased moral hazard and risk in the Japanese banking system, which in turn has reduced the quality and efficiency of the lending process.

Further magnifying the problem of moral hazard in Japan was a program of financial deregulation adopted during the 1980s. As in the United States and East Asia, when lending restrictions were weakened in Japan, the riskiness of bank lending immediately rose. Coupled with the excessive optimism of corporate executives and speculators, deregulation played a large part in creating incredible real estate and stock market bubbles in Japan during the late 1980s. To provide one extreme example of the size of this bubble economy, it has been reported that at one point real estate developers in Japan estimated that the square mile surrounding the Emperor's palace in the center of Tokyo was valued at more than all of the land in California (Krugman 1999).

WHAT IS RESPONSIBLE FOR THE GREAT RECESSION IN JAPAN?

The similarities between the Great Recession in Japan and the Great Depression of the 1930s are striking. In each case, the first obvious sign of a problem was a large stock market crash, which took place in Japan in December 1989. Falling inflation, and eventually deflation, subsequently followed. As output began to fall, the bad debts held by banks began to increase and financial intermediation began to slow considerably, leading to further falls in aggregate demand and output. The most significant difference between the Great Recession and the Great Depression is one of magnitude. While the Great Depression was absolutely devastating to the world economy, the Great Recession has been largely isolated to Japan, and even in Japan the falls in output and the increases in unemployment have been much smaller than those that occurred during the Great Depression.

Declines in aggregate supply created by structural inefficiencies in the Japanese economy have played a role in this recession, particularly in explaining why this recession has persisted for more than a decade. A number of factors have contributed to lower aggregate supply growth in Japan. One has been the inflexibility of the Japanese labor market, in large part because of its tradition of lifetime employment, which severely limits flexibility in hiring and firing decisions. Coupled with a significant amount of nominal and real wage rigidity in Japan, for the reasons suggested by New Keynesian models of wage inflexibility, deflation in Japan has led to higher real wages and unemployment levels unprecedented in Japanese postwar history. These high unemployment rates exist in spite of the fact that Japanese corporations continue to employ bloated labor forces and resist layoffs. Other factors constraining aggregate supply growth include the high degree of market concentration and lack of international competition within Japan's dual economy, both of which have slowed productivity and growth.

Finally, diminishing marginal returns have significantly reduced the productivity potential of new capital after decades of astronomical investment rates.

Despite all of these factors affecting aggregate supply, the existence of sustained deflation clearly indicates that this recession has been driven primarily by falling aggregate demand, not by reductions in aggregate supply. These persistent declines in aggregate demand have been driven by two primary factors.

Underconsumption

Japan has traditionally relied heavily on investment to generate enough aggregate demand to keep its economy at its natural rate of growth. It was easy to justify and maintain these high investment rates in the early postwar period when the economy was starved for capital and growing at 6 percent a year. However, as the Japanese economy grew larger, diminishing returns to capital began to set in and the productivity of newer investment projects began to fall. A big part of the transition from being a developing country to becoming a developed country involves saving less and consuming more while at the same time shifting demand from investment goods to consumption goods. This transition in the composition of aggregate demand, which also stabilizes aggregate demand because consumption is more stable than investment, has occurred in most western developed countries. In contrast, Japan has continued to save nearly 20 percent of its GDP throughout the postwar era. The pressure to find investment projects for all of this savings has led to overbuilding, overproduction, falling returns on capital, and a great deal of aggregate demand instability.

If this scenario sounds familiar, think back to the warnings of Underconsumptionist Theories, which were discussed in Chapter 3. These theories argued that the production of goods within rich economies would outpace the growth rate of consumption. Without adequate aggregate demand to absorb these goods, chronic overproduction would threaten future economic prosperity. Efforts to stimulate aggregate demand through increasing investment demand might help in the short run but hurt in the long run, as higher levels of capital led to even more excess supply.

A similar Underconsumptionist theme is an integral part of Keynesian theory, which argues that higher levels of savings do not guarantee full employment—in fact, just the opposite. In Keynes' model, investment may not be large enough to keep the economy at its potential rate of output because of low expectations. The Keynesian principle of the paradox of thrift suggests that countries can save too much relative to their investment levels, leading to chronic aggregate demand shortfalls and increasingly frequent economic contractions. Because of this, higher savings rates are largely self-defeating because more savings reduces aggregate demand and output, which in turn reduces savings.

The way to avoid lower output and the destabilizing effects of higher savings rates in the Keynesian and Underconsumptionist theories is for public policy to encourage consumption by increasing the percent of GDP devoted to government purchases and/or by taxing savings. This is the exact opposite of what the Japanese government has chosen to do. Instead, their policymakers have placed their sole focus on stimulating investment spending in an effort to maintain full employment. While this might have been the proper policy to follow for a capital-starved economy that had just lost a devastating war, it is not proper stabilization policy for an already prosperous economy. However, Japan seems unable and unwilling to abandon its postwar economic policies. In fact, the desire to sustain high investment rates was one of the principal reasons behind financial deregulation in Japan during the 1980s. The stock market crash of early 1990s signaled the end of a period of economic overconfidence and the beginning of a period of falling expectations, falling investment, falling aggregate demand, and recession.

Debt-Deflation

The second major reason that aggregate demand has fallen so significantly and so persistently is that a banking crisis threatened to strike Japan soon after the recession started. Two interrelated factors precipitated this banking crisis. First, crashes in the stock and real estate markets severely reduced the value of assets owned by banks and the collateral that backed many of their loans. As a result, banks immediately found themselves holding large amounts of bad loans. Second, and more important, the deflation of the late 1990s increased the real value of corporate debt relative to the value of their assets. As explained in the Debt-Deflation theory, discussed in detail in Chapter 10, deflation increases the real value of firm debt because debt contracts have fixed nominal values that do not adjust with the price level. However, the asset values of firms fall during a deflation. As the financial position of firms deteriorate, banks see the number of defaulted or delinquent loans in their portfolio rise, leading to the panic selling of assets. As panic selling spreads, asset prices are further depressed and both firms' and banks' financial positions are further weakened. Weak banks either fail or they *credit ration*, meaning they reduce the amount of new lending they undertake. Kenneth Kuttner and Adam Posen (2001) find evidence, similar to that found by Ben Bernanke (1983) in the United States during the Great Depression, that credit rationing has taken place during the Great Recession in Japan. This credit rationing occurred even though, contrary to what happened during the Great Depression, almost all banks in Japan have avoided closure. The result of this credit rationing has been lower investment and consumption, which has in turn reduced aggregate demand and output.

If this all sounds familiar, it should. The same scenarios that played themselves out within banking systems during the Great Depression and during the East Asian crisis have occurred within Japan as well (although in East Asia it was depreciation of the exchange rate and not deflation that precipitated the crisis). The only difference here is one of scale. To Japan's benefit, the Japanese economy was originally strong enough and their banking system sound enough to avoid massive bank failures, bank runs, and a complete collapse in financial intermediation. Some Japanese banks did fail, such as the second and fifth largest credit unions in 1995, followed in 1997 by several mid-sized banks. However, these banks are exceptions. Most Japanese banks have continued to operate for more than a decade (with the help of periodic bailouts) even though the Japanese banking system lingers on the brink of crisis. Merrill Lynch estimates that if the number of non-performing loans is measured correctly, 40 percent of Japanese banks are currently insolvent (i.e., bank liabilities are greater than their assets). Estimates of non-performing loans in Japanese banks are staggering, ranging between $1.2 trillion and $2.5 trillion dollars, or upward of 50 percent of Japanese GDP (*The Economist* 2001).

It is the sheer size of this number that explains the inability of Japanese policymakers to put an end to this enduring banking crisis. Briefly consider the problems associated with a government bailout of banks of this magnitude. Where would all of this money come from? What price should the government pay for these bad loans? Who gets bailed out first? Won't a bailout lead to even more moral hazard in the future? Should the government nationalize banks? For banking reform to work, isn't corporate and structural reform needed first to stabilize the financial position of corporations? These questions are only a small indication of the size and the scope of the problems that have left Japan and its policymakers paralyzed with indecision.

STABILIZATION POLICY IN JAPAN

If modern business cycle theory, particularly Keynesian and New Keynesian theory, explains the Great Recession in Japan so well, then why hasn't Keynesian stabilization policy been able to end the contraction? The reasons behind the failure of stabilization policy in Japan are multifaceted and the result in many ways from the same factors responsible for the recession.

Monetary Policy in Japan

The Bank of Japan, the central bank of Japan, is relatively independent and insulated from political considerations. This is true of many of the powerful ministries that run the Japanese government. These ministries are heavily bureaucratic, and policy is formed in a top-down process directed by lifelong government insiders. While this independence from politics can be a good thing in terms of discouraging shortsighted public policies aimed only at advancing special interests, it also makes Japanese decision-making highly conservative and slow to respond to changes in economic conditions. As deflation has persisted in the Japanese economy, the Bank of Japan has been reluctant to abandon its restrictive price-level targets that have played a key role in driving prices lower and reducing aggregate demand.

Kuttner and Posen (2001) conducted an extensive review of Japanese monetary policy in the 1990s. They found that the Bank of Japan made only weak efforts to increase the monetary base during most of this period because of, unbelievably, worries about inflation. However, even when the Bank of Japan has increased the monetary base more aggressively, as it has since 2000, it has not been able to generate significant increases in the money supply. For example, between March 2001 and July 2003 the Bank of Japan increased the monetary base by 40 percent but the money supply increased by only 6 percent. The reason is that the money multiplier has fallen dramatically since the recession began. The M2 multiplier has fallen from roughly 13 in 1992 to 10 in 1997 to below 8 in 2002. This drop in the money multiplier has been driven by large increases in the currency-to-deposit ratio, which has risen from .68 in 1992 to .85 in 1997 to 1.06 in 2002 (Bank of Japan 2002). Clearly, Japanese citizens are hoarding more currency as the recession lingers, dampening the money multiplier process and reducing the ability of the Bank of Japan to increase the money supply.

Why have currency holdings risen so dramatically in Japan? The weak positions of Japanese banks have definitely played a role. For obvious reasons, Japanese savers are reluctant to place their money in banks that are technically bankrupt, even if deposit insurance is available. However, an even more important reason why currency holdings have increased during this recession harkens back to the Keynesian model and its arguments regarding the ineffectiveness of monetary policy during economic contractions. Keynes believed that households and banks tend to increase their holdings of money as a precautionary measure during bad times. This is particularly true when interest rates are low because there is a low opportunity cost of holding money and not placing it in a bank account. Low interest rates also make purchasing bonds unattractive because interest rates are likely to increase, which will reduce the value of any bonds being held. Because of these considerations, Keynes believed that any change in the money supply during recessions is likely to be hoarded, severely restricting the ability of monetary policy to manipulate interest rates, investment, and aggregate demand. Keynes referred to this as a *liquidity trap*. As we saw in Figure 15.2, nominal interest rates in Japan have been near zero since 1995, indicating that the economy could be caught in such a trap. What is worse, even if the Bank of Japan could find a way to increase the money supply significantly, nominal interest rates are so close to zero that they cannot be driven down any further without eliminating any incentive to hold money in banks. As a result, any future increases in the money supply in Japan are likely to be hoarded, and the ability of monetary policy to stimulate investment and aggregate demand through further reductions in interest rates appears to be extremely limited, given current conditions.

However, even if monetary policy cannot increase the money supply and drive nominal interest rates any lower than they currently are, it does not mean that monetary policy is necessarily powerless to stimulate aggregate demand. Many economists have argued that the Bank of Japan now has to dramatically increase the monetary base in ways that could stimulate aggregate demand more directly. One option would be for the Bank of Japan to expand the monetary base by buying up long-term government debt. This would reduce worries about the size of the public debt in Japan and allow for more expansionary fiscal policy in the future. Another option would be to increase the monetary base by lending money to firms or buying corporate financial assets in an effort to stimulate investment spending directly without relying on banks. Finally, the Bank could buy non-performing loans, which would not only provide liquidity to banks but also stabilize their financial position so that these new reserves would be lent out. However, the monetary base is expanded, if it is increased enough, inflation will eventually rise. If the public views the Bank's commitment to higher inflation as credible, higher expected inflation will increase nominal interest rates, encourage the holding of financial assets, discourage the hoarding of money, and stabilize banks' balance sheets. Once the health of the financial system has improved, traditional monetary policy will once again be effective. To this point, unfortunately, the Bank of Japan seems reluctant to engage in such a radical break from conventional, conservative monetary policy actions and make a commitment to higher inflation. Instead, it seems content to let deflation gradually eat away at the country's financial position.

Fiscal Policy in Japan

Kuttner and Posen also examined the effects of fiscal policy in Japan since the recession began. They conclude that while fiscal policy has helped stabilize output somewhat, it has been too timid to have large benefits. This is primarily because the Japanese government has been reluctant to increase government spending and cut taxes simultaneously due to worries about the size of its deficit, which is currently 8 percent of GDP, and the size of its outstanding debt, which is currently more than 140 percent of GDP. For example, a 10-year/$500 billion spending package for public works projects (which is small relative to the size of the Japanese economy) was enacted in 1995, but in 1997 an increase in the level of consumption taxes was implemented to cover growing budget deficits (this is just another example of the Japanese government favoring capital projects over consumption). As a result, little net stimulus to aggregate demand was created, and Japan was left with more capital in an economy that was already overbuilt. Another example of misguided Japanese fiscal policy was the Coupon Issuance Program adopted in 1998. Under this program, roughly $170 of coupons were given to each qualifying Japanese citizen in an effort to stimulate consumption. Of course, just as microeconomic theory would predict, this temporary tax cut simply encouraged consumers to spend their coupons and save more of their income. It had little impact on aggregate demand, but significantly increased Japan's budget deficit. Even more troubling, Japan's budget deficits are expected to explode in the near future as its population rapidly ages and the ratio of the elderly to the working-age population increases dramatically, placing further restrictions on the future use of discretionary fiscal policy.

CONCLUSIONS

Two lessons can be learned from the Great Recession in Japan. First, modern macroeconomic theory, particularly Keynesian and New Keynesian theory, can explain many important aspects of the Japanese recession quite well. Specifically, these theories have explained the effects of Japanese policies that encourage savings and discourage consumption, the effects of deflation on wages and the balance sheets of banks, the reasons that banking system fragility leads to credit rationing and lower financial intermediation, and how Japan has slipped into a low interest rate liquidity trap that can render traditional monetary policy ineffective. If these characteristics of the Great Recession in Japan sound familiar, they should. Many of these same factors played important roles in the Great Depression of the 1930s and in the East Asian Crisis of 1997–1999, particularly deflation (or depreciation of the exchange rate in the case of the East Asian crisis) and its role in creating banking crises that initiated severe economic contractions. Economists have learned from these earlier crises, which has led to a better understanding of the economic situation in Japan.

The other lesson that can be learned from the Great Recession is that macroeconomic knowledge does not mean a thing if policymakers do not follow sound economic advice. Toshihiko Fukui, the new governor of the Bank of Japan, has recently said that macroeconomics textbooks offer no solution to the problem of ending deflation in Japan. He obviously has not read (or understood) very many macroeconomics textbooks. Economists have come to a general consensus on three broad reforms that must take place within Japan in order to end the deflation and allow its economy to begin to grow its way out of this long recession.

Aggressive monetary policy and fiscal policy are needed in Japan, and at the same time. Japanese policymakers have been reluctant to significantly loosen monetary policy because of their preoccupation with low inflation. However, a commitment to higher inflation is exactly what Japan needs right now. Even if Japan is in a liquidity trap and future increases in the monetary base will not lead to further reductions in interest rates, this does not mean that monetary policy is necessarily ineffective. The Bank of Japan should immediately make a credible commitment to increasing the monetary base by buying government debt, buying corporate assets, or even directly lending money to corporations. Not only will aggressive monetary policy stimulate aggregate demand but also the inflation created will help bank balance sheets and encourage households to spend now, as opposed to waiting for lower prices in the future. The buying of long-term government debt will also remove a major constraint on fiscal policy, which is the fear that expansionary fiscal policy will lead to excessive government debt levels. With this constraint gone, Japanese policymakers will be freer to aggressively cut taxes and increase government spending (preferably taxes and spending that encourage private consumption) at the same time.

Japan needs to resolve its non-performing loan crisis as soon as possible so that financial intermediation can begin again. The threat of a banking collapse has hung like a storm cloud over the Japanese economy since 1997, leading to a protracted period of credit rationing that has severely dampened investment lending, consumer lending, and aggregate demand. However, in the seven years that this crisis has been building, the Japanese government has been completely unwilling to tackle most of the difficult issues associated with banking reform. Instead, the government periodically bails out large banks in a piecemeal process. Japan must immediately commit itself to a comprehensive bailout program involving buying up bad debts at fair but highly discounted prices (possibly by using new money created by expansionary monetary policy). To avoid future problems with moral hazard incentives created by these bailouts, the Japanese government has to conduct bailouts in conjunction with imposing new banking regulations that more closely limit the lending practices of banks and also begin to sever the close ties between Japanese banks and corporations. The Japanese government also needs to encourage more direct finance in the form of better and more efficient stock and bond markets, which are underdeveloped compared to those of major economies outside the region. Finally, the quickest and maybe the best way to introduce more competition into the system and make these banks more efficient is to allow foreign ownership of Japanese banks and give foreign banks the right to operate within Japan's closed financial markets.

Japan needs to undertake substantial structural reform aimed at increasing the efficiency of its economy. The Japanese economy is too strong for this recession to last forever. But when it is over, the errors of the 1990s will be replayed once again unless Japan engages in significant reform at the microeconomic level aimed at increasing competition and economic efficiency in its economy. This includes opening Japanese domestic markets to international goods. It also includes allowing more immigration or more women into the workforce to stem the contraction of its labor supply. Finally, Japan must reduce its reliance on investment to generate aggregate demand and instead switch production toward more consumer goods. The best way to achieve this final objective is to remove the incentives in Japanese fiscal policy that favor savings and investment over consumption.

Why have Japanese policymakers failed to enact these reforms? Why haven't they learned the proper lessons from modern macroeconomic theory, the Great Depression, and the East Asian Crisis? The answer rests in Japan's insulated, inflexible, and bureaucratic political system, which has resisted both internal and external pressure to reform. The biggest issue facing Japan may not be a liquidity trap but a political trap. The political tide seemed to be turning in 2001 when a tough-talking new prime minister, Junichiro Koizumi, was elected. However, since his election no significant economic reforms have been put in place within Japan.

Economic reform can work. The remarkable recovery of South Korea after the East Asian Crisis, which enacted many of the economic reforms needed today in Japan (see Chapter 14), attests to this. However, as long as Japan resists reform it will have to settle for lower growth and lower standards of living. Growth in Japan was slightly higher at 2.7 percent in 2003 and is expected to be 2 percent in 2004, which is higher than it has been but still extremely low for a country that is far below its natural rate of output. Unfortunately, things will probably have to get worse before political circumstances force policymakers to deal seriously with the economic and financial problems facing Japan. However, in the words of Keynes, "If we do nothing long enough, there will in the end be nothing else that we can do" (Keynes 1931).

SUGGESTED READINGS

Paul Krugman, "It's Baaack: Japan's Slump and the Return of the Liquidity Trap" (1998): A comprehensive review of the liquidity trap and the failure of stabilization policy within Japan.

Paul Krugman, *The Return of Depression Economics* (1999): Chapter 4 includes a general discussion of Japan's boom in the 1980s and slowdown in the 1990s.

Kenneth N. Kuttner and Adam S. Posen, "The Great Recession: Lessons for Macroeconomic Policy from Japan" (2001): A comprehensive review of the roles played by monetary policy, fiscal policy, and the financial crisis during the Japanese recession.

Adam S. Posen, "The Looming Japanese Crisis" (2002): A description of the potential financial and economic crises that could occur within Japan in the future without significant policy reform. Included is a discussion of the role of the U.S. government in creating the political impetus for economic reform in Japan.

Conclusions: What We Do and Do Not Know about Business Cycles

A QUICK TRIP THROUGH BUSINESS CYCLE THEORY

Mimicking the subject itself, the study of business cycles has undergone periods of remarkable progress and unexpected regression, of irrational confidence in our knowledge and unjustified skepticism in the ability of economists to make economies work better. However, the best way to judge our understanding of recessions and depressions, just like the best way to judge economies themselves, is to evaluate their long-run record of growth. By this measure there has been real and significant progress. All one has to do is look back at the first models of business cycles, which centered around things such as sunspots and weather fluctuations, to understand just how far the study of economic contractions has come. These early models were simple (comfortingly so) and focused on a single cause of business cycles. Both experience and research have taught us, however, that there is nothing simple about recessions and depressions. Their characteristics are variable, their fundamentals complex, and their transmission unclear.

The first modern theories of business cycles, the Keynes/Keynesian and Monetarist models, agree that fluctuations in aggregate demand are the source of business cycles. What these different aggregate demand theories do not agree upon is what causes these fluctuations. Keynesians believe the culprit is unstable expectations that lead to investment and consumption volatility. Coupled with wage and price inflexibility, these fluctuations in investment and consumption lead to large swings in aggregate output. Because these fluctuations represent lost output, there is a responsibility for the government to improve welfare by using countercyclical fiscal and monetary policy to stabilize aggregate demand and output.

Monetarists, on the other hand, assert that monetary policy is responsible for business cycles because central bankers insist on conducting just the kind of stabilization policy that Keynesians advocate. Monetarists believe that wages and prices are perfectly flexible, and they believe in the natural rate hypothesis, or the principle that aggregate supply determines output in the long-run and changes in aggregate demand only affect output only in the short-run. Because policymakers have limited information, especially about what the natural rate of the economy actually is, central bankers often aim too high in an effort to stimulate output in the short-run, creating excessive inflation in the long run. When faced with the fact that higher and higher levels of inflation are necessary to keep output at or above the natural rate, the central bank is eventually forced to reverse course and create a recession in order to reduce inflation. This means that monetary policy becomes a destabilizing, not a stabilizing, factor in the economy.

The Rational Expectations model, with its assertion that only unexpected changes in policy can have real effects on output, both supports and diverges from the Monetarist model. Like the Monetarists, Rational Expectations proponents believe that stabilization policy is destabilizing and inflationary. However, by asserting that only unexpected changes in monetary policy have real effects, the Rational Expectations model raises significant questions about how monetary policy can be the primary source of business cycles in a world where economic information is widely available, especially in terms of explaining the source of large economic contractions such as the Great Depression.

The 1970s illustrated that aggregate demand shocks are not the only potential source of business cycles. The oil price spikes associated with the OPEC oil embargo created stagflation that could only be consistent with a decrease in aggregate supply. Likewise, the 1980s and 1990s were generally characterized by robust growth and falling inflation, which are consistent with an increase in aggregate supply. These events fed a neoclassical resurgence in business cycle theory that emphasized perfectly flexible prices and aggregate supply-driven business cycles. This is best exemplified by Real Business Cycle models, which argue that changes in aggregate productivity create fluctuations in aggregate supply that are the primary determinant of fluctuations in output. Because business cycles are optimal responses to changes in the real fundamentals of an economy, laissez-faire policies are preached by Real Business Cycle economists. While Real Business Cycle models have the appealing feature of being built upon microfoundations and can explain many aspects of the 1970s, 1980s, and 1990s, such as countercyclical prices and procyclical real wages, they have no plausible explanation for the cause of major economic contractions such as the Great Depression, the East Asian Crisis, or the Great Recession in Japan.

The term *New Keynesian* has been used to refer to a group of models that examine the microeconomic foundations of imperfect competition, in the form of wage inflexibility, price inflexibility, or imperfect information and risk. New Keynesian models incorporate both rational expectations and the natural rate hypothesis, and both aggregate demand and aggregate supply shocks. As a result, they are consistent with a broad range of business cycle behaviors and episodes. Most important, these models provide insight into the role that financial institutions play in economic contractions, which has been crucial to our understanding of the Great Depression as well as modern economic crises in East Asia, Argentina, and Japan. This is especially true regarding New Keynesian research on the effects of risk on the financial position of firms, how risk creates moral hazard and affects the quality of bank loans, and how risk leads to credit rationing during recessions. These New Keynesian models represent the best and most insightful descriptions of how business cycles get started and the mechanisms by which they have real and persistent effects on an economy. However, their biggest drawback is that they are still more of a collection of related models than a single, coherent, and comprehensive model of business cycles. As a result, New Keynesian models provide multidimensional explanations of recessions and depressions that appear to be close to the complex reality of business cycles, but do not provide any simple explanations or prescriptions.

WHAT WE KNOW ABOUT BUSINESS CYCLES

As the preceding section illustrates, quite a bit of ground, both theoretical and empirical, has been covered in this book. Clearly, significant progress has been made in our understanding of recessions and depressions. It is worth the time and effort to briefly review conclusions on which economists have reached some consensus. These key findings can be summarized in five statements.

Both aggregate demand and aggregate supply shocks are important sources of business cycle fluctuations. The first empirical fact about business cycles covered in this book is that business cycles are not cyclical, meaning that they do not exhibit a regular pattern. This suggests that recessions have multiple causes. The U.S. and international case studies covered in this book support this idiosyncratic view of business cycles. As emphasized by Keynesians and Monetarists, fluctuations in aggregate demand are clearly important sources of fluctuations in output.

The cyclical behaviors observed during the Great Depression, during postwar business cycles in the United States before the 1970s, during the 2001 recession in the United States, during the East Asian Crisis, and during the Great Recession in Japan are all consistent with aggregate demand-driven business cycles, with prices moving procyclically and real wages moving countercyclically. On the other hand, the 1970s, 1980s, and 1990s in the United States were periods of countercyclical price and procyclical real wage movements that are consistent with shifts in aggregate supply, such as the productivity shocks emphasized by Real Business Cycle models. Thus, a comprehensive model of business cycles must incorporate both demand and supply shocks. This is one of the primary objectives of New Keynesian research.

Expectations play a key role in initiating business cycles. Even the very first business cycle theories recognized the importance of expectations, and expectations have played a significant role in every modern business cycle theory since. However, these modern theories believe that expectations are important for different reasons.

The idea that expectations could be self-fulfilling was first proposed by the Sunspot theory in the 1800s. This idea later was incorporated into Keynes' concept of animal spirits, where he argued that unstable expectations lead to volatile investment and aggregate demand. In Keynes' mind, expectations are largely irrational, and the volatility they create necessitates a role for government in offsetting fluctuations in aggregate demand using countercyclical monetary and fiscal policy.

Other theories have focused on the role of price expectations and how mistaken expectations can lead to market disequilibria. The early Cobweb theory, which postulated that business cycles are the result of backward-looking price expectations, was largely adopted by the Monetarist model, which asserts that price expectations are slow to adjust to changes in the price level created by changes in monetary policy. This causes changes in monetary policy to have real effects on output. In contrast, the Rational Expectations model argued that if agents use the rational choice model and balance marginal benefits and marginal costs when making their decisions to consume, work, or invest, they must do the same thing when forming their expectations. As a result, expectations should be forward-looking, meaning that people will anticipate and act to offset any changes in policy that are observable. This Rational Expectations model highlighted two important ways that expectations affect fiscal and monetary policy. The first is policy irrelevance, which states that predictable policy, such as stabilization policy, cannot have real effects on an economy if markets are perfectly competitive. The second is the Lucas Critique, which states that the effects of any specific policy are unpredictable unless policymakers know exactly how expectations will change in response to this change in policy. Both of these concepts raise serious questions about the effectiveness of using government policy to stabilize output.

Finally, New Keynesian models also emphasize the role of expectations, especially as it pertains to peoples' perceptions of risk. Unlike the Keynesian model, where expectations are largely irrational, New Keynesians emphasize how changes in risk perception are rational responses to changes in the financial position of firms and the fundamentals of an economy. As a result, changes in expectations and risk can lead to rational actions such as banks and firms engaging in riskier behavior during economic expansions (moral hazard) or banks restricting lending during recessions (credit rationing), both of which can magnify the size of business cycle fluctuations.

Imperfectly competitive labor markets play a key role in propagating business cycles. Unemployment has long been one of the most reliable and sensitive indicators of business cycle trends. It is clear that most cyclical unemployment is involuntary because unemployment moves too much relative to the acyclical behavior of real wages for it to be entirely voluntary. This can only be the result of imperfect competition in labor markets.

There is considerable evidence that both nominal wage and real wage inflexibility exists in labor markets because of efficiency wages, implicit and explicit contracts, coordination failure, and other imperfections highlighted by New Keynesian models. What is interesting about these models is that wage inflexibility does not necessarily mean that real wages have to be consistently countercyclical, as argued by Keynes. Instead, different market imperfections within labor markets and between labor and goods markets can interact to generate procyclical or even the acyclical real wage behavior we observe in the data.

Understanding monetary policy and the natural rate hypothesis are crucial to understanding business cycles. The primary concept that defines the study of modern macroeconomics is the natural rate hypothesis, which states that changes in the money supply and aggregate demand influence output only in the short-run and not in the long-run. As a result, a tradeoff is inherent in monetary policy between stimulating growth in the short-run and the inflationary effects of such a policy in the long-run.

The postwar history of monetary policy in the United States can be viewed as a tug of war between these two competing objectives of increasing output and maintaining low inflation. On numerous occasions the Federal Reserve has used timely monetary policy to prevent or minimize recessions, such as after the 1987 stock market crash and during 2001, when the Federal Reserve prevented a significant recession after the 9/11 terrorist attacks. On the other hand, the Fed has also fallen into the trap of excessively relying on monetary policy to sustain growth, even when the natural rate of output growth has fallen. The result of this, as seen during the 1970s, was accelerating inflation that eventually forced the Fed to contract money growth and the economy in order to bring inflation back in line. Inflationary fears have preceded numerous economic contractions in the United States, including the Great Depression, the severe 1981 recession, and the 1990–1991 recession during the Gulf War. Thus, while monetary policy has stabilized output as compared to the prewar period and has prevented some recessions, the gains have not been as large as they could have been. In fact, the active use of monetary policy has led to an era in which business cycles have been largely policy driven.

Deflation or depreciation (from macroeconomic policy mistakes) and weak financial systems (from microeconomic policy mistakes) turn recessions into depressions. Each of the major depressions of the twentieth century has had two distinguishing characteristics. First, they were each initiated by major macroeconomic policy mistakes that led to either deflation or depreciation. During the Great Depression, the primary policy mistake was the naïve adherence of central banks to a flawed gold standard, which led to lower money growth even as prices and GDPs began to fall worldwide. During the Great Recession in Japan it was adherence to low inflation targets, even in the face of a recession and contractionary fiscal policy, that led to deflation. In East Asia and Argentina, the critical macroeconomic policy mistakes were inflexible commitments to fixed exchange rates with the dollar, even in the face of an unsustainable appreciation of their currency. Eventually this led to currency crises and steep depreciations of their currencies.

However, macroeconomic policy mistakes alone do not make depressions. Each of the major twentieth century economic crises also occurred within countries with banking systems that were financially troubled even before the contractions began. This is primarily because of a lack of bank regulation at the microeconomic level, particularly the absence of loan regulations aimed at limiting moral hazard. This includes a lack of limits on connected lending, minimal capital adequacy requirements, and a history of freely available government bailouts. Because of this lack of oversight, banks often exposed themselves to the kind of risk, in the form of exchange rate risk and default risk on their loan portfolios, that you usually see only on a casino table. This was true in the United States during the Great Depression, when the United States had a large number of small, undiversified banks with little or no protection from bank panics in the form of deposit insurance or lending from the Federal Reserve. This was also true in East Asia, Argentina, and Japan, where financial deregulation led to huge amounts of foreign investment, domestic lending booms, connected lending among conglomerates, and a history of easy government bailouts, which in turn led to unprecedented levels of non-performing loans even before these economic crises began.

It is when these events—deflation or depreciation and a banking crisis—strike simultaneously that depressions occur. Keynes recognized that deflation could lead to higher real wages and involuntary unemployment when nominal wage rigidity exists. However, economists have increasingly begun to emphasize the role of nominal debt rigidity as being even more important in generating financial crises and depressions. Deflation and/or depreciation increases the real value of debt (because its nominal value is fixed) relative to the value of assets (whose nominal value is not fixed). Because of this, firms see their financial positions deteriorate and begin to default on their bank loans. These higher default rates lead many banks to become insolvent and stop lending altogether, especially if they were in a weak financial position to begin with. As banks close, it leads to panic among depositors that can weaken other banks as well. Those banks that manage to stay open protect against additional deposit outflows and bad loans by selling their assets, placing further downward pressure on prices and further weakening the financial system. They also credit ration, or restrict the amount of new lending they undertake. As all of these things occur, financial intermediation grinds to a halt, investment and durable consumption spending free-fall, and a downturn that could have remained a recession becomes a depression.

Depressions end after two changes take place. First, countries have to reverse their policy mistakes and end the deflation and depreciation. During the Great Depression, deflation ended in the United States when it abandoned the gold standard and Roosevelt expanded fiscal policy under the New Deal. In East Asia, the IMF initially asked crisis countries to restrict their monetary and fiscal policies even further in an effort to re-attract the foreign investment that fled their countries once the contraction began. This made the economic situation even worse and failed to end the depreciations of their exchange rates. It was not until the IMF saw the error of its ways and reduced the austerity conditions in their bailout programs that these countries' exchange rates stabilized. Japan has still not taken significant action to stimulate aggregate demand and stop their deflation, which is one reason that their economy still remains in a 13 year slowdown (the fact that they have not fallen into a depression is a testament to the importance of wealth in withstanding negative shocks).

The second part of the solution is to resolve the banking crises and restore lending. This can be accomplished by the government providing bailouts in conjunction with implementing better bank regulation aimed at improving the soundness of the financial system. This process took place in the United States after the Depression and in Korea after the East Asian crisis. However, in other countries bailouts and reform have been slow. This is one of the principal reasons that lending and investment remains low and economic contractions linger on in Argentina and Japan.

In business cycle theories such as the Keynesian and Monetarist models, financial collapse was a symptom, not the cause, of recessions and depressions. Keynes believed that investment demand fell during depressions because of pessimistic expectations, not because of constraints on the supply of credit. Monetarists believed that the supply of credit decreased during recessions because of monetary policy, not because of the credit rationing of banks. However, newer theories, such as New Keynesian theories, have placed the spotlight directly on the role of financial systems in generating contractions, and economists have increasingly come to realize that banks play an integral role in any realistic explanation of why economies experience recessions and especially depressions. This has led to dramatic improvements in our theory, and has been the most important advance in our understanding of recessions and depressions during the last 20 years.

WHAT WE DO NOT KNOW ABOUT
BUSINESS CYCLES

On many issues, debate among economists persists and research continues to take place. Here are four questions about business cycles that economists are still grappling with, questions that serve as a roadmap to future progress in our understanding of recessions and depressions.

Is the use of stabilization policy stabilizing or destabilizing? The Keynesian model makes a clear and persuasive argument for the use of countercyclical monetary and fiscal policy as the only means of protecting capitalist economies, which Keynes believed were inherently unstable, from collapse. So persuasive was Keynes's argument that economists have spent the last 70 years poking holes in it. Monetarists argue that in addition to having an inflationary bias, stabilization policy suffers from imperfect information, a lack of accurate forecasting, and policy lags that make it just as likely to make things worse as it is to make them better. As an alternative, they espouse money growth rules that are non-discretionary. Rational Expectations proponents believe that stabilization policy only has real effects if it is unpredictable, in other words, if it is destabilizing. In addition, any forecast of the impact of a change in policy is only as reliable as our understanding of how expectations will change as policy changes (the Lucas Critique). Consequently, they too argue for money growth rules. Real Business Cycle advocates argue that business cycles are optimal responses to real changes in the economy and as a result should be ignored in accordance with a commitment to laissez-faire policies. Finally, New Keynesians sit on the fence. While they accept that there is market failure and a role for government policy to stabilize output, they recognize that there are significant practical difficulties with the active use of monetary and fiscal policy. As a result, they tend to argue either for the restrained use of stabilization policy or for less restrictive policy rules such as a nominal GDP target.

The empirical evidence suggests that recessions have been less frequent in the United States during the postwar era than before and that stabilization policy has played a role in this increased stability. However, it is also clear that stabilization policy has led to higher levels of inflation that have initiated policy and output contractions, wiping out much of its potential benefits. Most of this increased stability has taken place over the last 20 years, a period of time in which policymakers have been more conservative in their use of monetary and fiscal policy. This indicates that policymakers have learned about both the potential benefits and the costs of stabilization policy and have been able to use it more judiciously. However, two decades is too short a period of time to feel confident that this increased stability will continue in the future.

This argument over the proper role of policy does not stop at the border. Economists have increasingly engaged in a debate over the policies that the IMF should advocate in response to economic crises in developing countries. Should the IMF focus on policies aimed at increasing the efficiency and productive capacity of these economies by pushing structural reform and austerity programs at the cost of abandoning Keynesian stabilization policy? Or should the IMF encourage stabilization policy intended to calm the economic situation so that future economic reform has more solid ground to take root? To this point, the IMF has followed the first path with mixed results. It appears that the IMF has become the primary stage on which the advocates of Keynesian stabilization policies and the proponents of neoclassical laissez-faire policies will have their future debates.

Just how imperfect are markets? How far away from the simplifying assumptions of perfect competition do we have to move to be able to model business cycles accurately? For most of the postwar era there has been a neoclassical movement in macroeconomics that reestablished representative agent models with perfectly flexible prices in business cycle research. However, it appears that these kinds of models have been taken as far as they can go and that the momentum has shifted

toward models of imperfect competition built on solid microfoundations.

However, at this point there is no consensus as to how important
different market imperfections are. Labor markets are imperfectly competitive, but just how inflexible are real wages? Which factors are most
important in explaining this inflexibility? These same questions can be
asked about price inflexibility in the goods market, although there is
considerably less agreement about its importance in explaining business cycles. Finally, a substantial amount of research has been conducted on the role of imperfect information and how people form their
expectations. However, there remains little consensus about what constraints exist on the rationality of expectations and on the availability
of information. Given their ethereal nature and the difficulties in measuring them, the study of expectations represents an important but
daunting challenge for economists.

*Can economists develop more accurate methods of forecasting business
cycles?* It has been said that an economist is someone who explains why
something happened after it has happened. Economists will never be
great forecasters because there is so much variance inherent in economic activity. However, their ability to forecast the future would be
greatly improved if economists had a unified, coherent, and simple
model to rely upon. This is the primary reason, along with the Lucas
Critique, that forecasting has fallen upon such hard times and is currently viewed so skeptically both inside and outside of the profession
of economics. On the other hand, there are reasons to think that our
theory is improving, and hope that better theory will eventually bring
about better forecasting. In particular, the new emphasis on the role of
financial systems in driving contractions may provide new avenues for
forecasters to improve both their models and their data.

Are the last 20 years in the United States a trend or an aberration? The
2001 recession and its slow-growth aftermath notwithstanding, the last
20 years have been a remarkable period of economic stability, with two
of the longest-recorded expansions taking place back-to-back in the
1980s and 1990s. The 1990s were especially prosperous, with high
productivity growth that led to higher real wages across all segments
of society. The question now is whether the 1990s were the result of a
New Economy, characterized by permanently faster productivity
growth and higher growth in standards of living, or whether the 1990s
were a bubble economy like what occurred in Japan during the 1980s,
where over-inflated stock markets and over-spending temporarily ob-
scured a fundamentally flawed economy. Most economists' best guess
is that it will be neither of these extreme alternatives and that the U.S.
economy will slowly rebound from the growth recession it has been

stuck in during the 2000s. However, it is unlikely that the U.S. economy will return to the growth rates reached in the late 1990s anytime soon.

CONCLUDING CONCLUSIONS

If failure is a necessary element of learning, then it is little wonder that our understanding of business cycles has progressed as far as it has. Again and again, economists have developed theories, have had these theories contradicted by the facts, and have then developed new theories based on these new facts. When a critic once charged Keynes with being inconsistent and always changing his mind, Keynes pointedly responded, "When the facts change, I change my mind. What do you do, sir?" This mindset of hypothesis and revision is at the heart of the scientific method of study and is clearly evident in business cycle research. For example, the current trend in research on recessions and depressions is toward the use of open-economy models that incorporate imperfect competition, particularly in financial markets. This research is a direct response to the mistakes made during the East Asian crisis, when economists failed to predict the crisis and initially pushed harsh and destabilizing policies based on a failure to understand the full ramifications of the crisis.

Chances are that some of the things that we hold true today will be proven wrong in the future. But after a careful reading of this book, it should be clear that our knowledge of business cycles is improving. Just like falling down is evidence that a child is learning to walk, economists' failures, both in the past and in the future, indicate that they are converging toward a fuller understanding, however complicated, of why economies experience costly recessions and depressions.

Appendix: A Brief Comparison of Major Business Cycle Theories

	Classical	Keynes	Keynesians	Monetarism
Perfect Competition?	Yes, among representative agents	No, particularly in labor markets	No, not in labor and goods markets	No, because of imperfect information and adaptive expectations
Price flexibility?	Perfectly flexible prices and wages	Nominal wages are inflexible because of coordination failure	Both prices and wages are fixed	Prices and wages are perfectly flexible
Source of changes in output?	Permanent changes in aggregate supply from exogenous changes in capital, labor, or productivity	Temporary changes in aggregate demand from changes in investment (animal spirits), monetary policy, or fiscal policy	Like Keynes, but focuses on unstable investment and consumption demand	Temporary changes in aggregate demand from changes in money growth
Can monetary policy stabilize output?	No, money neutrality always holds	Monetary policy has real effects but is limited during recessions because of	Monetary policy is effective and should be based upon the Phillips	No, because it affects output only temporarily and is subject to imperfect

(Continued)

	Classical	Keynes	Keynesians	Monetarism
		the liquidity trap	curve	information, lags, and inflationary biases
Can fiscal policy stabilize output?	No, laissez faire	Government spending is very effective, but tax cuts are not effective during recessions	Both government spending and tax policy are effective	No, because of imperfect information, lags, and inflationary biases
Behavior of inflation?	Countercyclical	Procyclical	Procyclical	Procyclical
Type of unemployment?	Voluntary	Involuntary	Involuntary	Voluntary
Behavior of real wages?	Procyclical	Countercyclical	Countercyclical	Countercyclical
Perfect Competition?	No, imperfect information exists despite rational expectations	Yes, among representative agents	No, not in labor, goods, or financial markets	No, not in financial markets
Price flexibility?	Prices and wages are perfectly flexible	Prices and wages are perfectly flexible	Wages and prices are inflexible because of a number of microeconomic factors	The nominal price of debt is fixed
Source of changes in output?	Temporary changes in aggregate demand from unexpected changes in money growth	Permanent changes in aggregate supply from exogenous changes in productivity	Temporary changes in aggregate demand and supply from changes in monetary and fiscal policy, expectations, and risk.	Small initial changes in aggregate demand are magnified as deflation leads to higher default risk, credit rationing, and falling investment
Can fiscal policy stabilize output?	No, because of policy irrelevance	Only through its effects on aggregate supply	No, because of political constraints and policy lags	N/A

	Classical	Keynes	Keynesians	Monetarism
Behavior of inflation?	Procyclical	Counter-cyclical	Could be pro-cyclical, coun-tercyclical, or acyclical	Procyclical
Type of unem-ployment?	Voluntary	Voluntary	Involuntary	N/A
Behavior of real wages?	Counter-cyclical	Counter-cyclical	Could be pro-cyclical, coun-tercyclical, or acyclical	N/A
Can mone-tary policy stabilize output?	No, not if monetary policy is predictable	No, money neutrality always holds	Yes, but only on a limited basis, and broad policy rules should be used whenever possible	Yes, if aimed at stabilizing prices to end deflation

Glossary

Acyclical: a variable that has no consistent correlation with changes in GDP.

Adaptive expectations: individuals are not forward-looking but backward-looking and change their expectations only gradually, based on what they have observed in the past.

Animal spirits: the existence of volatile expectations that are in no way related to economic fundamentals.

Austerity conditions: the imposition of severe budget cuts and new taxes by a country in return for IMF funding. Austerity conditions are typically aimed at cutting a country's budget deficits in order to reduce future pressures to increase the money supply and inflation.

Beggar-thy-neighbor: a policy of attempting to run trade surpluses at the expense of other countries.

Calibration: the process of choosing values for the parameters of a model so that it behaves in a way consistent with the long-run properties of the economy.

Chaebol: refers to one of the 30 large corporate conglomerates in South Korea, similar to the Keiretsu in Japan.

Coincident indicator: a variable that peaks or troughs at the same time as GDP.

Constant returns to scale: a property of a production function in which a doubling of both capital and labor will double output.

Coordination failure: if agents are reluctant to adjust wages or prices without seeing others do so first, then these wages and prices will be slow to adjust, resulting in wage or price inflexibility.

Countercyclical: a variable that has a constant negative correlation with GDP, meaning it rises when GDP falls and falls when GDP rises.

Credit rationing: when banks respond to higher bankruptcy and credit risk by restricting the amount of their lending to firms.

Currency board: a monetary system, such as the one adopted in Argentina, in which each Argentinean peso was backed on a one-to-one basis with reserves of U.S. dollars. Under a currency board, Argentina committed itself to maintaining a fixed exchange rate of one with the dollar.

Depression: informally, while there is no formal definition, it is an economic contraction in which output falls by more than 10 percent.

Diminishing marginal returns: refers to a property of production function such that if the quantity of one of the inputs to production is fixed, the additional units of output produced by increasing the other input will get smaller as the quantity of that input rises. In other words, holding capital constant the marginal product of labor falls as the quantity of labor rises. Likewise, holding labor constant the marginal product of capital falls as the quantity of capital rises.

Duration stabilization: the observation that recessions have become less frequent, and expansions longer, since World War II.

Econometrics: the use of statistical methods to address economic questions.

Economic forecasting: the methods of quantifying economic uncertainty.

Economies of scale: occur when the average cost of production falls as the quantity of the good produced rises. Economies of scale tend to exist in industries with large fixed costs because higher production allows these fixed costs to be spread out over more units, reducing average cost.

Endogenous: determined within the model. For example, endogenous business cycle models are generated from within the model and not by outside shocks.

Exogenous: determined outside of the model. For example, exogenous business cycle models are driven by external shocks that are outside of the model.

Expansion: defined as two or more consecutive quarters of positive GDP growth.

Export promotion: a development strategy focused on building manufacturing industries that produce goods to be exported abroad.

Fiat money: money not backed by a commodity, so that its supply can be determined at the discretion of monetary authorities.

GDP (Gross Domestic Product): The market value of all final goods and services produced within a country's borders over a given period of time, usually a year. GDP measures aggregate income, aggregate output, and aggregate expenditure within an economy.

Globalization: increased cultural and economic integration among individuals, markets, and nation states.

Gold standard: an international monetary system that required the amount of paper currency in circulation within each country to be backed by a fixed amount of gold. As a result, a country's gold holdings would place an upper limit on the quantity of money supplied within that country.

Growth recessions: periods of positive but below average, or trend, GDP growth.

Hedge funds: large investment funds financed by very large investors or banks, typically requiring minimum deposits of $100 million or more. Hedge funds engage in highly risky behavior and attempt to make large returns by speculating on changes in asset prices, either positive or negative.

Indexed: assets with contractual clauses that adjust the value of payments for changes in measured inflation.

Involuntary unemployment: the existence of workers who are willing to work at the current wage but are unable to find a job, even at a slightly lower wage.

Keiretsu: large corporate/banking conglomerates in Japan, similar to the Chaebols in South Korea.

Labor hoarding: when firms agree to smooth workers' employment in exchange for workers changing their effort during busy and slack times.

Lagging indicator: a variable that peaks (or troughs) after GDP peaks (or troughs).

Laissez-faire: the classical hypothesis that the best government policy is generally one that does little to interfere in the operations of markets.

Leading indicator: a variable that peaks (or troughs) before GDP peaks (or troughs).

Liquidity trap: Keynes' hypothesis that any change in the money supply during recessions is likely to be hoarded, leading to little change in interest rates, investment, and aggregate demand.

Lucas Critique: the observation that without an understanding of how people adjust their expectations in response to changes in economic conditions, which in any given circumstance may be impossible to predict, any forecast of the future based on data from the past will be unreliable.

M1: a definition of money that includes currency in circulation, demand deposits (checking accounts), and travelers checks.

M2: a definition of money that includes M1, small savings deposits, small certificates of deposit, and money market mutual funds.

Maturity: the time at which the bond's principal is repaid.

Marginal product of labor: the change in output from a change in the quantity of labor.

Markup-pricing: choosing a price that is simply a constant percentage above the good's cost.

Menu costs: the costs of changing prices.

Monetary base: a measure of the money supply that includes reserves held by banks and currency in circulation. It is the portion of the money supply that a central bank directly controls.

Money multiplier: the ratio of the change in M1 to a change in the monetary base.

Moral hazard: exists when individuals are able to allocate some of the down-side risk of a project to others while keeping all of the up-side benefits of a project for themselves, thus encouraging these individuals to engage in riskier behavior than they otherwise would.

Multiplier effect: higher spending increases income, which in turn increases spending, which further increases income, and so on.

Natural rate hypothesis: the Monetarist proposition that in the long-run the economy returns to its natural rate of output and that changes in money growth only change the level of inflation.

Natural rate of unemployment: output level consistent with the full employment of capital, labor, and technology available in the economy, toward which the economy gradually moves in the long run.

Offshore banking: international banking conglomerates chartered in countries with little or no financial regulation.

Paradox of thrift: Keynes's hypothesis that any policy effort to increase aggregate savings rates would largely be self-defeating because higher savings would reduce aggregate demand and output, in turn leading to a fall in savings.

Peak of an expansion: the point in time at which the level of GDP reaches its maximum before it starts to decline. Thus, the peak of an expansion dates the beginning of a recession.

Phillips curve: illustrates the Keynesian hypothesis that a stable negative relationship should exist between inflation and unemployment.

Policy irrelevance: the hypothesis in the Rational Expectations model that all government policies that are observable will be completely ineffective.

Potential output: the level of output consistent with the full employment of all resources, which the economy in no way has to gravitate toward automatically.

Procyclical: a variable that has a constant positive correlation with GDP, meaning that it falls when GDP falls and rises when GDP rises.

Profit margin: the price of a good minus the average cost of producing it.

Rational expectations: the hypothesis that individuals form their expectations by making an optimal forecast of the future using all currently available information. This means that while the public can make errors, they do not make predictable, or systematic, errors.

Real rigidity: rigidity in prices that stems from the market fundamentals of supply and demand in which firms operate.

Recession: defined as two or more consecutive quarters of negative GDP growth.

Representative agents: a simplifying assumption that all individuals have the same preferences and act alike in every way.

Ricardian Equivalence: the hypothesis that deficits are irrelevant because deficit-financed fiscal policy will be matched by increases in household savings to pay for these deficits. As a result, total savings and aggregate demand would remain unchanged.

Securitization: the transformation of non-marketable assets (such as mortgages) into marketable assets (such as bonds).

Solow residual (or multifactor productivity): a measure of aggregate productivity calculated by subtracting the weighted contributions of capital growth and labor growth from measures of output growth.

Stagflation: rising unemployment and inflation occurring at the same time, created by a decline in aggregate supply.

Structural adjustment conditions: market reforms aimed at increasing productivity and efficiency in an economy, such as deregulating markets, improving legal systems, and baking reforms, that are imposed by the IMF in return for funding.

Subscriptions: the funds that member countries provide to the IMF that comprises the capital the IMF has to use.

Supply-Side economics: a movement that asserts that only aggregate supply determines output and that the primary focus of policymakers should be on the negative effects of government taxation and regulation.

Trough of a recession: the point in time at which GDP falls to its lowest level before it begins to rise again, meaning that a trough dates the beginning of an expansion.

Voluntary unemployment: only those workers who are not willing to work at the current real wage are unemployed, while everyone else who wants to work at the current wage can find a job.

Yield: a measure of the yearly return on holding an asset, typically a bond. It is calculated by determining the interest rate that equates the present value of future payments received from the bond with the current price of the bond.

Yield curve: a representation of how the yields on comparable bonds change as their maturity changes.

Bibliography

Altonji, Joseph G. (1986). "Intertemporal Substitution in Labor Supply: Evidence from Micro Data." *Journal of Political Economy,* 97: 507–522.

Artis, Michael J., Zenon F. Kontolemis, and Denise R. Osborn. (1997). "Business Cycles for G7 and European countries." *Journal of Business,* 70: 249–279.

Bailey, Martin Neil. (2002). "The New Economy: Post Mortem or Second Wind?" *Journal of Economic Perspectives,* 16: 3–22.

Ball, Laurence, N. Gregory Mankiw, and David Romer. (1988). "The New Keynesian Economics and the Output-Inflation Tradeoff." *Brookings Papers on Economic Activity,* no. 1, pp. 1–82.

Bank of Japan Research Paper. (2002). "How Should the Recent Increase in Japan's Monetary Base be Understood?" www.boj.or.jp/en/ronbun/02/data/ronbun0209a.pdf.

Basu, Susanto, and Alan M. Taylor. (1999). "Business Cycles in International Historical Perspective." *Journal of Economic Perspectives,* 13: 45–68.

Bernanke, Ben. (1983). "Nonmonetary Effects of the Financial Crisis in the Propagation of the Great Depression." *American Economic Review,* 73: 257–276.

———. (1990). "Clearing and Settlement During the Crash." *Review of Financial Studies,* 3: 133–151.

———. (1995). "The Macroeconomics of the Great Depression: A Comparative Approach." *Journal of Money, Credit, and Banking,* 27: 1–28.

Blanchard, Oliver, and John Simon. (2001). "The Long and Large Decline in U.S. Output Volatility." *Brookings Papers on Economic Activity,* no 1, pp. 135–174.

Blinder, Alan. (1988). "The Fall and Rise of Keynesian Economics." *Economic Record,* 64: 278–294.

———. (1991). "Why Are Prices Sticky? Preliminary Results from an Interview Study." *American Economic Review,* 91: 89–96.

———. (1998). *Central Banking in Theory and Practice.* Cambridge: MIT Press.

Braun, Nick. (2000). "Total Factor Measures for the G7 Countries." Economic and Social Research Council Working Paper, http://www.gla.uk/economics/TFP.

Cecchetti, Stephen. (1986). "The Frequency of Price Adjustment: A Study of the Newsstand Prices of Magazines." *Journal of Econometrics,* 31: 255–274.

Clark, John Maurice. (1917). "Business Acceleration and the Law of Demand: A Technical Factor in Economic Cycles." *Journal of Political Economy* 25: 217–235.

Corsetti, Giancarlo, Paolo Pesenti, and Nouriel Roubini. (1998). "What Caused the Asian Currency and Financial Crisis?: Parts I and II." National Bureau of Economic Research Working Paper Nos. 6833 and 6834.

De Long, Bradford. (2000). "The Triumph of Monetarism." *Journal of Economic Perspectives,* 14: 83–94.

———. (2002). "Productivity Growth in the 2000s." NBER Macroeconomic Annual, forthcoming.

——— and Lawrence H. Summers. (2001). "The 'New Economy': Background, Historical Perspective, Questions, and Speculations." *Economic Review, The Federal Reserve Bank of Kansas City,* fourth quarter, pp. 29–59.

Diebold, Francis X. (1998). "The Past, Present, and Future of Macroeconomic Forecasting." *Journal of Economic Perspectives,* 12: 175–192.

——— and Glenn D. Rudebusch. (1999). *Business Cycles: Durations, Dynamics, and Forecasting.* Princeton: Princeton University Press.

Dornbusch, Rudiger. (1997). "How Real Is U.S. Prosperity?" Column reprinted in *World Economic Laboratory Columns,* Massachusetts Institute of Technology, December.

Economist, The. (2001). "Out for the Count." October 13, pp. 65–66.

Edwards, Sebastian. (1998). "Capital Flows, Real Exchange Rates, and Capital Controls: Some Latin American Examples." National Bureau of Economic Research Working Paper No. W6800.

Estrella, Arturo, and Frederic S. Mishkin. (1998). "Predicting U.S. Recessions: Financial Variables as Leading Indicators." *Review of Economics and Statistics,* 80: 45–61.

Ezekial, Mordecai. (1938). "The Cobweb Theorem." *Quarterly Journal of Economics,* 52: 255–280.

Feldstein, Martin. (2002). "Argentina's Fall: Lessons from the Latest Financial Crisis." *Foreign Affairs,* 81: 8–15.

Fischer, Irving. (1933). "The Debt-Deflation Theory of Great Depressions." *Econometrica,* 1: 337–357.

Fischer, Stanley. (1977). "Long-Term Contracts, Rational Expectations, and the Optimal Money Supply Rule." *Journal of Political Economy,* 85: 191–205.

Friedman, Milton. (1968). "The Role of Monetary Policy." *American Economic Review,* 58: 1–17.

——— and Anna Schwartz. (1963). *A Monetary History of the United States, 1867–1960.* Princeton: Princeton University Press.

Froot, Kenneth A., Paul G. J. O'Connell, and Mark. S. Seasholes. (1999). "The Portfolio Flows of International Investors." Harvard Business School Working Paper.

Goldstein, Morris. (2000). "IMF Structural Conditionality: How Much Is Too Much?" Institute for Intenational Economics Working Paper No. 01-04.

Gordon, Robert J. (1976). "Recent Developments in the Theory of Inflation and Unemployment." *Journal of Monetary Economics,* 2: 185–220.

———. (2000). "Does the 'New Economy' Measure up to the Great Inventions of the Past?" *Journal of Economic Perspectives,* 14: 49–74.

Greenwald, Bruce, and Joseph Stiglitz. (1993). "New and Old Keynesians." *Journal of Economic Perspectives,* 7: 23–44.

Greenspan, Alan. (1998). "The Current Asian Crisis on the Financial Resources of the IMF." Testimony Before the Committee on Agriculture, U.S. House of Representatives.

Hall, Robert E. (1993). "Macro Theory and the Recession of 1990–1991." *American Economics Association Papers and Proceedings,* 83: 275–279.

Hanes, Christopher. (2000). "Nominal Wage Rigidity and Industry Characteristics in the Downturns of 1893, 1929, and 1981." *American Economic Review,* 90: 1432–1446.

Haubrich, Joseph G., and Ann M. Dombrosky. (1996). "Predicting Real Growth Using the Yield Curve." *Economic Review,* 32: 26–35.

Hawtrey, Robert George. (1913). *Good and Bad Trade.* London: Constable & Co.

Heilbroner, Robert L. (1986). *The Worldly Philosophers.* New York: Simon and Schuster.

Heisenberg, W. (1971). *Physics and Beyond.* London: George Allen & Unwin Ltd.

Hicks, John R. (1937). "Mr. Keynes and the 'Classics': A Suggested Interpretation." *Econometrica,* 5: 147–159.

Hobson, John A. (1922). *The Economics of Unemployment.* London: George Allen & Unwin Ltd.

Hoover, Herbert. (1952). *The Memoirs of Herbert Hoover: The Great Depression.* London: Macmillan.

Jevons, William Stanley. (1884). *Investigations in Currency and Finance.* London: Macmillan.

Katz, Richard. (2000). "Helping Japanese Economic Reform." *The Washington Quarterly,* 23: 135–153.

Keynes, John Maynard. (1920). *The Economic Consequences of Peace.* New York: Harcourt, Brace.

———. (1923). *A Tract on Monetary Reform.* London: Macmillan.

———. (1931). *Essays in Persuasion.* London: Macmillan.

———. (1936). *The General Theory of Employment, Interest, and Money.* London: Macmillan.

Kiley, Michael. (2000). "Endogenous Price Stickiness and Business Cycle Persistence." *Journal of Money, Credit, and Banking,* 32: 28–53.

Knoop, Todd A. (2003). "Business Cycles and the Cyclical Behavior of Profits," Working Paper.

Kondratieff, Nikolai D. (1935). "The Long Waves in Economic Life." *Review of Economics and Statistics.* 27: 105–115.

Krueger, Anne O. (1998). "Whither the World Bank and the IMF?" *Journal of Economic Literature,* 36: 1983–2020.

———. (2000). "IMF Stabilization Programs," Stanford Center for International Development Working Paper Series, December 2000.

Krugman, Paul. (1998). "It's Baaack: Japan's Slump and the Return of the Liquidity Trap." *Brookings Papers on Economic Activity,* no. 2, pp. 137–205.
———. (1999). *The Return of Depression Economics.* New York: W.W. Norton.
Kuttner, Kenneth N., and Adam S. Posen. (2001). "The Great Recession: Lessons for Macroeconomic Policy from Japan." *Brookings Papers on Economic Activity,* no. 2, pp. 93–160.
Kydland, Finn E., and Edward C. Prescott. (1982). "Time to Build and Aggregate Fluctuations." *Econometrica,* 50: 1345–1370.
Levy, Daniel, Mark Bergen, Shantanu Dutta, and Robert Venable. (1997). "The Magnitude of Menu Costs: Direct Evidence from Large U.S. Supermarket Chains." *Quarterly Journal of Economics,* 112: 791–825.
Long, John B., Jr., and Charles I. Plosser. (1983). "Real Business Cycles." *Journal of Political Economy,* 91: 39–69.
Lucas, Robert E. (1972): "Expectations and the Neutrality of Money." *Journal of Economic Theory,* 4: 103–124.
———. (1973). "Some International Evidence on Output-Inflation Tradeoffs." *American Economic Review,* 63: 326–334.
———. (1978). "Unemployment Policy." *American Economic Review: Papers and Proceedings,* 68: 353–357.
———. (1980). "Rules, Discretion, and the Role of the Economic Advisor." In *Rational Expectations and Economic Policy,* ed. Stanley Fischer. Chicago: University of Chicago Press.
——— and Thomas J. Sargent. (1978). "After Keynesian Economics." In *After the Phillips Curve: Persistence of High Inflation and High Unemployment.* Boston: Federal Reserve Bank of Boston.
Maddock, Rodney, and Michael Carter. (1982). "A Child's Guide to Rational Expectations." *Journal of Economic Literature,* 20: 39–51.
Malthus, Thomas R. (1798). *An Essay on the Principle of Population.* London: W. Pickering.
Mandel, Michael J. (2001). "Restating the '90s." *Business Week,* April 1, pp. 50–58.
Mankiw, N. Gregory. (1990). "A Quick Refresher Course in Macroeconomics." *Journal of Economic Literature,* 28: 1645–1660.
———. (1985). "Small Menu Costs and Large Business Cycles." *Quarterly Journal of Economics,* 100: 529–537.
———. (1989). "Real Business Cycles: A New Keynesian Perspective." *Journal of Economic Perspectives,* 3: 79–90.
———. (1992). "The Reincarnation of Keynesian Economics." *European Economic Review,* 36: 559–565.
Mayer, Thomas. (1975). "The Structure of Monetarism." *Kredit and Kapital,* 8: 292–313.
McKinsey Global Institute. (2001). "U.S. Productivity Growth 1995–2000." *McKinsey Global Institute,* October.
McNees, Steven K. (1986). "Forecasting Accuracy of Alternative Techniques: A Comparison of Macroeconomic Forecasts." *Journal of Business Economics and Statistics,* 4: 5–15.
Mishkin, Frederic S. (2000). "Financial Policies and the Prevention of Financial Crises in Emerging Market Countries." National Bureau of Economic Research Working Paper No. 8087.

Mitchell, Wesley. (1927). *Business Cycles: The Problem and Its Setting*. New York: National Bureau of Economic Research.

Muth, John. (1961). "Rational Expectations and the Theory of Price Movements." *Econometrica*, 29: 37–43.

Oliner, Stephen D., and Daniel E. Sichel. (2000). "The Resurgence of Growth in the Late 1990s: Is Information Technology the Story?" *Journal of Economic Perspectives*, 14: 3–22.

Peregrine. (1997). "Peregrine Sees Asian Ex-Japanese Bad Debts at $500B." NY: Bloomberg, L.P. November 11–12.

Phillips, Arthur W. (1958). "The Relation between Unemployment and the Rate of Change in Money Wage Rates in the United Kingdom, 1862–1957." *Economica*, 25: 283–299.

Plosser, Charles. (1989). "Understanding Real Business Cycles." *Journal of Economic Perspectives*, 3: 51–78.

Pomerleano, M. (1998). "The East Asian Crisis and Corporate Finances: The Untold Micro Story." World Bank Policy Research Working Paper #1990.

Posen, Adam. (2002). "The Looming Japanese Crisis." *International Economic Policy Briefs*, 5: 1–11.

Ranciere, Romain, Aaron Tornell, and Frank Westermann. (2003). "Crises and Growth: A Re-evaluation." NBER Working Paper No. 10073.

Romer, Christina D. (1993). "The Nation in Depression." *Journal of Economic Perspectives*, 7: 19–39.

———. (1999). "Changes in Business Cycles: Evidence and Explanations." *Journal of Economic Perspectives*, 13: 23–44.

——— and David H. Romer. (1994). "What Ends Recessions?" *NBER Macroeconomics Annual*, 9: 13–57.

Romer, David. (1993). "The New Keynesian Synthesis." *Journal of Economic Perspectives*, 7: 5–22.

———. (2001). *Advanced Macroeconomics*. Boston: McGraw Hill.

Sachs, Jeffery. (1997). "The IMF Is a Power unto Itself." *The Financial Times*, December 11.

Samuelson, Paul. (1964). "The General Theory: 1946." In *Keynes' General Theory: Reports of Three Decades*, ed. Robert Lekachman. New York: St. Martin's Press.

Sargent, Thomas. (1986). "The End of Four Big Inflations." In *Rational Expectations and Inflation*, ed. Thomas Sargent. New York: Harper Collins.

Schumpeter, Joseph. (1939). *Business Cycles*. New York: McGraw-Hill Book Co.

Smith, Adam. (1776). *An Inquiry into the Nature and Causes of the Wealth of Nations*. London: W. Strahan & T. Cadell.

Solow, Robert M. (1956). "A Contribution to the Theory of Economic Growth." *Quarterly Journal of Economics*, 70: 65–94.

Stiglitz, Joseph E. (1997). "Reflections on the Natural Rate Hypothesis." *Journal of Economic Perspectives*, 11: 3–10.

———. (2002). *Globalization and Its Discontents*. New York: W.W. Norton.

Stock, James H., and Mark W. Watson. (2002). "Has the Business Cycle Changed and Why?" *NBER Macroeconomics Annual*, forthcoming.

Summers, Lawrence. (1989). "The Ishihara-Morita Brouhaha." *International Economy*, 52: 1–15.

Sumner, Scott, and Stephen Silver. (1989). "Real Wages, Employment, and the Phillips Curve." *Journal of Political Economy*, 97: 706–720.

Temin, Peter. (1989). *Lessons from the Great Depression*. Cambridge: MIT Press.

Tobin, James. (1993). "Price Flexibility and Output Stability: An Old Keynesian View." *Journal of Economic Perspectives*, 7: 45–65.

Volcker, Paul A., and Toyoo Gyohten. (1992). *Changing Fortunes: The World's Money and the Threat to American Leadership*. New York: Times Books.

Wicksell, Knut. (1936). *Interest and Prices: A Study of the Causes Regulating the Value of Money*. London: Macmillan.

Williamson, John, and Molly Mahar. (1998). "A Survey of Financial Liberalization." *Princeton Essays in International Finance*, no. 211.

Yamaguchi, Yutaka. (2002). "Monetary Policy in a Changing Economic Environment." *Jackson Hole Symposium Sponsored by the Reserve Board of Kansas City*, pp. 241–251.

Zarnowitz, Victor. (1985). "Rational Expectations and Macroeconomic Forecasts." *Journal of Business and Economic Statistics*, 3: 293–311.

———. (1992). "Chapter 14: An Analysis of Annual and Multiperiod Quarterly Aggregate Forecasts." In *Business Cycles: Theory, History, Indicators, and Forecasting*. Chicago: University of Chicago Press.

Index

About the Author

TODD A. KNOOP is associate professor of economics and business at Cornell College, where his primary research and teaching interests include macroeconomic theory, tax reform, and monetary policy. He has published many articles in such journals as *Economic Inquiry* and the *Southern Economic Journal*.